Gallimaufry

A Quiddity of Collective Nouns & Other Profundities

Sue Ellery

*For Tegen and Aaron
from Damawyn
with love*

© 2012 Sue Ellery

All rights reserved.

ISBN 978-1-291-15774-1

Sue Ellery has asserted her right under the Copyright Designs and Patent Act, 1988 to be identified as the author of this work.

This book is sold subject to the condition that it shall not, by way of trade or otherwise, be lent, resold, hired out, or otherwise circulated without the publisher's prior consent in any form of binding or cover other than that in which it is published and without a similar condition being imposed on the subsequent purchaser.

Also by Sue Ellery, 'Pantomime Stew', a privately printed collection of poetry and doggerel by the late Brenda Wootton – please checkout my online store on www.freewebstore.org/Quiddity1/. Contact me on that site for further information about either book, or to make (polite) suggestions for inclusion in possible later editions!

'There is little enough poetry in our speech (and lives) to continue to ignore such a rich vein as this.'

James Lipton
'An Exaltation of Larks'

Part One: An Introduction of Ideas

An exaltation of expressions i
An Introduction i
Four-word haiku iii

The trouble with terms – An Apologia iv
1. When is a collective noun not a collective noun? v
2. Quantity viii
   a. Foods viii
   b. Measurement ix
   c. Containment ix
   d. Generic terms x
   e. Habitat x
3. Quality xi
   a. States of being xii
   b. Characteristics xii
4. A Freedom of Expressions xiii
   a. A muse of wordsmiths xiv
   b. An antiquity of words xv
   c. An inspiration of idioms xvi
   d. A teapot of terms xviii
   e. And the 'Other Profundities'? xviii
   f. And finally … xix
5. A Field of Contenders xx
6. An Acknowledgement of Thanks xxiv
7. An Endnote xxv
How to use this book xxvi
Key to abbreviations xxvi

Part Two: A Treasure Trove of Terms

Ch 1 **A Nobility of Beasts**..1
    Animals 2

Ch 2 **A Flight of Fancy**..17
    Birds...18

Ch 3 **A Congregation of Creatures**................................33
    a. Insects, Arthropods & Micro-organisms................34
    b. Marine life 39
    c. Reptiles 45

Ch 4 **A Grotto of Greenery** 49
    Plant life, Gardening, Crops & Agriculture..............50

Ch 5 **A Clutch of Characters**...57
    People 58

Ch 6 **A Broadside of Belligerents** 89
    a. Military, Naval & Warfare 90
    b. Transport & Vehicles 98

Ch 7 **A World of Wonder**..103
    a. Architectural & Built Landscape..........................104
    b. Astronomical 109
    c. Geographical & Geological..................................112
    d. Weather, Light & Colour......................................116

Ch 8 **A Banality of Bric-a-Brac**....................................123
    a. Domestic..124
    b. Food & Drink 142
    c. Sports, Games & Pastimes 157

Ch 9 **A Play of Words** 163
    a. Theatrical & Dance...164
    b. Musical & Sounds 168
    c. Literary & Printing..173
    d. Popular Culture..179
    e. Religion..182
    f. Myth & Magic...187

Ch 10 A Comedy of Errors 191
    a. Intangibles (Ideas, Idioms, Clichés, Abstract Concepts) 192
    b. Communication & Language 206
    c. Emotions & Characteristics 212
    d. Time 219

Ch 11 A Compound of Collectives 221
    a. Anatomical 222
    b. Computing, Scientific & Technical 225
    c. Medical 229
    d. Legal, Business, Economic & Political 233

Part Three: A Ragbag of References

- **Bibliography – Collections of collected nouns** 243
  - Other useful sources 244
  - Useful websites 245
- **List of Illustrations** 246
  - Sources of illustrations 265
  - Notes on the principal illustrators 266
- **Index of collective nouns** 269

gal·li·mau·fry/ˌgaləˈmôfrē/
Noun:
- A confused jumble or medley of things.
- A hash made from diced or minced meat.

Middle French: *galimafree* stew
First known use: circa 1556

(Google)

"Every family had a few skeletons in their cupboards, but the Vanger family had an entire gallimaufry of them."

The Girl with the Dragon Tattoo, Stieg Larsson

Part One: An Introduction of Ideas

An Exaltation of Expressions

An Introduction

Over the ages, at different times and for various reasons, people have felt a need to devise special words for collections or groups of things. "Lots of" or "some" certainly doesn't do the trick. Your family is hungry, you see a group of animals, and you run back to your family with the news – what do you tell them? If there are only a *couple of rabbits*, and they're a *range of hills* away, then it's not worth the effort; but a whole *drift of wild swine* (or whatever the equivalent Neolithic term was) a few trees distant, means everyone can eat at last. There were many terms thought up purely for the hunters; food gathering was a far more pressing and bloody business in the early days. As time went on, and societies grew and cultures developed, new words were added to this *ragbag of terms*. Essentially and originally, the collective term needed to explain a little of the thing it was describing for purely practical reasons.

But, above and beyond the mundane needs of everyday existence: what mystic, awed at the beauty of their song from high in the heavens, first breathed reverently *an exaltation of skylarks*; or entranced at the tiny, jewel-like birds on the thistle-heads, *a charm of goldfinches*? What cynic, satiated with *a surfeit of religion*, described *'a superfluity of nuns'*, or *a skulk of friars*? What alert mind first described *a malapertness of pedlars* – (I presume pedlars are nothing if not malapert) – or *an incredibility of cuckolds*? (Having established [via the OED, who quote their source as *The Book of St Albans*] that the sense here is 'incredulity' – I imagine the cuckolds were incredulous as they could they not believe that their wives would be unfaithful to them.) The devisers of these terms were obviously colourful characters, with in many cases, vivid imaginations – and presumably with someone close by to listen and then be sufficiently interested to perpetuate their newly-devised phrase for posterity.

The phrases that have come down to us through the years echo of a different *way of life*, a different *set of priorities*. Yet they clearly demonstrate some of the illuminating *flashes of inspiration* which our forefathers must have had, and they show a versatility and a downright playfulness of the human intellect which still appeal to us today. The fact that some of these terms are still common currency over five hundred years later (such as *a school of fish*, and *a pride of lions*), and that these terms can still delight us or inspire us, speaks volumes across the years.

Many of the archaic words have long since left us – who now would understand *a badelynge of ducks* (a paddling), *a subtiltie of sergeants* (a subtlety), or *a fesnying of ferrets* (apparently a 19th century miscopy of busy-ness)? (Come to that, are ducks so called because they do? – 'Duck', that is.) Some seem to be simply alliterative: *a kindle of kittens, a lepe of leopards*; some are onomatopoeic: *a gaggle of geese, a gobble of turkeys*; some display assonance: *a herd of curlews, a croak of toads*. Others are anthropomorphic, ascribing to animals perceived human characteristics: *a sloth of bears, a shrewdness of apes*, or *a skulk of foxes*. Some simply mean a collection of domesticated creatures or things: *a herd of cows, a tribe of goats* or *a pack of hounds*. There was also obviously a need for a term to express a group of working animals: *a drove of kine*, and *a team of oxen*. The kine were indeed driven, and the oxen needed to work as a team. And the sheep, happily for the shepherd, flocked.

Most groups of wild animals and birds seem to feel the need to live in a gregarious community – witness especially: *a colony of gulls, a troop of monkeys* and *a muster of storks*. Yet some terms seem ludicrous, such as *a singularity of boars* and *a stud of mares* (surely a mare is the opposite of a stud?).

It is probably no accident that monkeys and baboons form a troop, like the strolling players of old; their antics are indeed very similar. How descriptive of their natures and habits is *a labour of moles* and *a concentration of kingfishers*! How descriptive of their appearance is *a flamboyance of flamingos*! *A barren of mules* is also no more than the truth. Some make you think deeper about the nature of the creature – why *a pod of killer whales*, unless there is in their temperament a natural mothering and protective instinct? Not the first trait of killer whales that would spring to mind, if you were looking for a descriptive term for them.

And as for *a watch of nightingales* – what an imaginative scene that brings to mind. And *a dazzle of hummingbirds* – why yes, of course it is!

Four word haiku

You may be familiar with the form of Japanese poetry known as haiku. It works on the principle 'less is more', and has a strict form of seventeen syllables in three unrhymed lines of five, seven and five syllables (Encarta World English dictionary definition). Lytton Strachey, in 1912, wrote, 'Omission is the beginning of all art', and although the form of our collective expressions is nowhere so rigid as haiku, yet they have an element of the same spirit within them. The clarity they contain within their four-word structure is an essence of an idea, a distillation of a thought, passed on to us from someone else's *flight of imagination*.

Collective nouns and Haiku seem so similar in essence to me that I cannot help but compare the forms. Several creatures seem to merit more than one collective term: geese, for example, on the ground, definitely 'gaggle'; while on the wing, they weave like *a skein of silk*. The Japanese poet Yasui noticed the difference:

"Wild geese! I know
   that they did eat the barley:
      yet, when they go ..."

Herons come in a 'sedge' (a miscopy, or from the reed beds where they feed?) or a 'siege' – possibly from their habit of lying in wait for fish. What circumstance had put this word in the mind of the instigator of this four word haiku? Had a group of herons been seen laying siege to a pond? And Chiyo is conveying the same message as the unidentified creator of *a whiteness of swans*, with this haiku:

"Had they no voice
   The herons would be lost –
      this morning's snow!"

A few of the more obscure words were certainly the result of some creative spelling and short-sighted copyists in earlier centuries. *A lepe of leopards* is very likely *a leap*, and *a covert of coots* may well be *a cover*.

As for the ducks a-badelynge, this is what Joso has to say:
"*I've just come from a place
    at the lake bottom!" – that is the look
        on the little duck's face.*"

The mystic I spoke of, enchanted by the song of the skylarks high in the blue, was trying to convey to others the feelings of extreme joy and reverence which the music inspired in him, and he succeeded most wonderfully.

The trouble with terms - an Apologia

'There's another one!', I said triumphantly, hearing the expression *a sea of debts* on a television programme, and busily scribbling it down in my notebook. "You can't have that," said my learned friend – "that's a metaphor, not a collective noun." This preamble is not for the faint-hearted. We are talking serious semantics here. But hang in there, it's worth the struggle.

The first point I need to make is, the English language is a deeply complex and wonderful thing, and I am rambling in what is, for me, relatively uncharted territory – the land of grammar. But I am seeking *a blessing of unicorns* – it has to be worth falling into a few *quagmires of syntax* along the way.

Secondly, this book is not intended solely for purists or experts of any kind – if they approve of the contents or find them useful, so much the better. It is intended for laymen like me, the labourers and bricklayers of the world of words, for amusement, for wonderment, for practical application and for inspiration.

We have *a delight of descriptive terms* available to us when we need to give a fuller description of something we are observing, and in classifying these terms, I acknowledge I am taking upon myself the roles of judge and jury. All such lists must be subjective – and as I am discovering many new examples every day (as will you, once you become addicted and focus in on them), I cannot begin to call the lists comprehensive, lengthy though they are.

In fact, I must own up to many of the expressions listed here being trawled from my own imperfect memory. Here are phrases you too will recognise, used daily by people from all *walks of life*, and, from my own research, few of the domestic variety are ever given the exalted status of inclusion in lists such as this.

John Bunyan, in The Pilgrim's Progress, offered this suggestion to his detractors:
If that thou wilt not read, let it alone;
Some love the meat, some love to pick the bone.

1. When is a collective noun not a collective noun?

Let's get this troublesome definition out of the way at the start. There is no grammatically correct term for the phrases that are popularly known as 'collective nouns'. The lists of interesting and archaic phrases which are often printed in reference books and crossword dictionaries are lists of phrases, not lists of individual nouns. A noun is essentially a single word, even if it is describing a group – in the phrase, *a pride of lions*, *a pride* is a (singular) collective noun, and *lions* is a plural noun; but the whole four-word construct is a phrase or expression, not a̲ collective noun.

Researching these lists, I became bewildered by the *plethora of choices* available. Are the phrases which I have compiled all, strictly speaking, collective nouns, I wondered? I suspected not. So exactly what constitutes a collective noun? The term itself has been described in several different ways:
- collective nouns
- collective terms
- collectives
- company terms
- group nouns
- group terms
- nouns of assemblage
- nouns of multitude
- terms of venery (archaic, relating to hunting).

Here are some definitions:

Fowler's Modern English Usage describes 'collectives' thus: *'a noun singular in form is used with a plural implication'*.

The New Encarta World English Dictionary says a collective noun is: *'a noun that refers to a group of people or things considered as a single unit'*.

So here is a list of collective nouns:
- committee
- family
- flock
- group
- orchestra
- school
- tribe.

These individual nouns can be interesting in themselves, but that is not what this book is essentially about. What I have compiled here are lists of the four-word phrases describing quantities (or qualities – more of this later) of different groups of creatures, people, objects and ideas.

Fowler gives an example of *a flock of sheep*, and explains the further complication that *collectives*, (as he calls them), can in themselves be given either singular or plural forms (as in *a flock of sheep*, and *flocks of sheep*). And to plunge deeper into this *morass of words*, *flock* is also a collective noun in the sense of woollen waste – but would not be spoken of as *a flock of woollen waste*, as this would be a tautology (it would be like saying *a woollen waste of woollen waste*, which is plainly nonsense). Some tautologies are (mistakenly) used in everyday speech, such as *a consensus of opinion*, when *consensus* actually means *unanimity of opinion* – but I'm sure you will discover tautologies, and clichés, a-plenty, inadvertently added to my lists – mea culpa.

So, as we are at liberty to do so, what are we going to call these essential parts of our colourful language? The word 'term' could be used, the word 'phrase' is technically correct, and James Lipton opts for 'venereal terms', but I am happiest with the word 'expression'. According to Encarta, an expression 'communicates an idea', or 'conveys a thought or feeling'. This seems to me entirely appropriate – the beauty and poetry of these phrases, especially some of the more archaic, is that they <u>are</u> so expressive. It would be far simpler to use one simple, generic, term for a group of anything – a *flock* for example, for all groups of birds, or a *school* for all groups of fish – but how prosaic, how unimaginative! It was its very expressiveness that first attracted me to *an exaltation of larks*, and ensnared me in the *mesh of words* collectively known as collective nouns. So let us call them 'collective expressions' – phrases with the format of *a [collective noun] of [plural noun]*.

And what is the correct collective expression for a collection of collective expressions? (Try saying that fast.) Again, there isn't one. What an oversight. Well – my offering, for what it's worth, is *a quiddity of collective expressions*. I had agonised and fretted over this issue for many months, trying out various delicious terms (a salmagundi? a gallimatias?), consulting reference books and search engines, when one day the word *quiddity* popped into my brain. I had no idea what it meant, but it must have drifted past my tired eyes and into the brain cell at some point. Quiddity, apparently, means both:
- the essence that makes something the kind of thing it is and makes it different from any other thing, and
- an evasion of the point of an argument by raising irrelevant distinctions or objections.

[Princeton University's Electronic Lexical Database at www.cogsci.princeton.edu/cgi-bin/webwn]

Or alternatively:
- the essence, nature, or distinctive peculiarity of a thing.
- a hair-splitting distinction; a trifling point; a quibble.
- an eccentricity; an odd feature.

[dictionary.com]

Well alleluia! There you are – a brace (or a leash) of useful explanations that seems to cover pretty much what I've been talking about throughout this Apologia.

2. Quantity

Collective expressions generally seem to amount to a description for a quantity of something. This seems indisputable – but not everything is easily quantifiable. Quantities of animals, objects and people are straightforward enough – but what about intangibles such as water and air, feelings and emotions, ideas and abstract concepts? Can these be quantified? Apparently such distinctions have now resulted in the classification of nouns as either count nouns, or mass (or non-count) nouns. (This is a new one since my schooldays!) As I understand it, these terms can be loosely categorised as follows:

Count nouns are tangible things or objects that can be counted (such as books, tools, cows, lawyers etc.). No problem.

Mass (or non-count) nouns are quantities 'en masse', as it were, (such as water, butter, air, etc.). Mass nouns are uncountable by a number, but can be quantified by a noun that signifies amount – some materials, foods, metals, liquids, gases, and many abstract nouns such as beauty, ignorance, serenity, patriotism etc., fall into this category. Hence, to measure or quantify mass nouns, we need a collective noun in front, together with 'of' – for example:
- a pail of water
- a pat of butter
- a surge of patriotism
- a welter of ignorance

It seems to me that one of the ways to decide if a phrase can be called a collective expression is to decide whether or not the noun it describes can be sub-divided.

a. Foods

Foods are a case in point – as all recipes are, of necessity, a combination of ingredients, and will be served in portions, are meals such as *a carbonade of beef*, or *a pot-au-feu*, classifiable as collective expressions? And as joints of meat must be cut to be served, are *a*

Part 1: An Introduction of Ideas

saddle of venison and *a loin of pork* collective expressions? *A bottle of champagne* may be of a standard size, but *a jeroboam of champagne* is significantly larger (equivalent to four bottles, in fact). On the principle that any such mass can be composed of a number of ingredients, or be of varying size (and hence quantity), I have recklessly included such terms in my lists.

b. Measurement

By definition, all individual words which describe a measurement of something – no matter how small those measurements are – can (in my book, which this is!) be called collective nouns; and all manner of things can be measured. Therefore, quantities of time, space, length, breadth, width, distance, volume, area, numbers, height, weight, extent, force, pressure, intensity, energy, mass, and so on, are all collectives. Hence, all nouns relating to quantities of measurement are collective nouns – such as: four (*a four of bridge*), kilo, score (as in *a score of apples*), centennial, tenth, ton, mile, light year, quarter. (I have resisted the temptation to list all such nouns here – they are more than adequately covered by Roget's Thesaurus, so they may appear somewhat arbitrarily!)

c. Containment

Containers of objects can, in effect, be sub-divided into their constituent parts. *A box of biscuits* is a collective expression, and obviously if some of the biscuits are eaten individually, and some remain, we are still left with *a box of biscuits*. *A barrel of oil* can also have some of the oil poured out, and yet still remain *a barrel of oil* – so it can be sub-divided. Yet when all the biscuits have been eaten, we are left with just a biscuit-box, and this empty box is clearly not a 'collective' of anything – there are no contents left to be sub-divided. (A collection of biscuit-boxes, is, however, another matter.) But a collection of biscuits is not necessarily always known as a box – it could be a packet, a plate, a pile, a tin or a tray, for example; it is a matter of the form the objects take, or the container used. So, are all containers (with contents) classifiable as collective expressions? Once again, I have been liberal in my judgement on such matters.

Collective expressions referring to containers can be 'nested' – for example, *a pair of earrings* can be placed in *a casket of jewellery*, which may be packed in *a T-chest of household goods*, then stored in *a container-load of boxes*, which is listed on *a manifest of ship's cargo*.

d. Generic terms

Some group names are so common and can be used with such a variety of plural nouns as to be ubiquitous. Virtually all cloven-hooved animals can be called a herd, most species of birds form flocks, many small flying insects swarm, and many different groups of people can be called a crowd. Likewise, a box (depending on size) can contain an almost limitless variety of items, and a forest could be made up of any number of different trees. In compiling these lists, I have used such common collectives where they are specifically associated with particular plural nouns (*a box of matches*, or *a herd of cows*, for example), but have not attempted to list everything that could be contained in a box, or to list 'a forest of …' every type of tree – an impossible and pointless task. In addition, any group of creatures related by blood and living communally, can be called a family. (Although Australians seem happy enough to describe almost any group of their indigenous creatures as *a mob* – kangaroos, wallabies, wombats, sheep, turkeys, emus, and people, as well as books [!], are all classified as such.)

e. Habitat

Some animal groups are defined collectively in terms of their place of residence or operation, such as *a hive of bees*, *a nest of fledglings*, or *a faculty of teaching staff*. These are also, in effect, containers – the hive contains bees, the nest, fledglings, and the faculty, teaching staff. So is it legitimate to use buildings as well as containers as collective expressions? In some cases I have, where that is the normal domicile or container associated with those objects or people. But note that if you wanted to tell someone that you had a lot of house guests, you would be more likely to say you had *a houseful of people* rather than *a house of people*, or to use the phrase *a truckload of cows*, rather than *a truck of cows*. (A house full of guests has a slightly different connotation, as the focus is on the house, rather than the people.)

The suffixes '-ful' and '-load', can be added to any number of words to form collective expressions. Here are some examples:
- *a spoonful of medicine*
- *a handful of coins*
- *a bellyful of food*
- *a lorry-load of bricks*
- *a container-load of furniture.*

3. Quality

I am no grammarian, and I am not a purist. For me, expressions which convey ideas, thoughts and feelings must be included in my lists, whether they are commonly regarded as 'collective nouns' or not. The 'acceptable' collective nouns I have listed here can cover a *range of ideas*. James Lipton (who is rightly regarded as something of an expert), in his delightful book 'An Exaltation of Larks – or, The Venereal Game', has opted for six categories of collectives:

- Onomatopoeic *a murmuration of starlings, a gaggle of geese*
- Characteristic *a leap of leopards, a skulk of foxes*
- Appearance *a knot of toads, a bouquet of pheasants*
- Habitat *a shoal of bass, a nest of rabbits*
- Comment pro or con, reflecting the observer's point of view – *a richness of martens, a cowardice of curs*
- Error resulting from an incorrect transcription by a scribe or printer, faithfully preserved in the corrupted form by subsequent compilers – *a school of fish*

Many other sub-divisions and categories are possible – I am not sure where some nouns of measurement, for example, would fit into this list. James Lipton himself does not categorise each term, leaving it to the reader to decide. But this is too dry a process for me – and the wit and inventiveness of some of the expressions defy easy classification.

Many collective expressions are also alliterative, as in *a husk of hares*, or *a shiver of sharks*. These may simply be further examples of someone's delight in the *play of words* – as in *a play of sunlight* – on the ear.

a. States of being

Some 'acceptable' collective expressions are used to describe objects or people in different states, or with different qualities or characteristics. Hawks, for example, can have (at least) five different collective nouns attached to them, depending on the actions they are undertaking at the time:

- *a cast of hawks* (two, let fly)
- *a kettle of hawks* (riding a thermal of air)
- *a leash of hawks* (three, unleashed)
- *a screw of hawks* (in migrating swarms)
- *a stream of hawks* (flying out of a 'kettle').

I have identified dozens of terms for groups of people, again depending on their actions, collective mood, or reasons for grouping together.

b. Characteristics

Amongst the more traditionally accepted and archaic collective nouns, *a shrewdness of apes* appears to describe a quality of the apes' characters, and *a barren of mules* describes the animals' inability to breed. So can collective expressions be used to describe different qualities of something abstract, such as emotions? You will have already guessed my answer.

Look at these ...

- *a roar of laughter*
- *an outburst of laughter*
- *a guffaw of laughter*
- *a cackle of laughter*
- *a snigger of laughter*
- *a snort of laughter*
- *a ripple of laughter*
- *a tinkle of laughter*
- *a peal of laughter*

I am sure the linguistic purists would feel that 'laughter' is a 'non-count noun', and hence unquantifiable. But to me, these phrases not only describe the quality, and sometimes the sound, of the laughter, they also tell you something of the amount of laughter – a ripple and a snigger are obviously less than a roar, for example. An *outpouring of grief* is obviously a significantly more powerful emotion than is *a smattering of tears* – and *a glimmer of sunlight* will pale against *a blaze of sunshine*.

All of these phrases used above are common currency, and would instantly be understood by any English speaker. They describe a wide *range of emotions*, or a wide *span of light* – and I would argue that they are all collective expressions.

4. A freedom of expressions

The trouble (or blessing, depending on your point of view – here come the unicorns) is that we have complete *freedom of expression*, and can say just what we like. Laws of grammar are not legally binding, and there is no court that sits in judgement over whether or not a term is a 'collective noun' (other than *a pan of reviewers*, of course). The terms are certainly rarely covered in ordinary dictionaries – look up 'obstinacy' in most dictionaries and you are unlikely to find the explanation 'a collective term for a group of buffalo'. However, there will certainly be critics, and there will inevitably be grammatical pitfalls I will have lurched into headlong. But it will be pointless you telling me that one or other of these terms I offer "is not, strictly speaking, a collective expression". I am not speaking strictly, and there's the rub.

While I am discussing my failings, I might mention in passing that my in-depth knowledge on matters scientific, technical, medical, anatomical, legal, military, political (you get the picture), leaves much to be desired. Hence the lists of collective expressions within these specialist subjects may be somewhat anachronistic and odd. Until those who are experts in such fields supply me with some more appropriate terms, I will have to ask you to bear with me. You will be able to see where the gaps are – I would be happy for you to fill them in.

The essential point about all of the collective expressions listed here, is that at some point each phrase has been invented by somebody – whether for practicality or amusement is usually unknown, as the authors of virtually all collective terms are anonymous – see ** on page xxiv below. (In the few cases where I can identify an author or particular source, I have added a footnote.)

a. A muse of wordsmiths

Surfing around the various web-sites on 'collective nouns' trawled up by the search engines has revealed that people are fascinated by the group terms for things. So much so, that they are prone to making up their own – perhaps within or relating to their particular profession or interest group. (I have listed in Part III some of the websites with the most extensive collections.) So how does a collective expression become 'legitimised'? At what point is it acceptable to add a particular new term to a list of collective expressions with some sense of authority – given that there is no authority that deals with such matters?

Being somewhat obsessed with the subject, I rarely miss examples of the genre in the media. There are those who have a certain penchant for this sort of thing who continually delight me: Billy Connolly (a hero of mine), is reported, in wife Pamela Stephenson's book, Bravemouth, as suggesting a *saturnalia of wee bevies*, and Michael Foot, speaking on proposed parliamentary reform, once said an appointed Chamber would be *a seraglio of eunuchs*. Joseph Heller's Catch 22 richly contributed the expression *argosies of plenty* for Milo Minderbender's supply planes.

And the American Dialect Society a few years ago awarded its prize for 'Most Outrageous (new) Word of the Year' to *a cliterati of feminist writers*.

Language is such a fluid thing. In the mid-1970s a leader in the study of nuclear magnetic resonance reportedly proposed that if Hertz was the term used for cycles per second, then Avis should be the appropriate term for radians per second (apparently a unit of convenience in NMR). The editors of the appropriate journal balked. A few months later this same author wrote an elegant paper on

Proton Enhanced Nuclear Induction Spectroscopy, which was referred to by its acronym. An editor later remarked ironically, "You should'a let him have Avis".

This is perhaps what first fascinated me about collective expressions – who coined a phrase in the first place, and why? And how did that phrase then become common currency in the language? There are fashions in language just as much as in anything else, and many of the archaic terms, such as those listed in Dame Juliana Barnes' *Book of St Albans* (1486), have long since left the vocabulary of ordinary citizens, and now appear only as curiosities in lists such as these (*a superfluity of nuns, a malapertness* [cheekiness] *of pedlars, a piteousness of doves,* or *an incredibility of cuckolds,* for example). My feeling is that they are more than curiosities – they demonstrate the richness and flexibility both of the English language, and of people's creativity and imagination. Such terms are also windows into the minds and lifestyles of our ancestors in antiquity – but I would like to think they are of more than passing historical interest. Maybe we should be enriching our vocabularies by re-discovering and using such terms a little more often in our speech and writings – though I appreciate there is a limit as to how often one may find such terms as *a malapertness of pedlars* useful in everyday conversation. But *a charm of finches* and *an exaltation of skylarks* are well worth resurrecting. At the very least such terms should be inspirational.

b. An antiquity of words

With regard to the archaic terms – all those expressions from Dame Juliana and others of her ilk are at least 500 years old, and one imagines they must have acquired *a patina of respectability* from their very antiquity. The earliest surviving list of such terms is *The Egerton Manuscript*, dating from around 1450, which contains 106 terms (although the claim to the first ever published list may lie with Edward II's Huntsman, Master William Twici, who wrote *Le Art de Venery*, in Norman French in the 1320s). This was followed in 1476 by John Lydgate's *Debate between the Hors, Shepe and the Ghoos* – published within one year of the establishment of the printing process in Britain. *The Book of St Albans*, otherwise known as *The Book of Hawking and Hunting*, was published in 1486 by Dame Juliana Barnes (or Berners), a redoubtable prioress of the nunnery of Sopewell – though there is dispute as to her exclusive authorship. With 164 terms, it was the definitive list for over 400 years, being reprinted in 1496, and with no less than twelve editions appearing in the 16th century; it has been in print ever since, and is still available today. Other manuscripts appeared in the sixteenth century with further (though shorter) lists.

Dame Juliana listed what were called 'terms of venery' or 'venereal terms', and as she was a prioress, you can imagine that she was not writing the 15th century equivalent of an English Kama Sutra. Today we associate 'venereal' with sexually-transmitted diseases, but 'venery' means 'pertaining to hunting', and the Latin root gives us the connection of 'to desire (and therefore) to pursue'.

James Lipton quotes a wonderfully illuminating dialogue, penned by Sir Arthur Conan Doyle in his 1906 novel, 'Sir Nigel', between a tutor (Sir John Buttesthorn, Knight of Duplin) and his pupil (Sir Nigel). Sir John is tutoring Nigel on the hunt, and is anxious that his student should be familiar with the terms of the craft. "It is sooth," he says, "that for every collection of beasts of the forest, and for every gathering of birds of the air, there is their own private name so that none may be confused with another… In truth," he continues, "none can say that they know all, though I have myself picked off eighty and six for a wager at court, and it is said that the chief huntsman of the Duke of Burgundy has counted over a hundred – but it is in my mind that he may have found them as he went, for there was none to say him nay", says Sir John. It is true that many of the early terms were devised as part of the language of the hunt, but as many again related to groups of tradesmen or people generally, and all are serendipitous insights into the natures of both creatures and people.

c. **An inspiration of idioms**

So there is nothing to stop us inventing new collective expressions – indeed, new terms are being coined and used everyday in the media. *A raft of measures* (in the sense of *a package of measures*) is a relative late-comer to the scene, but is now heard (and more importantly, understood) frequently on the news.

So does publishing a collective term, or using it in the media, authenticate it? (I have included expressions from such *a dazzle of luminaries* as James Joyce, Wordsworth and Dylan Thomas on that premise.) If so, does an internet web-site count as media, and are the lists which I have found on the net therefore automatically authenticated as a result – or is this just a case of 'vanity publishing'? **An example has been cited of the expression *a whistle of modems*, which I have included in my lists, and appears to have become acceptable since being printed in an article in a computer magazine called *Byte*. Such contributions are often very clever or witty, and some seem logical (such as *an aarmoury of aardvarks* from one of Lipton's contributors); others seem to me trite, too contrived or just plain boring. Working on the somewhat hazardous assumption that those that appeal to me may also appeal to others, I have included some 'contributions' to web-sites (and to me personally) – together with some of my own invention – in italics. By the same token, and at the risk of appearing arbitrary, I have omitted those on other lists that seemed to me unsatisfactory for some reason. Hopefully, if others find these newly-minted terms attractive and worth repeating, they may well start using them themselves, and a new breed of collective terms may start appearing in any new lists which are published.

There is a lovely, if apocryphal, story of a group of four Oxford dons who pass a highly visible group of prostitutes on the street. Each don represents a different academic discipline, and therefore a different viewpoint. The first don comments, *"A jam of tarts"*. The second don (obviously a Music Fellow) retorts "No, *a flourish of strumpets!"* The third don (something of an expert on nineteenth-century English literature), not to be outdone, comes back with, "Not at all ... *an essay of Trollope's."* The fourth don (Modern English literature) settles the score with *"An anthology of English pros"*.

Lipton argues that, witty though these expressions are, they cannot be allowed, as they do not meet the criteria for a collective term in that they should illuminate or evaluate some quality of the thing described (though he almost allows *a flourish of strumpets*). I see his point, but I have allowed them all for no other reason than that they made me laugh. He goes on to contribute some of his own, for a group of homosexuals, which he likewise dismisses for the same reason: *a charm of fairies*, *a basket of fruit* and *a basket of faggots*. Apart from these terms being outrageously homophobic, I agree with him here – this may be witty word play, but it is not helpful or descriptive of the natures of homosexuals. Having said that, every homosexual I know is charming, so I'll allow *a charm of fairies*. (And some expressions can be cruel as well as witty – I've recently heard of *a shortage of dwarves*.)

d. A teapot of terms

Many collective expressions are terms of necessity or practicality, or describe the mundane and the commonplace (such as *a hod of bricks*, or *a mountain of ironing*), and therefore are often excluded from lists such as these. I have decided however, that my list should not be exclusive, and again I have erred on the side of generosity in my selection. More importantly, I feel it may be only through realising how often such collective expressions are used in our everyday speech, and in noticing what other (more exciting?) terms may be possible, that some of the more intrepid adventurers may be encouraged to experiment with the new, and to venture into deeper linguistic waters to try out their new-found knowledge.

So we have here not only the lyrical and the poetic, but also the legal and the political; not just the sonorous or the witty, but also the scientific and the technical, the banal and the domestic, the intangible, and the harsh slang of today's youth cultures. In another 500 years or so, our descendants may well find terms such as *a shitload of problems*, or *a stash of weed*, as quaint as we now find some of Dame Juliana's offerings, and smile, as we do.

e. And the 'other Profundities'?

As you whiffle, like the Jabberwock, through the tulgey wood of terms stretching from here to … the index (it only *seems* like eternity), and then stand back in uffish thought, you may reflect that certain of these terms are not 'collective' at all. You may have read my excuses, you may even be sympathetic to some of my wheedling arguments, and you may still, quite legitimately, come to the conclusion that there is indeed nothing collective about certain of these terms at all. (By this time, if you've read them all, you will of course be burbling gently.) OK – I agree with you. After several years of banging my brain cell against this great and wonderful *wall of words*, I did occasionally lose the plot. In fact I passed 'burbling' very early on, and graduated through 'dribbling' to 'gabbling incoherently' – which I passed with colours flying. "Is that the subject, or the object? Object ... or subject?" I would murmur to myself as I dropped off to sleep. If I can make an argument for *a shadow of doubt* (a shadow as a small quantity of doubt), what's wrong with *a gesture of solidarity*? What's that telling me? Is it about a certain type of gesture, or is it illuminating the strength of the solidarity? Or both? Beats me.

So if these troublesome terms are not collective expressions, what sort of expressions are they? Some are definitely metaphors, some are idioms – well, that's fine, but it's not enough. Even my learned friends drew a blank. But I can hear some of you word wizards out there now – "What is she banging on about? Of course the correct term is a ...". Well, do, please tell. Shine the light of your superior knowledge in my direction and help me out here.

In the meantime I decided to cover my considerable ass (as our friends across the pond have it) and added to the title "and other profundities". This is my get-out clause, my equivalent of a pre-nuptial agreement. So, any terms you feel are not collective expressions – well, of course they're not – they're profundities. As explained in the title. And snicker-snack to you too.

f. And finally ...

Cultures and their languages are never static, and as new situations, forms, structures, concepts, and ideas are formed, new words need to be coined to describe them. When I told a friend that I was compiling a book of collective nouns, he said "Oh, you mean like *a trip of hippies*?" – a phrase which was probably coined in the sixties or seventies, and which seems entirely appropriate. I had heard it some time ago, but had long forgotten it. Another friend's daughter recently cried out, "Daddy, look, there's *a block of seagulls!*". Technically, she used a collective term, and while it might not be satisfactory, it is not necessarily incorrect.

So it seems to me we are limited only by the scope of our imaginations. Effectively, any phrase which meets the criteria of including 'a noun singular in form used with a plural implication', is a collective expression in <u>my</u> book – so if the muse strikes you – go for it! Who's to say you're wrong?

Although you <u>may</u> want to avoid the 'block of seagulls' syndrome, and suffer the fate of the 'churl', as Sir John says to Sir Nigel, … *"lest you should make some blunder at table, so that those who are wiser may have the laugh of you, and we who love you may be shamed"*. Armed with this book, you will be well prepared to meet all comers.

5. A Field of Contenders

In the realm of collective nouns, there are possibly only two current contenders for the role of 'Master Collector' – James Lipton and Ivan G Sparkes. Rex Collings and Steve Palin (see the Bibliography for details) have useful and attractive collections of animals and birds, and there are several beautifully illustrated collections for children (*A Cache of Jewels, A Rattle of Bones*). However, with the exceptions of the afore-mentioned children's books and Steve Palin's, none of the others are readily available in bookshops today.

Having already written the foregoing preamble, I recently acquired (from the States) the most recent edition of James Lipton's *An Exaltation of Larks – The Ultimate Edition*, which came out nearly 20 years ago in 1993, and does not appear to have been superseded. The first printing came out in 1968, the book has now run to 12 editions, and in 25 years it has never been out of print. So, winner of the 'greatest number of collective noun books sold' award (although available only in the States) undoubtedly goes to Lipton. Despite this, Lipton is possibly second-in-line for the 'largest printed collection of collective nouns' award, though the earlier and reputedly more extensive *Dictionary of Collective Nouns and Group*

Terms by Ivan G Sparkes is now out of print and obtainable only from libraries or second-hand shops.

Having taken my existing Lipton references from a much earlier (1977) edition from my local library – which even then had to be ordered in – I was eager to see how Lipton had progressed with his opus. I was astonished. The man's scholarship and dedication are extraordinary. For 23 years he has researched the orthography of 'venereal terms' like a man possessed, and his sections on the archaic 'terms of venery' is exemplary, witty and highly illuminating.

As a taster, and an illustration of the tortuous route that must be followed to understand the sometimes impenetrable language of the archaic terms, here is Lipton on '*a cutting of cobblers*':

"*The key to this term lay at the end of a labyrinthine path [...]. The Book of St Albans was printed just ten years after the date that is generally taken as the dividing line between Middle and Modern English, and, to the inexpert eye, some of these terms can appear indecipherable. Take this one: what would you make of a Trynket of Corueseris? Well you would begin with Corueseris. The 'is' you know is a fifteenth century plural form. And you take the 'u' for a 'v' because until the 1820s, 'u' and 'v' were identical. Now you have the singular 'corveser', and this is where you begin in the Oxford English Dictionary, which says that 'corveser' is a variant of 'corviser'. Very well, you move on to 'corviser', and search through all the orthographic shapes it has taken through the centuries, coming finally to 'coruerseris', from French 'courvoisier', shoemaker. We seem to have half our term, but why a 'trynket'? Quickly enough you discover that the OED has 'tryn' as a variant spelling of 'trin', and then you come to the coup de foudre. Under 'trinket', the OED says 'From the similarity of form, it has been suggested that this is the same word as 'trenket' or' trynket', a small knife, specifically a shoemaker's knife'. Bingo!*"

So from *A Trinket of Corueseris*, Lipton finally reaches *A Cutting of Cobblers*. My learned lodger however, faced with the above, came up with an alternative solution. Firstly, given the tendency in 15th century Britain for wildly creative spellings, perhaps 'corueseris' was intended as a 'cordwainer' or shoemaker; now a cobbler was a lowly soul who just repaired shoes, whereas a shoemaker was a much more highly exalted trade. Secondly, in the 16th century, shoes – especially those for high-ranking noblemen or gentlewomen – were often ornate and highly decorated, possibly with pretty little 'folderols' or 'trinkets'. Voila – *a trinket of shoemakers*. So one man's 'cutting?' is another man's 'cobblers'? All of which just goes to show how difficult it is to be definitive when making statements about the intentions of a wordsmith who's been dead for over 500 years.

Dame Juliana is frequently as obscure, as the following list of a few of her original terms, together with Lipton's extrapolations, demonstrates:

Dame Juliana	James Lipton
a bleche of sowteris	*a blackening of shoemakers*
a ffraunch of mylneris	*a gobble of millers*
a credens of seweris	*a credence of tasters*
an unbrewing of kerueris	*a mess of carvers*

I now appreciate a little better how easy it is to read these 500-year old terms with a 21st century eye, and to get horribly confused. For example, my endearing *charm of finches*, may in fact be only a 'chirm', a word apparently meaning the sounds they make – but happily it is now too late. *A charm of finches* is now confidently appearing in all printed lists and at a web-site near you.

Lipton consults a dozen or more ancient books for reference, with several more recent scholarly publications for verification. And each of these older sources is likely to have a different spelling of each term, one from the other. Thank you, James, for saving the rest of us the effort of pinning these terms down into a form we can understand today. I have amended my lists accordingly, and annotated briefly where necessary. But if you want the nitty-gritty, the real low-down on these archaic terms, then Lipton is your man.

But the best bit of all about both Lipton and Sparkes, is that they care not a jot or a whit for count or non-count nouns. The terms do not appear in either book. In fact Lipton plunges straight in in his first listing with the eminently uncountable (and apt) *a baptism of fire* and gets up to speed with the amorphous *a head of steam*. As for Sparkes, he plods along happily through *knots of idioms* and *mobs of metaphors*, sprinkling *tumults of passions* and *faggots of improbabilities* along the way. So thanks for that, boys. If it matters not to the masters, then why should the pupil fret?

But I'm afraid I must be a little picky. Sparkes' lists, though sensibly categorised into 'Collective Nouns' in Part 1, and 'Subjects' in Part 2, are unrelieved by a single illustration, and often distinctly odd. ('Heavenware' as a group term for the 'inmates' of heaven? 'A camp' for a ridge-shaped heap of potatoes? [Surely that should be 'a clamp'?] *A girdle of din*? *A plump of pain*? [What?] And not a reference to back them up? Well, I ask you ...) In his defence, most of his nouns seem to have had at least some previous existence – though I feel there may be some cross-fertilisation between Sparkes and Lipton.

And then there is Lipton. The first third of his latest edition covers, as comprehensively as one could wish, the archaic terms, and some others commonly used in everyday speech. It is in the second part of his book that I drift away dissatisfied. When I first started investigating collective expressions I hunted in vain for a comprehensive, cross-referenced listing, not just of living creatures, people, and a few objects, but a thesaurus of all such common terms – in the same way as any good grammarian may (I imagine!) have dictionaries of acronyms, synonyms and slang on their bookshelves, for example. Lipton does not come up trumps for me here. Instead he opts to play his own 'venereal game', inviting inventions from his readers and devising many of his own. Laudable, but ultimately this can become formulaic and a tad predictable – and over half of his 1100 venereal terms fall into this category.

Yes, I know I have invented a few of my own here, (and borrowed some of Lipton's for my lists), but usually where I felt a need as no other suitable term was presenting itself (rainbows, ladybirds and balloons are cases in point). And I am, you will already have noticed, always eager to encourage others to share my obsession, but there is a limit to how much I can take of *'a tabula rasa of empiricists', 'a stratum of geologists', 'a gout of rheumatologists',* and so on. Although some of these are very clever or witty, in some cases they are merely contrived or convoluted (and with terms like *'a glossolalia of pentecostals'*, almost as impenetrable as Dame Juliana.) Unfortunately Lipton devotes the remainder of his book to these contributions, missing out on a whole *gallimaufry of expressions* that already exist and are in common use, such as *a plume of feathers, an archipelago of islands* or *a pearl of wisdom*. And of course many of the expressions he has accepted are from enthusiasts of American professions or sports terms meaningless to me – and his cross-referencing is non-existent.

But enough; James and Ivan are still my heroes, and had it not been for their dogged determination and unflagging enthusiasm – and their omissions – I would not have felt driven to bridge that gap with the span of my own untutored odyssey. It was the discovery that they claim over 1000 collective nouns apiece (although it is almost impossible to count them) that led me to realise that my own humble, early efforts, topping as they then did, over 2000, may not have been that humble after all. With the final count now well in excess of 3000, even if as many as a third of them were disputable, then – dammit, I, too, could'a been a contender!

6. An Acknowledgement of Thanks...
...and a *salvo of bravos* to friends Sandy Angove, Dot Campbell, Cathy Lake, Ruth Lewarne and (sadly, the late) Steve Adler for their encouragement and support, particularly to Steve for his literary allusions. Also to my long-suffering and endlessly supportive partner, Chris, and my sons: Davy for nagging and urging me on, and Jan for his forbearance and coffee-making services, and to all three, from me, my undying love.

7. An Endnote ...

Spotted on an internet website:
[From BW] *This question has bothered me on a kind of conceptual, rather than a linguistic, level. The word "fesnyng" is the collective noun given to ferrets. A fesnyng of ferrets is one of those idiomatic and endearing terms now facing extinction. [...] So, there is the rough Saxon term "fesnyng", heavy with both alliteration and assonance: "a fesnyng of ferrets". Lovely. Here, though, is the problem. Ferrets are fiercely solitary animals. They are no more likely to get together in a fesnyng than you or I are. So how, or why, does this word exist? How can you label something which does not ever happen? The argument: make your own fesnyng. Put a group of ferrets together (I believe that a bathtub is usually used for this purpose), and one might claim to be entitled to say "there's a fesnyng in my bath". However, I disagree. You do not have a fesnyng any more than several lions from different prides constitute one pride when put together. Any thoughts??*

   [Reply from ghanka] I have something much better than mere thoughts. Last night, in the spirit of scientific research, I invited several people over for a few beers. In my bathtub upstairs I installed 12 ferrets. Then, whenever anyone returned from using the bathroom I asked them, "Did you notice anything unusual in the bathroom?" Not a single individual said he noticed anything unusual, but when I pressed further two or three of them did say, "Well, there was a fesnyng in your bathtub...." Now I completely agree with your contention that just gathering together a few lions from different prides would not constitute a new pride any more than gathering together a random bunch of people would result in a family, but what the above ferret experiment seems to show is that, since ferrets do not naturally form fesnyngs, the fact that I formed one unnaturally – so to speak – in my bathtub, does not make it any less a fesnyng, since there is no more genuine fesnyng to compare it to. In a further spirit of scientific research I plan to put 8 or 10 unrelated people of various genders in my bathtub and see if that results in a family ... I hope this clears up the mystery.

[Courtesy of newsgroup: alt.usage.English]

How to use this book

1. The lists are displayed alphabetically by noun in the left-hand column of each page, and alphabetically by collective or descriptive term in each right-hand column – so, for example, you can look up a number of descriptions for groups of monkeys, or a number of groups for whom the collective term 'troop' can be used.
2. The numbering of the columns is designed to count the total number of different nouns (to the left), as against the total number of different collective nouns (to the right).
3. 'A' or 'An' is understood to prefix each collective noun.
4. Italicised terms denote expressions submitted to internet websites, or inventions of my own.
5. Every collective or descriptive term used in the book is included in the index in Part 3, for ease of reference.
6. A few collective expressions may have inadvertently sneaked into more than one chapter, especially in relation to people.

Key to abbreviations used in the book:

arch .... archaic	Austr ..... Australian	b .... bottle
dial. .... dialect	Fr. .... French	gall .... gallons
lbs .... pounds (weight)	ltr .... litres	tog .... together
yds .... yards		

Chapter One

A Nobility of Beasts

'a panoply of elephants'

Gallimaufry

'a mischief of rats'

1. Animals

Sorted by noun	Sorted by collective noun
1. *aarmoury of aardvarks*	1. *aarmoury of aardvarks*
2. bag of (shot) animals	2. ambush of tigers
cage of animals	3. *armament of armadillos*
circus of animals	4. array of hedgehogs
community of animals	5. *aurora of polar bears*
cull of animals	6. bag of (shot) animals
farmyard of animals	7. band of coyote
genus of animals	band of gorillas
phylum of animals	8. barrel of monkeys
polyzoarium (colony) of animals	9. barren of mules
sanctuary of animals	10. *belfry of bats*
species of animals	11. *bellow of bulls*
vivarium of (small) animals	12. bench of (show) dogs
zoo of animals	13. bevy of otters
3. *durante of anteaters*	bevy of roes/roe deer (6 head)
4. cluster of antelopes	14. bloat of hippopotami [b]
herd of antelopes	15. bobbery of (hunting) dogs
5. shrewdness of apes	16. boogle of weasels
6. *armament of armadillos*	17. bow of cattle

Chapter 1: Animals

fez of armadillos	18. brace of bucks (2)
hoover of armadillos [g]	brace of foxes (2)
7. coffle of asses	brace of geldings (2)
drove of asses	brace of greyhounds (2)
herd of asses	brace of hares (2)
pace of asses	19. buffoonery of orangutans
8. congress of baboons	20. bunch of cattle
flange of baboons	21. burden of mules [a]
rumpus of baboons	22. burrow of gophers
troop of baboons	burrow of rabbits
9. cast of badgers	23. bury of conies
cete of badgers	bury of rabbits
colony of badgers	24. business of ferrets
litter of badger cubs	25. busyness of ferrets
sett of badgers	26. byre of cattle
10. *waddle of basset hounds*	27. cackle of hyenas
11. *belfry of bats*	28. cage of animals
cloud of bats	29. *candle of tapirs*
swarm of bats	30. caravan of camels
12. *maul of bears*	31. cartload of monkeys
sleuth of bears	cartload of chimpanzees
sloth of bears	32. cast of badgers
13. *nobility of beasts*	cast of lambs
14. colony of beavers	33. cavayard of mules
family of beavers	34. cete of badgers
lodge of beavers	35. chine of polecats
society of beavers	36. circus of animals
15. herd of bison	37. citadel of mole burrows
16. sute of bloodhounds [e]	38. clan of hyenas
	39. clash of bucks
	40. *clipping of geldings*
	41. cloud of bats
	42. clowder (or clouder) of cats
	43. cluster of antelopes
	cluster (or clutter) of cats
17. singular (or singularity) of	44. coalition of cheetahs

3

      boars
      sounder of wild boar
18. brace of bucks (2)
      clash of bucks
      leash of bucks (3)
19. herd of buffalo
      gang of buffalo
      obstinacy of buffaloes
      stampede of buffalo
20. drove of bullocks
21. *bellow of bulls*
      ring of bulls
22. caravan of camels
      flock of camels

      train of camels
23. herd of caribou
24. dray of carthorses
25. clowder (or clouder) of cats
      cluster (or clutter) of cats
      glaring of cats
      glorying of cats
      intrigue of cats
      pounce of cats [b]
      rain of cats and dogs
26. bow of cattle
      bunch of cattle
      byre of cattle
      creaght of cattle (Gaelic
         'drove')
      drift of cattle (dial)

45. coffle of asses
46. cohort of zebra
47. colony of beavers
      colony of badgers
      colony of chinchillas
      colony of meerkats
      colony of rabbits
      colony of voles
48. column of iguanodon
49. community of animals
50. company of moles
51. confusion of weasels
52. congress of baboons
53. corps of giraffe
54. corral of horses
55. coterie of prairie dogs
56. couple of conies
      couple of foxhounds
      couple of harriers
      couple of impala
      couple of sheep (ewe + 1
         lamb)
      couple of spaniels
57. court of kangaroos [d]
58. cowardice of curs

59. crash of hippopotami
      crash of rhinoceros

Chapter 1: Animals

    drive of cattle
    drove of cattle
    flote of cattle
    herd of cattle
    kraal of cattle
    mob of cattle (US & Austr)
    muster of cattle (Austr)
    roundup of cattle
    stampede of cattle
27. herd of chamois
28. coalition of cheetahs
29. cartload of chimpanzees
30. colony of chinchillas
31. rag of colts
    rake of colts
32. bury of conies
    couple of conies
33. flink of cows (12 or more)
    herd of cows
    kine of cows
    lorry-load of cows
34. band of coyote
    pack of coyotes
    run of coyotes [b]
    shift of coyotes
    wiliness of coyotes
35. litter of cubs
36. cowardice of curs
37. great herd of deer (80 head)
    herd of deer
    leash of deer (3)
    little herd of deer (20 head)
    middle herd of deer (40)
    mob of deer
    parcel of deer
    rangale (rabble) of deer

60. creaght of cattle (Gaelic 'drove')
61. crèche of (young) dinosaurs
62. cry of hounds
63. *cuddle of koalas*
64. cull of animals
65. curiosity of mongooses
66. den of foxes
    den of wolves
67. destruction of wildcats
68. double couple of sheep (ewe + 2 lambs)
69. dout (or dowt) of wildcats
70. down (don or dun) of hares
    down of sheep

71. doylt of tame swine
72. dray of carthorses
    dray (or drey) of squirrels
73. drift of cattle (dial)
    drift of hogs
    drift of sheep (dial)
    drift of wild swine
74. drive of cattle
75. drove of asses
    drove of bullocks
    drove of cattle
    drove of donkeys

5

Gallimaufry

38. crèche of (young) dinosaurs
    herd of (plant-eating) dinosaurs
    pack of (carnivorous) dinosaurs
39. bench of (show) dogs
    bobbery of (hunting) dogs
    pack of dogs
    kennel of dogs
    patrol of (guard) dogs
40. drove of donkeys
41. herd of eland
42. herd of elephant
    panoply of elephants
    parade of elephants
    rampage of elephants
    tribe of elephants
43. gang of elk (US)
    herd of elk
44. refugium of endangered species
45. business of ferrets
    busyness of ferrets
    fesnying of ferrets
46. brace of foxes (2)
    den of foxes
    earth of foxes
    leash of foxes (3)
    skulk of foxes
    troop of foxes
47. couple of foxhounds (2)
    relay of foxhounds (2 or 3 couples)
48. brace of geldings (2)
    clipping of geldings
49. horde of gerbils

    drove of hares
    drove of kine
76. *durante of anteaters*
77. earth of foxes
78. fall of lambs
79. family of beavers
    family of meerkats
    family of otters
80. fare of pigs
81. farmyard of animals
82. farrow of piglets
83. fesnying of ferrets

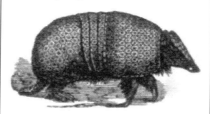

84. fez of armadillos
85. field of pigs
    field of racehorses
86. flange of baboons
87. fleet of greyhounds
88. flick of hares
89. flink of cows (12 or more)
90. flock of camels
    flock of goats
    flock of sheep
91. flote of cattle
92. fold of Highlanders (cattle)
    fold of sheep
93. fortress of moles
94. gallop of greyhounds
95. gam of weasels
96. gambol of lambs

50. corps of giraffe
    herd of giraffe
    journey of giraffes
    totter of giraffes

    tower of giraffes
51. implausibility of gnus [b]
52. flock of goats
    herd of goats
    tribe of goats
    trip of goats
53. burrow of gophers
    pocket of gophers
54. band of gorillas
    whoop of gorillas
55. brace of greyhounds (2)
    fleet of greyhounds
    gallop of greyhounds
    leash of greyhounds (3)
56. group of guinea pigs
    laboratory of guinea pigs
57. horde of hamsters
58. brace of hares (2)
    down (don or dun) of hares

97. gang of buffalo
    gang of elk (US)
    gang of moose
    gang of weasels
98. gaze of racoons [b]
99. genus of animals
100. giggle of hyenas
101. glaring of cats
102. glorying of cats
103. great bevy of roe deer (12)
104. great herd of roe deer (80)
105. group of guinea pigs
     group of lemurs
106. grumble of pugs
107. harras of (breeding) horses
108. herd of antelopes
     herd of asses
     herd of bison
     herd of buffalo
     herd of caribou
     herd of cattle
     herd of chamois
     herd of cows
     herd of deer
     herd of (plant-eating)
       dinosaurs
     herd of eland
     herd of elephant
     herd of elk
     herd of giraffe
     herd of goats
     herd of hartebeest
     herd of horses
     herd of ibex
     herd of llamas
     herd of moose

Gallimaufry

drove of hares	herd of pigs
flick of hares	herd of reindeer
husk (or huske) of hares	herd of sheep
lease (leash) of hares	herd of swine
lie of hares	herd of wildebeest
madness of March hares	herd of yaks
trace of hares	herd of zebra
trip of hares	109. hide of tigers
59. couple of harriers	110. hirsel of sheep (entire stock of a farm)
60. herd of hartebeast	
61. array of hedgehogs	111. hoover of armadillos ^g
prickle of hedgehogs	112. horde of gerbils
62. fold of Highlanders (cattle)	horde of hamsters
63. parcel of hinds	horde of rats
64. bloat of hippopotami ^b	113. huddle of hippos
crash of hippopotami	114. hurtle of sheep
huddle of hippos	115. husk (or huske) of hares
regular-army of hippopotami ^f	husk of jackrabbits
thunder of hippos	116. hutch of rabbits
65. drift of hogs	117. implausibility of gnus ^b
parcel (or passel) of hogs	118. intrigue of cats
66. corral of horses	119. journey of giraffe
harras of (breeding) horses	120. kennel of dogs
herd of horses	kennel of hounds (raches) ^h
ramuda of horses (large group)	121. kindle of kittens
	kindle of leverets
	kindle of rabbits
	122. kine of cows
	123. kraal of cattle
	124. laboratory of guinea pigs
	125. labour of moles
	126. leap (or lepe) of leopards
span of horses (pair harnessed together)	127. lease (leash) of hares (3)
	128. leash of bucks (3)
stable of horses	leash of deer (3)
stampede of horses	leash of foxes (3)

Chapter 1: Animals

    stud of (breeding) horses
    team of (working) horses
      (dial)
67. cry of hounds
    kennel of hounds (raches) [h]
    leash of hounds (3)
    mute of hounds
    pack of hounds (raches) [h]
68. team of huskies
69. cackle of hyenas
    clan of hyenas
    giggle of hyenas
70. herd of ibex
71. column of iguanodon
72. couple of impala
73. husk of jackrabbits
74. court of kangaroos [d]
    mob of kangaroos
    troop of kangaroo
75. drove of kine
76. kindle of kittens
    litter of kittens
77. cuddle of koalas
    mob of koalas
78. cast of lambs
    fall of lambs
    gambol of lambs
    rack of lambs
79. group of lemurs
    troop of lemurs
80. leap (or lepe) of leopards
    prowl of leopards
81. kindle of leverets
82. pride of lions
    sawt (or sault) of lions
    sowse of lions

    leash of greyhounds (3)
    leash of hounds (3)
129. lie of hares
130. litter of badger cubs
    litter of cubs
    litter of kittens
    litter of piglets/pigs
    litter of pups
    litter of whelps

131. little herd of deer (20 head)
132. lodge of beavers
133. lorry-load of cows
134. machination of monkeys
135. madness of March hares
136. mask of racoons
137. maul of bears
138. meet of racehorses
139. meinie of oxen
    meinie of sheep
140. menace of mongooses
141. menage of mongrels

Gallimaufry

troop of lions	142. menagerie of wild animals
83. truckload of livestock	143. middle bevy of roe deer (10)
84. herd of llamas	144. middle herd of deer (40)
85. order of mammals	145. migration of reindeer
86. stud of mares	146. mischief of mice
87. richesse of martens	mischief of rats
richness of martens	147. mission of monkeys
88. colony of meerkats	148. mob of cattle (US & Austr)
family of meerkats	mob of deer
mob of meerkats	mob of kangaroos (Austr)
89. mischief of mice	mob of koalas (Austr)
nest of mice	mob of meerkats
90. citadel of mole burrows	mob of sheep (Austr)
91. company of moles	mob of wallabies (Austr)
fortress of moles	mob of wombats (Austr)
labour of moles	149. movement of moles
movement of moles	150. mulada of mules
mumble of moles	151. mumble of moles
92. curiosity of mongooses	152. muster of cattle (Austr)
menace of mongooses	muster of sheep (Austr)
93. menage of mongrels	153. mute of hounds
94. barrel of monkeys	154. nest of mice
cartload of monkeys	nest of rabbits
machination of monkeys	nest of trotters (pigs)
mission of monkeys	155. nobility of beasts
tribe of monkeys	156. nursery of racoons
troop of monkeys	157. obstinacy of buffaloes
wilderness of monkeys	158. order of mammals
95. gang of moose	159. pace of asses
herd of moose	160. pack of coyotes
96. remuda of mounts (cowboy)	pack of (carnivorous)
97. barren of mules	dinosaurs
burden of mules [a]	pack of dogs
cavayard of mules	pack of hounds (raches) [h]
mulada of mules	pack of mules
pack of mules	pack of polar bears

Chapter 1: Animals

    rake of mules
    span of mules
98. buffoonery of orangutans
99. bevy of otters
    family of otters
    romp of otters [b]
100. meinie of oxen
    rake of oxen
    team of oxen
    yoke of oxen
101. pandemonium of pandas
102. pomp of pekingese
103. fare of pigs
    farrow of piglets
    field of pigs
    herd of pigs
    litter of piglets/pigs
    sty of pigs
    trip of pigs
104. purr of platypuses
105. *aurora of polar bears*
    pack of polar bears
106. chine of polecats
107. string of ponies
108. salon of poodles
109. prickle of porcupines
110. passel of possum
111. coterie of prairie dogs
    town of prairie dogs
112. grumble of pugs
113. piddle of puppies [b]
    litter of pups
114. burrow of rabbits
    bury of rabbits
    colony of rabbits
    hutch of rabbits

    pack of rats
    pack of stoats
    pack of weasels
    pack of wolves
161. pandemonium of pandas
162. panoply of elephants
163. parade of elephants
164. parcel of deer
    parcel of hinds
    parcel (or passel) of hogs
165. passel of possum
166. patrol of (guard) dogs
167. pen of sheep
168. phylum of animals
169. piddle of puppies [b]

170. plague of rats
171. pocket of gophers
172. polyzoarium (colony) of animals
173. pomp of Pekingese
174. pop of weasels
175. pounce of cats [b]
176. prickle of hedgehogs
    prickle of porcupines
177. pride of lions
178. prowl of leopards

kindle of rabbits
nest of rabbits
rabbitry of (breeding) rabbits
trace of rabbits
warren of rabbits
wrack of rabbits (kittens)
115. gaze of racoons ᵇ
mask of racoons
nursery of racoons
116. field of racehorses
meet of racehorses
string of racehorses
117. horde of rats
mischief of rats
pack of rats
plague of rats
rabble of rats
swarm of rats
118. herd of reindeer
migration of reindeer
119. crash of rhinoceros
stubbornness of rhinoceros
120. bevy of roes/roe deer (6 head)
great bevy of roe deer (12)
middle bevy of roe deer (10)
121. couple of sheep (ewe + 1 lamb)
double couple of sheep (ewe + 2 lambs)
down of sheep
drift of sheep (dial)
flock of sheep
fold of sheep
herd of sheep
hirsel of sheep (entire stock

179. purr of platypuses
180. rabbitry of (breeding) rabbits
181. rabble of rats
182. rack of lambs
183. rag of colts
184. rain of cats and dogs
185. rake of colts
rake of mules
rake of oxen
186. rampage of elephants
187. ramuda of horses (large group)
188. rangale (rabble) of deer
189. refugium of endangered species
190. relay of foxhounds (2/3 couples)
191. regular-army of hippopotami ᶠ
192. remuda of mounts (cowboy)
193. reserve of wild animals
194. richesse of martens
195. richness of martens
196. ring of bulls
197. romp of otters ᵇ
198. roundup of cattle
roundup of sheep
199. rout (or route) of wolves
200. rumpus of baboons
201. run of coyotes ᵇ
202. salon of poodles
203. sanctuary of animals
204. sawt (or sault) of lions
205. scurry of squirrels ᵇ
206. sett of badgers
207. shift of coyotes
208. shrewdness of apes

Chapter 1: Animals

of a farm)
hurtle of sheep
meinie of sheep
mob of sheep (Austr)
muster of sheep (Austr)
pen of sheep

roundup of sheep
trip of sheep (dial)
122. stench of skunks
surfeit of skunks
123. slumber of sloths
124. couple of spaniels
125. dray (or drey) of squirrels
scurry of squirrels ᵇ
126. pack of stoats
127. doylt of tame swine
drift of wild swine
herd of swine
sounder of (tame) swine ᶜ
128. candle of tapirs
129. terror of terriers
130. ambush of tigers
hide of tigers

209. singular (or singularity) of boars
210. skulk of foxes
211. sleuth of bears
212. sloth of bears
213. slumber of sloths
214. sneak of weasels
215. society of beavers
216. sounder of (tame) swine ᶜ
sounder of wild boar
217. sowse of lions
218. span of horses (pair harnessed together)
span of mules
219. species of animals
220. stable of horses
221. stampede of buffalo
stampede of cattle
stampede of horses
222. stench of skunks
223. streak of tigers
224. stretch of giraffes
225. string of horses
string of ponies
226. stripe of zebras
227. stubbornness of rhinoceros
228. stud of (breeding) horses
stud of mares
229. sty of pigs
230. surfeit of skunks
231. sute of bloodhounds ᵉ
232. swarm of bats
swarm of rats
233. team of (working) horses (dial)
team of huskies

streak of tigers
131. nest of trotters (pigs)
132. colony of voles
133. mob of wallabies

134. boogle of weasels
   confusion of weasels
   gam of weasels
   gang of weasels
   pack of weasels
   pop of weasels
   sneak of weasels
135. litter of whelps
136. menagerie of wild animals
   reserve of wild animals
137. dowt (or dout) of wildcats
   destruction of wildcats
138. herd of wildebeest
139. den of wolves
   pack of wolves
   rout (or route) of wolves
   troop of wolves
140. mob of wombats
   warren of wombats
   wisdom of wombats
141. herd of yaks
142. cohort of zebra
   herd of zebra
   stripe of zebras
   zeal of zebra

team of oxen
234. terror of terriers
235. thunder of hippos
236. totter of giraffes
237. tower of giraffes
238. town of prairie dogs
239. trace of hares
   trace of rabbits
239. train of camels
241. tribe of elephants
   tribe of goats
   tribe of monkeys
242. trip of goats (dial)
   trip of hares
   trip of pigs
   trip of sheep (dial)
243. troop of baboons
   troop of foxes
   troop of kangaroo
   troop of lemurs
   troop of lions
   troop of monkeys
   troop of wolves
244. truckload of livestock
245. vivarium of (small) animals
246. waddle of basset hounds
247. warren of rabbits
   warren of wombats
248. wilderness of monkeys
249. wiliness of coyotes
250. whoop of gorillas
251. wisdom of wombats
252. wrack of rabbits (kittens)
253. yoke of oxen
254. zeal of zebra
255. zoo of animals

Chapter 1: Animals

Notes

a. Archaic, from one of the 16th century manuscripts (most commonly, The Book of Hawking & Hunting', by Dame Juliana Barnes, 1486).
b. From James Lipton: 'An Exaltation of Larks'.
c. The Book of St Albans says of this term: 'Twelve make a sounder of wild swine, sixteen a middle sounder and twenty or more a great sounder.'
d. The phrase "A court of kangaroos" is frequently thought to be legitimate, given the (quite unrelated) expression "a kangaroo court".
e. Probably from 'pursuit'.
f. From Flanders & Swann 'The Hippopotamus Song'
g. Believed to have originated during the Great Depression in America. Armadillos were often eaten instead of the "chicken in every pot" promised by President Herbert Hoover. (From Alon Shulman's book)
h. Raches are hounds that hunt by scent.

'a stubbornness of rhinoceros'

Gallimaufry

'a mission of monkeys'

'a ring of bulls'

Chapter Two

A Flight of Fancy – Birds

'a battery of quails'

Gallimaufry

'a cast of hawks'

2. Birds

Sorted by noun	Sorted by collective noun
1. rookery of albatross	1. ascension of larks
2. colony of auks (on land)	2. asylum of loons
flock of auks (at sea)	3. aviary of birds
loomery of auks	4. badelynge (or badling) of ducks
raft of auks (on water)	5. bag of (shot) birds
3. colony of avocets	6. *ballet of swans*
4. bag of (shot) birds	7. band of jays
5. aviary of birds	8. bank of swans
dissimulation of (small) birds	9. battery of chickens
fleet of (small) birds	battery of quails
flight of (small) birds	10. bazaar of guillemots
flock of (small) birds	11. bellowing of bullfinches
parcel of birds (dial)	12. bevy of larks (a company of)
pilmer of birds (dial)	bevy of partridges
pod of birds (small flock)	bevy of quail

Chapter 2: A Flight of Fancy

sanctuary of birds	bevy of swans
volary (or volery) of birds (in an aviary)	13. bew of partridges
	14. *bob of wagtails*
woodchoir of birds (chorus)	15. boil of hawks (2 or more spiralling in flight)
6. sedge of bitterns	
7. brood of black game	16. bouquet of pheasants
8. chain of bobolinks [b]	17. brace of grouse
9. chatter of budgerigars	brace of pheasant
10. bellowing of bullfinches	18. brood of black game
11. flock of bustards	brood of chickens
12. wake of buzzards [b]	brood of grouse (single family)
13. tok of capercailzies (arch.)	
14. mews of capons	brood of hens
15. *radiance of cardinals*	19. brook of pheasants
16. battery of chickens	20. building of rooks
brood of chickens	21. bunch of ducks
cletch of chickens (dial)	bunch of teal
clutch of chickens	bunch of waterfowl
flock of chickens	bunch of wildfowl
peep of chickens	22. cargo of eagles
17. hatch of chicks	23. carpet of vultures
18. chattering of choughs	24. cast of falcons (2)
clattering of choughs	cast of hawks (2, let fly)
19. *posse of cock-turkeys*	cast of vultures
20. commotion of coots	25. caucus of crows
covert (or cover) of coots	26. cete of finches
fleet of coots	27. chain of bobolinks [b]
rasp of coots	28. charm of falcons
	charm of finches
	charm of goldfinches
	charm of hummingbirds
	29. chatter of budgerigars
	chatter of starlings
	30. chattering of choughs
21. flight of cormorants	chattering of goldfinches
gulp of cormorants [b]	chattering of hummingbirds

22. herd of cranes
    sedge (or sledge) of cranes
23. caucus of crows
    clan of crows
    hoard of crows
    hover of crows
    murder of crows
    storytelling of crows
24. *squat of cuckoos*
25. head of curlews
    herd of curlews
26. murder of currawongs [e]
27. trip of dotterel
28. columbarium (dovecote) of doves
    cote of doves
    dole (or dule) of doves
    duet of doves (pair)
    flight of doves (migrating)
    piteousness of doves
    prettying of doves
29. clatch of ducklings (off nest)
    clutch of ducklings (on nest)
    fleet of ducklings (on water)
30. badelynge (or badling) of ducks
    bunch of ducks
    column of (wild) ducks
    dopping of ducks (diving)
    fleet of (wild) duck
    flush of ducks (brood)
    paddling of ducks (on water)
    plump of ducks (in flight)
    raft of ducks
    safe of ducks
31. chime of wrens
32. chirm of finches
33. chyne of seabirds (dial)
34. circus of puffins
35. clamour of rooks
36. clan of crows
37. clatch of ducklings (off nest)
38. clattering of choughs
39. cletch of chickens (dial)
40. cloud of dunlin
    cloud of sea fowl
41. cluster of knots
42. clutch of chickens
    clutch of ducklings (on nest)
    clutch of partridges
43. clutter of starlings
44. coil of teal
45. colony of auks (on land)
    colony of avocets
    colony of gulls (community)
    colony of ibises
    colony of penguins
46. columbarium (dovecote) of doves
47. column of (wild) duck
48. commotion of coots
49. company of gannets
    company of parrots
    company of widgeon
50. concentration of kingfishers
51. concourse of seabirds
52. congregation of plovers
    congregation of rooks
53. conspiracy of ravens
54. *constable of ravens*
55. convocation of eagles

Chapter 2: A Flight of Fancy

sail of ducks team of wild ducks (in flight) 31. cloud of dunlin flight of dunlins fling of dunlins (or oxbirds) 32. cargo of eagles convocation of eagles eyrie (or aerie) of eagles 33. mob of emus 34. nest of fledglings 35. cast of falcons (2) charm of falcons 36. cete of finches charm of finches chirm of finches trembling of finches trimming of finches  37. flamboyance of flamingos flurry of flamingos pat of flamingos regiment of flamingos skein of flamingos stand of flamingos ᵇ 38. company of gannets *freefall of gannets* *plummet of gannets*	56. *corroboree of lyre birds* 57. cote of doves 58. council of rooks 59. covert (or cover) of coots 60. covey of grouse covey of partridges covey of ptarmigan covey of quail 61. crèche of penguins 62. crop of turkeys 63. crowd of ibis crowd of redwing 64. darkening of jackdaws 65. dazzle of hummingbirds 66. deceit of lapwings 67. descent of woodpeckers 68. desert of lapwing 69. dissimulation of (small) birds 70. doading of sheldrake 71. dole (or dule) of doves 72. dopping of ducks (diving) dopping of goosander dopping of merganser dopping of sheldrake 73. dread of terns ᵍ 74. drift of quail drift of swans 75. dropping of pigeons 76. drum of goldfinches drum of hummingbirds 77. drumming of grouse 78. duet of doves (pair) duet of turkeys 79. *durante of toucans* 80. *embarrassment of red-faced*

21

39. gaggle of geese
    nide of geese
    skein of geese (in flight)
    team of geese
    wedge of geese
40. charm of goldfinches
    chattering of goldfinches
    drum of goldfinches
    glister of goldfinches
    troubling of goldfinches
    vein of goldfinches
41. dopping of goosander
42. flight of goshawks
43. brace of grouse
    brood of grouse (single family)
    covey of grouse
    drumming of grouse
    lek of grouse
    pack of grouse (large group)
44. bazaar of guillemots
45. rasp of guineafowl
46. colony of gulls (community)
    flock of gulls
    pack of gulls
    screech of gulls
    squall of gulls
47. boil of hawks (2 or more spiralling in flight)

warblers
81. exaltation (or exalting) of larks
    exaltation of skylarks
82. eye of pheasants
83. eyrar of swans
84. eyrie (or aerie) of eagles
85. fall of woodcock/woodchucks
86. filth of starlings
87. flamboyance of flamingos
88. fleet of (small) birds
    fleet of coots
    fleet of (wild) duck
    fleet of ducklings (on water)
    fleet of mudhen (American coot)
89. flight of (small) birds
    flight of cormorants
    flight of doves (migrating)
    flight of dunlins
    flight of goshawks
    flight of pigeons
    flight of pochards
    flight of swallows
90. fling of dunlins (or oxbirds)
    fling of sandpipers
91. flock of auks (at sea)
    flock of (small) birds
    flock of bustards
    flock of chickens
    flock of gulls
    flock of pigeons
    flock of swifts
    flock of turkeys
92. flurry of flamingos

Chapter 2: A Flight of Fancy

cast of hawks (let fly)
kettle of hawks (riding a thermal)
leash of hawks
screw of hawks (in migrating swarms)
stream of hawks (out of a kettle)
48. brood of hens
49. sedge of herons
serge of herons
siege of herons
50. charm of hummingbirds
chattering of hummingbirds
dazzle of hummingbirds
drum of hummingbirds
hover of hummingbirds
shimmer of hummingbirds
troubling of hummingbirds
51. colony of ibises
crowd of ibis
52. darkening of jackdaws
train of jackdaws
53. band of jays
party of jays
scolding of jays
54. concentration of kingfishers
halcyon of kingfishers
55. cluster of knots
56. deceit of lapwings
desert of lapwing
57. ascension of larks
bevy of larks (a company of)
exaltation (or exalting) of larks
springful of larks [c]

93. flush of ducks (brood)
flush of mallard (on land)
94. *formality of penguins*
95. *freefall of gannets*
96. gaggle of geese
97. *gallon of petrels*
98. game of swans
99. gang of (wild) turkeys [d]

100. gatling of woodpeckers
101. glister of goldfinches
102. gobble of turkeys
103. gulp of cormorants [b]
gulp of magpies
gulp of swallows
104. halcyon of kingfishers
105. hatch of chicks
106. head of curlews
head of pheasants
107. hennery of poultry
108. herd of cranes
herd of curlews
herd of swans
herd of wrens
109. hill of ruffs

58. parcel of linnets
59. asylum of loons
60. *corroboree of lyre birds*
61. gulp of magpies
    tiding (or tidings) of magpies
    tittering of magpies
62. flush of mallard (on land)
    puddling of mallard (on water)
    sord of mallard
    sute/suit of mallard (landed)
63. dopping of merganser
64. fleet of mudhen (American coot)
65. match of nightingales
    pray of nightingales
    puddling of nightingales
    watch of nightingales
66. pitch of orioles
    split of orioles
67. pride of ostriches
68. parliament of owls
    stare of owls
    wisdom of owls

69. company of parrots
    pandemonium of parrots
    prattle of parrots
70. bew of partridges

110. hoard of crows
111. host of sparrows
112. *hover of hummingbirds*
     hover of crows
113. huddle of penguins
114. *improbability of puffins*
115. jug of quail
116. *kahuna of surf birds*
117. kettle of hawks (riding a thermal)
118. kit of pigeons (flying together)
119. knob of pintail
     knob of teal
     knob of waterfowl
     knob of wildfowl (fewer than 30)
120. lamentation of swans
121. leash of hawks
     leash of plovers
122. lek of grouse
123. loft of pigeons
124. loomery of auks
125. lute of wildfowl
126. mark of swans
127. match of nightingales
128. meinie of sparrows
129. mews of capons
130. mob of emus
     mob of turkeys
131. murder of crows
     murder of currawongs [e]
132. murmuration of starlings
133. muster of peacocks
     muster (or mustering) of storks

Chapter 2: A Flight of Fancy

bevy of partridges
clutch of partridges
covey of partridges
warren of partridges
71. muster of peacocks
ostentation of peacocks
pride of peacocks
splendour of peacocks
72. pod of pelicans
73. colony of penguins
crèche of penguins
formality of penguins
huddle of penguins
parade of penguins
parcel of penguins
raft of penguins (on water)
rookery of penguins
waddle of penguins (on land)
74. *gallon of petrels*
75. bouquet of pheasants
brace of pheasant
brook of pheasants
eye of pheasants
head of pheasants
nye (or nide) of pheasants
76. dropping of pigeons
flight of pigeons
flock of pigeons
kit of pigeons (flying together)
loft of pigeons
77. knob of pintail
78. congregation of plovers
leash of plovers
stand of plovers
wing of plovers

134. mutation of thrushes
135. nest of fledglings
136. nide of geese
137. nye (or nide) of pheasants

138. ostentation of peacocks
139. pack of grouse (large group)
   pack of gulls
140. paddling of ducks (on water)
141. pandemonium of parrots
142. parade of penguins
143. parcel of birds (dial)
   parcel of linnets
   parcel of penguins
144. parish of rooks
145. parliament of owls
   parliament of rooks
146. party of jays

79. flight of pochards
    rush of pochards (or
        dunbirds)
80. hennery of poultry
    run of poultry
81. covey of ptarmigan
82. circus of puffins
    improbability of puffins
    raft of puffins
83. battery of quails
    bevy of quail
    covey of quail
    drift of quail
    jug of quail

84. conspiracy of ravens
    constable of ravens
    unkindness of ravens
85. embarrassment of red-faced
        warblers
86. crowd of redwing
87. building of rooks
    clamour of rooks
    congregation of rooks
    council of rooks
    parish of rooks
    parliament of rooks
    shoal of rooks
    wing of rooks

147. pat of flamingos
148. peep of chickens
149. phalanx of storks
150. pil of seabirds (dial)
151. pilmer of birds (dial)
152. pitch of orioles
153. piteousness of doves
154. pitying of turtledoves
155. *plummet of gannets*
156. plump of ducks (in flight)
    plump of waterfowl
    plump of wildfowl
    plump of woodcock
157. pod of birds (small flock)
    pod of pelicans
158. *posse of cock-turkeys*
159. prattle of parrots
160. pray of nightingales
161. prettying of doves
162. pride of ostriches
    pride of peacocks
163. puddling of mallard (on
        water)
    puddling of nightingales
164. quarrel of sparrows
165. *radiance of cardinals*
166. raffle of turkeys
167. raft of auks (on water)
    raft of ducks
    raft of penguins (on water)
    raft of puffins
    raft of teal
    raft of widgeon
168. rafter of turkey
169. rasp of coots
    rasp of guineafowl

Chapter 2: A Flight of Fancy

88. hill of ruffs
89. scamper of sanderlings ᶠ
90. fling of sandpipers
91. chyne of seabirds (dial)
    concourse of seabirds
    pil of seabirds (dial)
    wreck of seabirds
92. cloud of sea fowl
93. squabble of seagulls
94. doading of sheldrake
    dopping of sheldrake
95. *strand of silky flycatchers*
96. exaltation of skylarks
97. walk of snipe (at rest)
    wisp of snipe (in flight)
98. host of sparrows
    meinie of sparrows
    quarrel of sparrows
    tribe of sparrows
    ubiquity of sparrows
99. chatter of starlings
    clutter of starlings
    filth of starlings
    murmuration of starlings
    scourge of starlings
100. muster (or mustering) of storks
     phalanx of storks
101. *kahuna of surf birds*
102. flight of swallows
     gulp of swallows
     rush of swallows
103. *ballet of swans*
     bank of swans
     bevy of swans
     drift of swans

170. *regatta of swans*
171. regiment of flamingos
172. rookery of albatross
     rookery of penguins
173. run of poultry
174. rush of pochards (or dunbirds)
     rush of swallows
175. safe of ducks
176. sail of ducks
177. sanctuary of birds

178. scamper of sanderlings ᶠ
179. school of turkeys
180. scolding of jays
181. scourge of starlings
182. screech of gulls
183. screw of hawks (in migrating swarms)
184. scry of wildfowl
185. sedge of bitterns
     sedge (or sledge) of cranes
     sedge of herons
186. serge of herons
187. shimmer of humming birds
188. shoal of rooks
189. siege of herons
190. skein of geese (in flight)
     skein of flamingos

eyrar of swans
game of swans
herd of swans
lamentation of swans
mark of swans
regatta of swans
sownder of swans
squadron of swans
team of swans
teeme of swans
wedge of swans (in the air)

whiteness (or whiting) of swans
104. flock of swifts
105. bunch of teal
coil of teal
knob of teal
raft of teal
spring of teal
106. dread of terns [g]
107. mutation of thrushes
108. *durante of toucans*
109. crop of turkeys
duet of turkeys
flock of turkeys
gang of (wild) turkeys [d]
gobble of turkeys
mob of turkeys
raffle of turkeys

191. sord of mallard
192. sownder of swans
193. splendour of peacocks
194. split of orioles
195. spring of teal
196. springful of larks [c]
197. squabble of seagulls
198. squadron of swans
199. squall of gulls
200. *squat of cuckoos*
201. stand of flamingos [b]
stand of plovers
202. stare of owls
203. storytelling of crows
204. *strand of silky flycatchers*
205. stream of hawks (from a 'kettle')
206. sute (or suit) of mallard (on land)
207. team of geese
team of swans
team of wild ducks (in flight)
208. teeme of swans
209. tiding (or tidings) of magpies
210. tittering of magpies
211. tok of capercailzies (arch.)
212. train of jackdaws
213. trembling of finches
214. tribe of sparrows
215. trimming of finches
216. trip of dotterel
trip of widgeon
trip of wildfowl
217. troubling of goldfinches

rafter of turkeys
school of turkeys
110. true love of turtle doves
pitying of turtledoves
111. carpet of vultures
cast of vultures
wake of vultures
112. *bob of wagtails*
113. bunch of waterfowl
knob of waterfowl
plump of waterfowl
114. company of widgeon
raft of widgeon
trip of widgeon
115. bunch of wildfowl
knob of wildfowl (fewer than 30)
lute of wildfowl
plump of wildfowl
scry of wildfowl
trip of wildfowl
116. fall of woodcock/woodchucks
plump of woodcock
117. descent of woodpeckers
gatling of woodpeckers

118. chime of wrens
herd of wrens

troubling of hummingbirds

218. true love of turtle doves
219. ubiquity of sparrows
220. unkindness of ravens
221. *vein of goldfinches*
222. volary (or volery) of birds (in an aviary)
223. *waddle of penguins (on land)*
224. wake of buzzards [b]
wake of vultures
225. walk of snipe (at rest)
226. warren of partridges
227. watch of nightingales
228. wedge of geese
wedge of swans (in the air)
229. whiteness (or whiting) of swans
230. wing of plovers
wing of rooks
231. wisdom of owls
232. wisp of snipe (in flight)
233. woodchoir of birds (chorus)
234. wreck of seabirds

Notes

a. Archaic, from one of the 16th century manuscripts (most commonly, The Book of Hawking & Hunting', by Dame Juliana Barnes, 1486).
b. From James Lipton: 'An Exaltation of Larks'.
c. From 'A Poem in October' by Dylan Thomas.
d. An old hunting term from the western US.
e. A currawong is a type of Australian magpie.
f. From 'Under Milkwood' by Dylan Thomas.
g. A dread of terns: immediately before beginning a migration, a noisy colony of birds suddenly becomes quiet; all then take to the air and fly away.

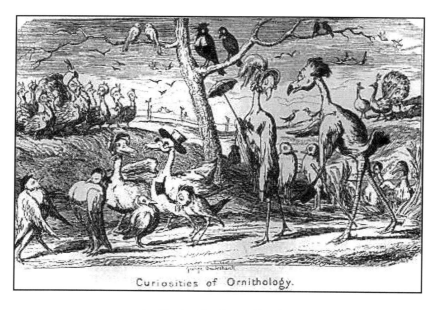

'a dissimulation of birds'

Chapter 2: A Flight of Fancy

'a regatta of swans'

'a sedge of cranes'

Gallimaufry

'a brood of chickens'

ZOOLOGY. [By *Charles Keene.*]
Railway Porter (to Old Lady travelling with a Menagerie of Pets). "'STATION MASTER SAY, MUM, AS CATS IS 'DOGS,' AND RABBITS IS 'DOGS,' AND SO 'S PARROTS ; BUT THIS ERE 'TORTIS' IS A INSECT, SO THERE AIN'T NO CHARGE FOR IT !"

'a menagerie of creatures'

Chapter Three

A Congregation of Creatures

a. *Insects, arthropods & micro-organisms*
b. *Marine life*
c. *Reptiles*

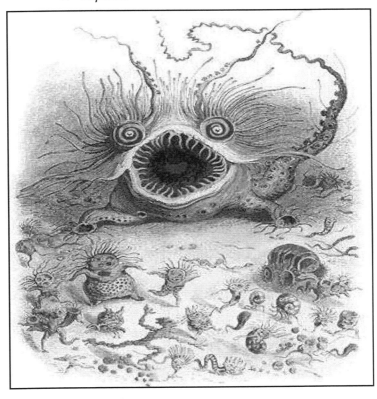

'a fraid of sea monsters'

Gallimaufry

'an army of wasps'

3a. Insects, arthropods & micro-organisms

Sorted by noun	Sorted by collective noun
1. army of ants	1. abscondance of fleas
bike of ants	2. apiary of bees
caste of ants	3. army of ants
colony of ants	army of caterpillars
farm of ants	army of wasps
formicary of ants	4. bed of scorpions
hill of ants	5. bike of ants
state of ants	bike of (wild) bees
swarm of ants	bike of hornets
trail of ants	6. bite of midges
2. colony of bacteria	7. business of flies
culture of bacteria	8. butt (hive) of bees
strain of bacteria	9. caste of ants
3. apiary of bees	caste of bees
bike of (wild) bees	10. category of organisms

Chapter 3: A Congregation of Creatures

butt (hive) of bees
caste of bees (2nd swarm)
chit of bees (alt. 3rd swarm)
cluster of bees (around the queen)
colony of bees
colt (or cote) of bees (3rd swarm)
drift of bees
erst of bees
fry of (young) bees
grist of bees
hive of bees
hum of bees
play of bees
rabble of bees

skep of bees
smart of bees (alt. 2nd swarm)
spew of bees (4th swarm)
spindle of bees (alt. 3rd swarm)
swarm of bees (1st swarm)
4. *scuttle of beetles*
5. flotilla of bluebottles
fluther of bluebottles
6. flock of butterflies
flutter of butterflies
kaleidoscope of butterflies
rabble of butterflies
rainbow of butterflies
swarm of butterflies
7. army of caterpillars
8. cluster of cells
	11. chit of bees (alt. 3rd swarm)
	12. *chorus of cicadas*
	    chorus of crickets
	13. circus of fleas
	14. class of organisms
	15. classification of organisms
	16. clat of worms
	17. clew of worms
	18. cloud of flies
	    cloud of gnats
	    cloud of grasshoppers
	    cloud of locusts
	    cloud of mayflies
	19. cluster of bees (around the queen)
	    cluster of cells
	    cluster of grasshoppers
	    cluster of spiders
	20. clutter of spiders
	21. cocoon of eggs
	22. colony of ants
	    colony of bacteria
	    colony of bees
	    colony of termites
	    colony of wasps
	23. colt (or cote) of bees (3rd swarm)
	24. community of microbes
	25. *cornucopia of slugs*
	26. *crash of cockchafers*
	27. culture of bacteria
	28. *dance of damselflies*
	29. delirium of flies [b]
	30. *dream of dragonflies*
	31. drift of bees
	32. erst of bees

9. *chorus of cicadas*
10. *crash of cockchafers*
11. infestation of cockroaches
    intrusion of cockroaches [b]
    swarm of cockroaches
12. *chorus of crickets*
    orchestra of crickets
13. *dance of damselflies*
14. *dream of dragonflies*
    hover of dragonflies
15. cocoon of eggs
16. abscondance of fleas
    circus of fleas
17. business of flies
    cloud of flies
    delirium of flies [b]
    scraw of flies
    swarm of flies
18. cloud of gnats
    horde of gnats
    rabble of gnats
19. cloud of grasshoppers
    cluster of grasshoppers
20. bike of hornets
    nest of hornets
    swarm of hornets
    vespiary of hornets
21. flight of insects
    insectarium of insects
    swarm of insects
22. *loveliness of ladybirds*
    luck of ladybirds
23. flock of lice [a]
    infestation of lice
24. cloud of locusts
    horde of locusts
33. escargatoire (nursery) of snails
34. farm of ants
35. flight of insects
36. flock of butterflies
    flock of lice [a]
37. flotilla of bluebottles
38. fluther of bluebottles
39. flutter of butterflies
40. formicary of ants
41. fry of (young) bees
42. grist of bees
43. herd of snails
44. hill of ants
45. hive of bees
46. horde of gnats
    horde of locusts
47. *hover of dragonflies*
48. *hum of bees*
49. infestation of cockroaches
    infestation of lice
50. insectarium of insects
51. intrusion of cockroaches [b]
52. kaleidoscope of butterflies
53. *knot of worms*
54. *loveliness of ladybirds*
55. *luck of ladybirds*
56. mound of termites
57. nest of hornets
    nest of scorpions
    nest of spiders
    nest of wasps
58. *orchestra of crickets*
59. *pail of wasps*
60. pladge of wasps
61. plague of locusts

Chapter 3: A Congregation of Creatures

     plague of locusts
     swarm of locusts
25. cloud of mayflies
     swarm of mayflies
26. community of microbes
27. bite of midges
     swarm of midges
28. scourge of mosquitoes
     swarm of mosquitoes
29. category of organisms
     class of organisms
     classification of organisms
30. bed of scorpions
     nest of scorpions
31. *cornucopia of slugs*
32. escargatoire (nursery) of snails
     herd of snails
     rout of snails

     walk of snails
33. cluster of spiders
     clutter of spiders
     nest of spiders
34. colony of termites
     mound of termites
35. army of wasps
     colony of wasps
     nest of wasps

62. play of bees

63. rabble of bees
     rabble of butterflies
     rabble of gnats
64. *rainbow of butterflies*
65. rout of snails
66. scourge of mosquitoes
67. scraw of flies
68. *scuttle of beetles*
69. skep of bees
70. smart of bees (alt. 2nd swarm)
71. spew of bees (4th swarm)
72. spindle of bees (alt. 3rd swarm)
73. state of ants
74. strain of bacteria
75. swarm of ants
     swarm of bees (1st swarm)
     swarm of butterflies
     swarm of cockroaches
     swarm of flies
     swarm of hornets
     swarm of insects
     swarm of locusts
     swarm of mayflies

Gallimaufry

pail of wasps	swarm of midges
pladge of wasps	swarm of mosquitoes
vespiary of wasps	76. trail of ants
31. clat of worms	77. vespiary of hornets
clew of worms	vespiary of wasps
knot of worms	43. walk of snails
wriggle of worms	44. *wriggle of worms*

Notes:

a. Cited from Caxton 1476.
b. Bill Bryson, 'Neither Here Nor There', 1991

'a swarm of midges'

Chapter 3: A Congregation of Creatures

'a garden of sea anemones'

3b. Marine Life

Sorted by noun	Sorted by collective noun
1. bloom of algae	1. aquarium of fish
2. host of angel fish	2. army of herring
3. company of archer-fish	3. array of eels
4. battery of barracuda	4. bale of turtles
5. fleet of bass	5. bally of fish (dial)
	6. battery of barracuda
	7. baulk of pilchards (dial)
	8. bed of clams
	bed of cockles
	bed of eels [d]
shoal of bass	bed of oysters
6. grind of blackfish	9. bind of eels (10 sticks / 250

39

Gallimaufry

7. school of butterfly fish
8. bed of clams
   bucket of clams
9. bed of cockles
10. lap of cod
11. colony of coral
    head of coral
    reef of coral
12. bushel of crabs
    cast of crabs
    trap of crabs
13. brood of dogfish
    troop of dogfish
14. *delight of dolphins*
    display of dolphins
    grind of (bottle-nosed)
       dolphins
    team of dolphins
15. swarm of dragonet fish
16. array of eels
    bed of eels ᵈ
    bind of eels (10 sticks / 250
       eels) ᵈ
    draft of eels (20 lbs.) ᵈ
    knot of eels
    slither of eels
    stick of eels (25) ᵈ
    swarm of eels
    wisp of eels
17. rookery of elephant seals
    team of elephant seals
    troop of elephant seals
18. aquarium of fish
    bally of fish (dial)
    catch of fish
    congregation of fish
	eels) ᵈ
	    bind of salmon
	10. bloom of algae
	11. bowl of goldfish
	12. breaking-school of pilchards
	    (dial)
	13. brimming of mackerel (dial)
	14. brood of dogfish
	15. bucket of clams
	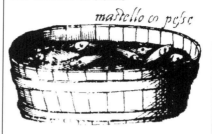
	16. bush of pilchards (dial)
	17. bushel of crabs
	18. cast of crabs
	19. catch of fish
	20. *cloud of plankton*
	21. clump of seaweed
	22. cluster of mussels
	    cluster of porcupine fish
	23. colony of coral
	    colony of seals
	24. company of archer-fish
	25. congregation of fish
	26. constellation of starfish
	27. cran of herring
	28. creel of prawns
	29. culch of oysters
	30. *delight of dolphins*
	31. den of octopuses
	32. display of dolphins

Chapter 3: A Congregation of Creatures

draught of fish	33. draft of eels (20 lbs.) [d]
drave of fish (a haul) [d]	34. draught of fish
drought of fish	draught of salmon
frail of fish	35. drave of fish (a haul) [d]
fray of fish	36. drought of fish
hatchery of fish	37. family of sardines
haul of fish	38. fever of stingrays
lane of fish (dial)	39. fleet of bass
leash of fish (3)	40. fleet of rays
net of fish	41. float of tuna
quota of fish	42. flote of tunny
run of fish (in motion)	flote of whales
scale of fish	43. flotilla of swordfish
school of fish	44. fluther of jellyfish
shoal of fish	45. *forest of seaweed*
stock of fish	46. frail of fish
take of fish	47. fray of fish
	48. gam of porpoises
	gam of whales
	49. *garden of sea anemones*
	50. glean of herrings
	51. glide of flying fish
	52. glint of goldfish [b]
	53. glut of parrs (young salmon)
	54. grind of blackfish
	grind of (bottle-nosed) dolphins
	grind of whales
	55. harem of seals
	56. harvest of salmon
	57. hatchery of fish
	58. haul of fish
	59. head of coral
	60. herd of porpoises
tally of fish (dial)	herd of seahorses
tank of fish	herd of seals
throw of fish	
yield of fish	

41

19. redd (nest) of fish eggs	herd of walruses
20. glide of flying fish	herd of whales
21. bowl of goldfish	61. hive of oysters
glint of goldfish [b]	62. host of angel fish
pond of goldfish	63. hover of trout
tank of goldfish	64. huddle of walruses
troubling of goldfish	65. knot of eels
22. army of herring	66. lane of fish (dial)
cran of herring	67. lap of cod
glean of herrings	68. lash (or last) of herring (dial)
lash (or last) of herring (dial)	69. leash of fish (3)
long hundred of herrings (120)	70. line of mackerel
	71. live-tank of lobsters
23. pod of killer whales	72. long hundred of herrings (120)
24. fluther of jellyfish	
medusa of jellyfish	73. *medusa of jellyfish*
quiver of jellyfish	74. net of fish
smack of jellyfish	75. nub of pilchards (dial)
smuth of jellyfish	76. oceanarium of marine life
studk of jellyfish	77. pack of perch
swarm of jellyfish	78. pail of shrimps
25. surfeit of lampreys [c]	79. party of rainbow fish
26. live-tank of lobsters	80. patch of seaweed
pound (as in 'pen') of lobsters	81. *pickle of sea cucumbers*
quadrille of lobsters [a]	82. pil of mackerel (dial)
squadron of lobsters	83. plum of seals
trap of lobsters	84. pod of killer whales
27. brimming of mackerel (dial)	pod of porpoises
line of mackerel	pod of seals (small herd)
pil of mackerel (dial)	pod of walrus
28. *wing of manta ray*	pod of whiting
29. oceanarium of marine life	85. pond of goldfish
30. steam of minnows	86. pound (as in 'pen') of lobsters
stream of minnows	87. quadrille of lobsters [a]
31. cluster of mussels	88. quantity of smelts [e]

Chapter 3: A Congregation of Creatures

32. arran of octopuses
    den of octopuses
    tangle of octopuses
33. bed of oysters
    culch (bed) of oysters
    hive of oysters
    set of (young) oysters
    wealth of oysters
34. glut of parrs (young salmon)
35. pack of perch
36. baulk of pilchards (dial)
    breaking-school of pilchards (dial)
    bush of pilchards (dial)
    nub of pilchards (dial)
    shermer of pilchards (dial)
    shoal of pilchards
37. *cloud of plankton*
38. cluster of porcupine fish
39. gam of porpoises
    herd of porpoises
    pod of porpoises
    school of porpoises
    turmoil of porpoises
40. creel of prawns
41. party of rainbow fish
42. fleet of rays
43. bind of salmon
    draught of salmon
    harvest of salmon
    run of salmon
44. family of sardines
45. *garden of sea anemones*
46. *pickle of sea cucumbers*
47. herd of seahorses
48. colony of seals

89. quiver of jellyfish
90. quota of fish
91. raft of sea otters
92. redd (nest) of fish eggs
93. reef of coral
94. rookery of elephant seals
    rookery of seals

95. run of fish (in motion)
    run of salmon
96. scale of fish
97. school of butterfly fish
    school of fish
    school of porpoises
    school of sharks
    school of whales
98. set of (young) oysters
99. shermer of pilchards (dial)
100. shiver of sharks [b]
101. shoal of bass
     shoal of fish
     shoal of pilchards
     shoal of shad
     shoal of sharks
102. slither of eels
103. smack of jellyfish

43

harem of seals
herd of seals
plum of seals
pod of seals (small herd)
rookery of seals
spring of seals
49. raft of sea otters
50. clump of seaweed
forest of seaweed
patch of seaweed
51. shoal of shad
52. school of sharks
shiver of sharks [b]
shoal of sharks
53. pail of shrimps
54. quantity of smelts [e]
55. constellation of starfish
56. spread of sticklebacks
57. fever of stingrays
58. flotilla of swordfish

scabbard of swordfish
59. hover of trout
60. float of tuna
61. flote of tunny
62. bale of turtles
turn of turtles
63. herd of walruses
huddle of walruses
pod of walrus
ugly of walruses

104. smuth of jellyfish
105. spread of sticklebacks
106. spring of seals
107. squadron of lobsters
108. steam of minnows
109. stick of eels (25) [d]
110. stock of fish
111. stream of minnows
112. studk of jellyfish
113. surfeit of lampreys [c]
114. swarm of dragonet fish
swarm of eels
swarm of jellyfish
115. take of fish
116. tally of fish (dial)

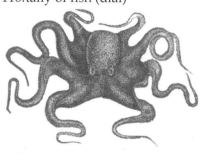

117. tangle of octopuses
118. tank of fish
tank of goldfish
119. team of dolphins
team of elephant seals
120. throw of fish
121. trap of crabs
trap of lobsters
122. troop of dogfish
troop of elephant seals
123. troubling of goldfish
124. turmoil of porpoises

Chapter 3: A Congregation of Creatures

64. flote of whales	125. turn of turtles
gam of whales	126. ugly of walruses
grind of whales	127. wealth of oysters
herd of whales	*128. wing of manta ray*
school of whales	129. wisp of eels
63. pod of whiting	130. yield of fish

Notes:

a. From 'Alice in Wonderland' by Lewis Carroll: The Lobster Quadrille.
b. From James Lipton: 'An Exaltation of Larks'.
c. King Henry I of England, in a fit of royal gluttony, is said to have died from eating a "surfeit of lampreys ...".
d. From Ivan G Sparkes, 'Dictionary of Collective Nouns & Group Terms'.
e. From Izaak Walton's 'Compleat Angler', 1676.

'a chorus of frogs'

3c. Reptiles

Sorted by noun	Sorted by collective noun
1. congregation of alligators	1. army of frogs
pod of (young) alligators	2. bale of turtles
2. *camouflage of chameleons*	3. bask of crocodiles ^c
3. quiver of cobras	4. bed of snakes
4. bask of crocodiles ^c	5. *camouflage of chameleons*

congregation of crocodiles float of crocodiles nest of crocodiles 4. army of frogs chorus of frogs [d] nod of frogs 5. mess of iguanas 6. *lounge of lizards* 7. rhumba of rattlesnakes 8. herpetarium of reptiles vivarium of reptiles 9. bed of snakes den of snakes knot of snakes nest of snakes pit of snakes *slither of snakes* trogle of snakes 10. wiggle of tadpoles 11. tank of terrapins 12. *croak of toads* knab of toads knot of toads *lump of toads* nest of toads 13. *creep of tortoises*  14. bale of turtles turn of turtles	6. chorus of frogs [d] 7. congregation of alligators congregation of crocodiles 8. *creep of tortoises* 9. *croak of toads* 10. den of snakes  11. float of crocodiles 12. generation of vipers 13. herpetarium of reptiles 14. knab of toads 15. knot of snakes knot of toads 16. *lounge of lizards* 17. *lump of toads* 18. mess of iguanas 19. nest of crocodiles nest of snakes nest of toads nest of vipers 20. nod of frogs 21. pit of snakes 22. pod of (young) alligators 23. quiver of cobras 24. rhumba of rattlesnakes 25. *slither of snakes* 26. tank of terrapins 27. trogle of snakes 28. turn of turtles

Chapter 3: A Congregation of Creatures

| 15. generation of vipers | 29. vivarium of reptiles |
| nest of vipers | wiggle of tadpoles |

Notes

a. Archaic, from one of the 16th century manuscripts (most commonly, The Book of Hawking & Hunting', by Dame Juliana Barnes, 1486).
b. From James Lipton: 'An Exaltation of Larks'.
c. From C E Hare 'The Language of Field Sports'.
d. The term 'a chorus of frogs' was probably first coined by Aristophanes in 405BC, in his comedy 'The Frogs', but has been used more recently by Paul McCartney in 'The Frog Chorus', and there is also a musical adaptation by Stephen Sondheim.

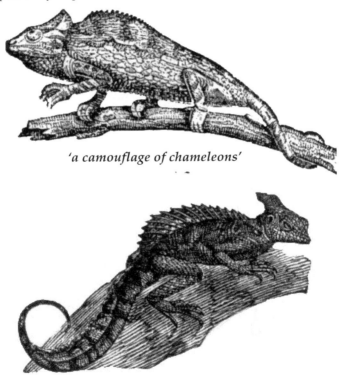

'a camouflage of chameleons'

'a lounge of lizards'

Gallimaufry

'*a quiver of cobras*'

'*a rhumba of rattlesnakes*'

Chapter Four

A Grotto of Greenery

*Including wild and cultivated plants,
trees, gardening, crops, and agriculture*

'a tussock of turf'

Gallimaufry

'a chain of daisies'

4. Plants

Sorted by noun	Sorted by collective noun
1. hang of apples (on the tree)	1. arboretum of trees
	2. arbour of trees or plants
	3. arrangement of flowers
	4. avenue of trees
	5. bale of hay
	6. bank of ferns
	bank of violets
	7. beat of flax ᶜ
	8. bed of flowers
	bed of leaves
	bed of nettles
	bed of reeds
2. stand of bamboo	bed of roses
3. carpet of bluebells	bed of rushes

Chapter 4: A Grotto of Greenery

4. rush of briars	bed of weeds
5. thicket of bushes	9. boll of cotton
6. field of buttercups	10. bolting of straw
7. crop of cabbages	11. bottle of furze
field of cabbages	bottle of hay
8. field of clover	12. boughpot of flowers [c]
9. pinetum of conifers	13. bouquet of flowers
plantation of conifers	14. bowl of fruit
10. crop of corn	15. browse of twigs (dial)
field of corn	16. bunch of flowers
knitch (bundle) of corn	bunch of teasels
neck of corn	17. burden of straw
sheaf of corn	18. buttonhole of flowers
shock of corn (10/15 sheaves)	19. calyx of sepals
11. boll of cotton	20. canopy of leaves
12. harvest of crops	canopy of trees
plantation of crops	21. carpet of bluebells
13. crowd of daffodils [a]	carpet of leaves
host of daffodils [a]	carpet of moss
14. chain of daisies	carpet of wild flowers
	22. cascade of flowers
	23. chain of daisies
	24. clod of earth
	25. clump of mistletoe
	clump of moss
	clump of reeds
	clump of trees
	clump of weeds
	26. cluster of nuts
	cluster of turnips
	27. colony of fungi
	colony of mushrooms
15. *pride of dandelions*	28. community of plants
16. herbarium of dried plants	29. conservatory of plants
17. clod of earth	30. copse of trees
sod of earth	31. cord of timber (cut)

18. bank of ferns
    grotto of ferns
    grove of ferns
19. beat of flax [c]
    head of flax (bundle) [c]
    lock of flax [c]
    shive of flax [c]
    stook of flax [c]
    strike of flax [c]
20. panicle of flowerlets
21. arrangement of flowers
    bed of flowers
    boughpot of flowers [c]
    bouquet of flowers
    bunch of flowers
    buttonhole of flowers
    cascade of flowers
    field of flowers
    garland of flowers
    nosegay of flowers
    patch of flowers
    posy of flowers
    vase of flowers
    wreath of flowers
22. jungle of foliage
    mass of foliage
    tod of foliage
23. expanse of forest
    swathe of forest
24. bowl of fruit
    crop of fruit
    truss of fruit (or flowers)
25. orchard of fruit trees
26. colony of fungi
27. bottle of furze
28. spray of gardenias

32. corolla of petals
33. corsage of orchids
34. coterie of orchids
35. crop of cabbages
    crop of corn
    crop of fruit
36. crowd of daffodils [a]
37. detritus of (dead) leaves
38. division of plants
39. drift of leaves
40. expanse of forest
    expanse of jungle
41. fascicle of plant parts
        (branches or stems)
    fascicle of pine needles (3-5)
42. field of buttercups
    field of cabbages
    field of clover
    field of corn
    field of flowers
    field of tulips
43. flurry of leaves
44. forest of trees
45. garb (sheaf) of wheat
46. garden of plants

47. garland of flowers
48. genus of plants
49. glade of grass
50. greenhouse of plants
51. grotto of ferns
52. grove of ferns

Chapter 4: A Grotto of Greenery

29. vinery of grapes
30. vineyard of grape vines
31. glade of grass
    lawn of grass
    tuft of grass
    tussock of grass
32. bale of hay
    bottle of hay
    lock of hay
    rick of hay
    stack of hay
    truss of hay
33. sprig of holly
34. stand of iris
35. tod of ivy
36. expanse of jungle
37. wreath of laurel
38. bed of leaves
    canopy of leaves
    carpet of leaves
    detritus of (dead) leaves
    drift of leaves
    flurry of leaves
    verticil of leaves
39. clump of mistletoe
    sprig of mistletoe
40. carpet of moss
    clump of moss
    colony of mushrooms
    troop of mushrooms
41. bed of nettles
    patch of nettles
    rush of nettles
42. corsage of orchids
    coterie of orchids
    spray of orchids

    grove of trees
53. hang of apples (on the tree)
    hang of plums (on the tree)
54. harvest of crops
55. head of flax (bundle) c
56. herbarium of dried plants

57. host of daffodils a
58. hothouse of (exotic) plants
59. jardinière of (house) plants
60. jungle of foliage
61. knitch (bundle) of corn
62. lawn of grass
63. lock of flax c
    lock of hay
64. logjam of tree-trunks
65. mass of foliage
66. meadow of wild flowers
67. neck of corn
68. nosegay of flowers
69. nursery of plants
70. orchard of fruit trees
71. pack of teasels (12 staves)
72. panicle of flowerlets
73. patch of flowers
    patch of nettles
74. pinetum of conifers
75. plantation of conifers
    plantation of crops
76. posy of flowers

43. cluster of nuts
44. corolla of petals
    whorl of petals
45. fascicle of pine needles (3-5)
46. fascicle of plant parts
    (branches or stems)
47. community of plants
    conservatory of plants
    division of plants
    garden of plants
    genus of plants
    greenhouse of plants
    hothouse of (exotic) plants
    jardinière of (house) plants
    nursery of plants
    rockery of plants
    terrarium of plants

48. hang of plums (on the tree)
49. bed of reeds
    clump of reeds
50. bed of roses
51. bed of rushes
52. calyx of sepals
53. stook of sheaves (corn)
54. bolting of straw
    burden of straw
55. bunch of teasels
    pack of teasels (12 staves)

77. *pride of dandelions*
78. quincunx of trees [b]
79. rick of hay

80. ring of toadstools
81. rockery of plants
82. rush of briars
    rush of nettles
83. sheaf of corn
84. shive of flax [c]
85. shock of corn (10/15 sheaves)
86. sod of earth
87. spinney of trees
88. spray of gardenias
    spray of orchids
89. sprig of holly
    sprig of mistletoe
90. stack of hay
91. stand of bamboo
    stand of iris
    stand of trees
92. stave of teasels (20 bunches)
93. stook of flax [c]
    stook of sheaves (corn)
94. strike of flax [c]
95. swathe of forest
96. tangle of weeds
97. terrarium of plants

Chapter 4: A Grotto of Greenery

stave of teasels (20 bunches)	98. thicket of bushes
56. thicket of thorns	thicket of thorns
57. cord of timber (cut)	thicket of trees
58. ring of toadstools	99. tod of foliage
59. arboretum of trees	tod of ivy
arbour of trees or plants	100. troop of mushrooms
avenue of trees	101. truss of fruit (or flowers)
canopy of trees	truss of hay
clump of trees	102. tuft of grass
copse of trees	103. tussock of grass
forest of trees	tussock of turf
grove of trees	104. vase of flowers
quincunx of trees [b]	105. verticil of leaves
spinney of trees	106. vinery of grapes
stand of trees	
thicket of trees	
wood of trees	
60. logjam of tree-trunks	
61. field of tulips	
62. tussock of turf	
63. cluster of turnips	
64. browse of twigs (dial)	
65. bed of weeds	
clump of weeds	
tangle of weeds	107. vineyard of grape vines
66. garb (sheaf) of wheat	108. whorl of petals
67. carpet of wild flowers	109. wood of trees
meadow of wild flowers	110. wreath of flowers
68. bank of violets	wreath of laurel

Notes:

a. Wordsworth: 'I wandered lonely as a cloud'.
b. An arrangement of five objects, usually trees, with one at each corner of a rectangle and one at the centre.
c. From Ivan G Sparkes, 'Dictionary of Collective Nouns & Group Terms'.

'a stook of corn sheaves'

'a bank of violets'

Chapter Five

A Clutch of Characters

'a catch of anglers'

Gallimaufry

'a Heep of creeps'

5. People

Sorted by noun	Sorted by collective noun
1. corroboree of aborigines	1. A-list of celebrities
moiety of aborigines ˣ	2. *abandonment of orphans*
2. colloquium of academics	3. *absence of waiters*
3. circle of acquaintance	4. academy of students
sphere of acquaintances	5. acne of adolescents ᶜ
4. retinue of admirers	6. *amalgamation of metallurgists*
5. acne of adolescents ᶜ	7. *amble of walkers*
6. camarilla of (secret) advisors	8. ambuscade of assailants
7. *bevy of alcoholics*	9. ambush of assailants
8. *catch of anglers*	ambush of widows ᶜ
drift of anglers	10. *anorak of train-spotters*
9. train of apothecaries	11. *anthology of (English) pros* ᶠ
10. *ascent of arborists*	12. arena of gladiators
11. team of archaeologists	13. army of fans
12. company of archers	army of volunteers
13. *conflagration of arsonists*	14. aroma of bakers ᶜ
14. cognoscenti of art experts	15. array of luminaries

Chapter 5: A Clutch of Characters

15. colony of artists	array of stars
school of artists	16. *ascent of arborists*
16. ambuscade of assailants	17. assembly of people
ambush of assailants	assembly of pupils
17. knot of astrologers	assembly of students
trine of astrologers c	18. *attitude of teenagers*
18. galaxy of astronomers c	19. audience of listeners
19. entourage of attendants	audience of viewers
meiny of attendants	20. *avalanche of skiers*
20. *lot of auctioneers*	21. B-list of celebrities
21. *clutch of auto mechanics*	22. babble of barbers c
22. goggle of aviators c	23. bacchanal of revellers
23. *bless of babies*	24. band of brothers p
24. debauchery of bachelors b	band of comrades
score of bachelors c	band of followers
25. *hostel of backpackers*	band of heroes
26. aroma of bakers c	band of men
tabernacle of bakers	band of pirates
27. leap of banderilleros u	band of robbers
28. *wunch of bankers*	band of savages
29. impi of Bantu warriors	25. banner of knights
30. horde of barbarians	26. *baring of W.I. members* g
31. babble of barbers c	27. baronage of barons
32. buzz of barflies c	28. baronetcy of baronets
33. promise of barmen	29. bellyful of bores c
34. baronage of barons	30. bevy of alcoholics
thought of barons	bevy of beauty/beauties
truth of barons	bevy of ladies
35. baronetcy of baronets	bevy of maidens
36. blarney of bartenders c	bevy of women
37. shower of bastards	31. *binder of women* z
38. squad of beaters (hunting)	32. *billow of smokers*
39. bevy of beauty/beauties	33. blackening of shoemakers
galaxy of beauty	34. blarney of bartenders c
40. fighting of beggars a	35. blast of hunters a
41. entourage of bodyguards	36. *blaze of pyromaniacs*

Gallimaufry

42. helotry of bondsmen	37. bleach of sutors (cobblers) [a]
43. bellyful of bores [c]	38. *bless of babies*
44. draught of bottlers [a]	39. blockade of protesters
45. company of bowmen	blockade of strikers
46. blunder of boys [i]	40. blunder of boys [i]
blush of boys	41. *blur of bicyclists*
leer of boys [c]	blur of impressionists [c]
mess of (little) boys	42. blush of boys
ogle of (office) boys [c]	43. board of directors
	board of governors
	board of regents [t]
	44. body of men
	body of pathologists
	45. *bond of (British) secret agents*
	46. booly of herdsmen
	(wandering with cattle)
rascal of boys [a]	47. bored of trustees [c]
47. company of boy scouts	48. bouquet of wine-tasters [c]
jamboree of boy scouts	49. brigade de cuisine (chefs)
troop of boy scouts	brigade of firemen
48. passel of brats	50. brood of children
49. feast of brewers [a]	brood of daughters
50. band of brothers [p]	51. brotherhood of men
51. pack of brownies	52. bundle of dukes [v]
troop of brownies	53. *bunch of drongos*
52. prevarication of bureaucrats	bunch of no-hopers
shuffle of bureaucrats	54. buzz of barflies [c]
53. cheat of bursars	55. C-list of celebrities
54. goring of butchers [a]	56. cabal of conspirators
55. draught of butlers	57. cajolery of taverners [a]
sneer of butlers [c]	58. camarilla of (secret) advisers
56. *blur of bicyclists*	camarilla of conspirators
57. drove of cabdrivers [c]	59. camp of refugees
58. rangale of camp followers	*camp of transvestites*
59. crusade of campaigners	60. caper of kids [c]
60. lash of carters [a]	61. caravanserai of merchants
61. *strip of cartoonists*	

Chapter 5: A Clutch of Characters

62. embruing of carvers
63. A-list of celebrities
    B-list of celebrities
    C-list of celebrities
    glitterati of celebrities
64. cycle of champions [v]
65. faction of charioteers
66. brood of children
    class of (school) children
    crèche of children
    ingratitude of children [c]
    protectory of (destitute) children
    tribulation of children [i]
67. clowder of churls [a]
    cluster of churls [a]
68. strangle of city dwellers [c]
69. gathering of the clans
    phratry of clans [w]
70. quest of clerks [v]
    school of clerks [a]
71. harlequinade of clowns
    pratfall of clowns [c]
72. cutting of cobblers [a]
    dronkship (drunkenship) of cobblers [a]
    trynket of cobblers [a]
73. kitsch of collectors [c]
74. dash of commuters [c]
75. forum of computer users
76. band of comrades
77. harem of concubines
    seraglio of concubines
78. cabal of conspirators
    camarilla of conspirators
    collaboration of conspirators

62. cartel of industrialists
63. caste of Hindus
    caste of warriors
64. catalogue of librarians
65. *catch of anglers*
66. cell of political activists
67. chain of house-buyers
68. chapter of knights
69. charm of fairies [c]
70. cheat of bursars
71. chiliarchy of (1000) men
72. circle of acquaintances
    circle of friends
73. clamour of cooks
74. clan of families
75. claque of sycophants
76. class of (school) children
    class of people
    class of students
77. click of photographers [c]
78. clique of friends
    clique of people
79. closing (glozing) of taverners [a]
80. *cloud of meteorologists*
    cloud of witnesses [m]
81. clowder of churls [a]
82. club of gentlemen
    club of members
83. cluster of churls [a]
    cluster of kindred
    cluster of twitchers (bird watchers)
84. *clutch of auto mechanics*
    clutch of kleptomaniacs
85. coach-load of supporters

61

Gallimaufry

league of conspirators	coach-load of tourists
79. network of contacts	86. coffle of slaves
80. panel of contestants	87. cognoscenti of art experts
81. clamour of cooks	88. cohort of people
hastiness of cooks ᵃ ᵈ	89. collaboration of conspirators
synod of cooks ˡ	90. collective of workers
temperance of cooks ᵃ	91. college of courtesans ᵛ
82. trinket of cordwainers	college of physicians
83. galaxy of cosmologists	92. colloquium of academics
84. diet of councillors	93. colony of artists
85. smere of couriers ᵃ	colony of lepers
smirk of couriers	colony of nudists
86. college of courtesans ᵛ	colony of people
harem of courtesans	colony of settlers
87. threatening of courtiers ᵃ	94. column of people
88. pack of cowards	95. commission of delegates
quake of cowards	commission of
run of cowards	representatives
89. saunter of cowboys ᶜ	96. committee of people
90. guild of craftsmen/women	97. commune of people
91. curse of creditors ᶜ	98. community of people
92. *Heep of creeps* ʸ	99. company of archers
93. shrivel of critics ᶜ	company of bowmen
94. incredibility (incredulity) of	company of boy scouts
cuckolds ᵃ	company of gentlemen
95. brigade de cuisine (chefs)	company of girl guides
96. smear of curriers ᵃ	company of people
97. queue of customers	100. complement of staff
98. legion of the damned	101. complex of psychoanalysts ᶜ
99. squat of daubers ᵃ	102. concourse of people
100. brood of daughters	103. confederacy of dunces ʲ
101. delirium of debutantes ᶜ	104. *conflagration of arsonists*
102. tantrum of decorators ᶜ	*conflagration of pyromaniacs*
103. commission of delegates	105. conglomerate of geologists ᶜ
convention of delegates	106. congress of lovers
104. wince of dentists ᶜ	107. conjunction of grammarians ᶜ

Chapter 5: A Clutch of Characters

105. posse of deputies	108. consternation of mothers [i]
106. family tree of descendants	109. convention of delegates
107. flotsam of destitute people	110. co-operative of workers
108. procession of dignitaries	111. cordon of guards
109. mess of diners (4 at table)	cordon of police
sitting of diners	112. corroboree of aborigines
110. board of directors	113. cortege of mourners
111. *desperation of divorcees*	114. coterie of friends
112. *dose of doctors*	coterie of people
113. obscuration of dons	115. coven of witches
114. frost of dowagers [c]	116. crèche of children
115. *swarm of (literary) drones*	
116. *bunch of drongos*	
117. *dribble of drunks*	
118. bundle of dukes [v]	
119. confederacy of dunces [j]	
120. erudition of editors [b]	
121. *dissent of egyptologists*	
122. grid of electrical engineers	117. credence of sewers (servers)[a]
123. ohm of electricians [c]	118. crocodile of people
124. workforce of employees	119. *crop of (daffodil) pickers*
125. *geek of engineers*	120. crowd of onlookers
126. prance of equestrians [c]	crowd of people
127. *fleet of (male) escorts*	121. crusade of campaigners
128. *seraglio of eunuchs* [s]	crusade of zealots
129. panel of experts	122. crush of reporters
team of experts	*crush of shoppers*
think-tank of experts	123. curse of creditors [c]
130. slew of exterminators [c]	curse of painters
131. charm of fairies [c]	124. cutting of cobblers [a]
132. clan of families	125. cycle of champions [v]
dynasty of (Hollywood) families	126. dash of commuters [c]
133. reunion of family members	127. dazzle of luminaries
134. gallery of famous names	128. debauchery of bachelors [b]
135. army of fans	129. délicatesse of gourmets [c]
	130. delicatessen of gourmands [c]

legion of fans
thrill of fans [c]
136. brigade of firemen
station of firemen
137. drift of fishermen
exaggeration of fishermen [b]
138. band of followers
school of followers
139. festival of fools
ship of fools
140. stalk of foresters
141. lodge of freemasons
142. circle of friends
clique of friends
coterie of friends
get-together of friends
league of friends
rendezvous of friends
143. practice of G.P.s
surgery of G.P.s
144. *knuckle of gangsters*
145. sprinkling of gardeners [c]
146. *pride of gays*
village of gays
147. club of gentlemen
company of gentlemen
league of gentlemen
148. conglomerate of geologists [c]
149. company of girl guides
150. giggle of girls [i]
151. arena of gladiators
procession of gladiators
school of gladiators
troupe of gladiators
152. *gleam of glitterati*
glint of glitterati

131. delirium of debutantes [c]
132. demonstration of protesters
133. den of opium addicts
den of thieves
134. descent of relatives [c]
135. *desperation of divorcees*
desperation of voters
136. diaspora of Jews
137. diet of councilllors
138. dilation of pupils [c]
139. diligence of messengers [a]
140. disguising of tailors
141. display of skydivers
142. *dissent of egyptologists*
143. disworship of Scots [a]
144. division of police
145. *dose of doctors*
146. draught of bottlers [a]
draught of butlers
147. *dribble of drunks*
148. *drift of anglers*
drift of fishermen
drift of lecturers [c]
149. dronkship (drunkenship) of cobblers [a]
150. drove of cabdrivers [c]
151. druck of people
152. dynasty of (Hollywood) families
dynasty of kings and queens
153. embruing of carvers
154. encampment of gypsies
155. enclave of people
156. entourage of attendants
entourage of bodyguards
157. erudition of editors [b]

Chapter 5: A Clutch of Characters

153. slaver of gluttons [c]
154. *gild of goldsmiths*
155. gaggle of gossips [a][e]
　　gathering of gossips [a]
156. delicatessen of gourmands [c]
157. délicatesse of gourmets [c]
158. board of governors
159. galaxy of governesses
160. unemployment of graduates[b]
161. conjunction of grammarians[c]
162. *wisdom of grandparents*
163. grope of groupies [c]
164. cordon of guards
165. levee of guests
　　party of guests
　　soiree of guests
166. encampment of gypsies
　　family of gypsies
　　troop of gypsies
167. swish of hairdressers [c]
168. salon of hairstylists
169. herd of harlots [a]
170. waywardness of haywards
171. booly of herdsmen
　　(wandering with cattle)
　　waywardness of herdsmen [a]
172. observance of hermits [a]
173. band of heroes
　　homage of heroes
174. gang of highwaymen
175. caste of Hindus
176. trip of hippies [c]
177. *magnum of hitmen*
178. guard of honour
179. gang of hoodlums

158. essay of trollops [f]
159. exaggeration of fishermen [b]
160. example of masters [a]
161. extreme unction of undertakers (an even larger group) [c]
162. faction of charioteers
　　faction of partisans
　　faction of rebels
163. faculty of teaching staff

164. faith of merchants [a]
165. fall of parachutists
166. family of gypsies
　　family of Mafiosi
　　family of people
167. family tree of descendants
168. feast of brewers [a]
169. fellowship of yeomen
170. festival of fools
171. *fidget of suspects*
172. *field of theoretical physicists*
173. fighting of beggars [a]
174. *fleet of (male) escorts*
175. *flight of refugees*
176. flock of people
　　flock of tourists
　　flock of twitchers (bird-watchers)

65

Gallimaufry

180. laughter of hostlers	177. *flood of plumbers*
181. chain of house-buyers	178. flotsam of destitute people
182. foresight of housekeepers ᵃ	179. flourish of strumpets ᶠ
183. blast of hunters ᵃ	180. flush of plumbers ᶜ
184. meet of huntsmen	181. fold of people
185. multiplying of husbands	182. folkmoot of people
unhappiness of husbands ᵇ	183. force of police
186. thicket of idiots	184. foresight of housekeepers ᵃ
187. blur of impressionists ᶜ	185. forum of computer users
188. cartel of industrialists	186. fraternity of men
189. prison of inmates	187. fraunch of millers ᵃ
190. vanguard of innovators	188. frost of dowagers ᶜ
191. ring of jewellers ᶜ	189. gaggle of gossips ᵃ ᵉ
192. diaspora of Jews	gaggle of onlookers
193. peal of Jezebels ᶠ	gaggle of women ᵃ
194. slant of journalists ᶜ	190. galaxy of astronomers ᶜ
195. neverthriving of jugglers ᵃ	galaxy of beauty
196. caper of kids ᶜ	galaxy of cosmologists
197. cluster of kindred	galaxy of governesses
198. dynasty of kings and queens	galaxy of starlets
199. clutch of kleptomaniacs	191. galère of undesirables
200. knot of knaves	192. gallery of famous names
netfull of knaves	gallery of rogues
rayful of knaves ᵃ	gallery of spectators
riffraff of knaves ᵃ	193. galley of slaves
sort of knaves	194. gam of whalers ᵃᵃ
201. banner of knights	195. gang of highwaymen
chapter of knights	gang of hoodlums
rout of knights ᵃ	gang of labourers
tourney of knights	gang of lovers
202. gang of labourers	gang of poets
203. bevy of ladies	gang of slaves
204. drift of lecturers ᶜ	gang of thieves
205. colony of lepers	196. gathering of gossips ᵃ
leprosarium (hospital) of	gathering of people
lepers	gathering of the clans

Chapter 5: A Clutch of Characters

206. catalogue of librarians
    shush of librarians ᶜ
    stack of librarians
207. audience of listeners
208. congress of lovers
    gang of lovers
    liaison of lovers
    trance of lovers ᶜ

    tryst of lovers
209. array of luminaries
    dazzle of luminaries
210. family of Mafiosi
211. bevy of maidens
    rage of maidens ᵃ
212. parade of mannequins
213. pummel of masseurs ᶜ
214. example of masters ᵃ
215. pavane of matadors ᶜ
216. set of mathematicians
217. torque of mechanics ᶜ
218. club of members
219. band of men
    body of men
    brotherhood of men
    chiliarchy of (1000) men
    fraternity of men
    host of men ᵃ

197. *geek of engineers*
198. generation of people
199. get-together of friends
200. ghetto of people
201. giggle of girls ⁱ
202. *gild of goldsmiths*
203. glaze of tourists ᶜ
204. *gleam of glitterati*
205. *glint of glitterati*
206. glitterati of celebrities
207. goggle of aviators ᶜ
208. goring of butchers ᵃ
209. *gossip of relatives*
210. graft of tree surgeons ᶜ
211. grid of electrical engineers
212. grip of porters ᶜ
213. grope of groupies ᶜ
214. group of people
    group of relations
215. grove of (old) women ⁿ
216. grub of (impoverished) writers ʳ
217. guard of honour
218. guild of craftsmen/women
    guild of tradesmen
219. gulag of political prisoners
220. gush of sycophants ᶜ
221. hack of smokers ᶜ
222. haggle of vendors ᶜ
223. *handful of palmists*
224. *hang-out of nudists*
225. harem of concubines
    harem of courtesans
    harem of slave-girls
226. harlequinade of clowns
227. hastiness of cooks ᵃ ᵈ

220. caravanserai of merchants
    faith of merchants [a]
221. diligence of messengers [a]
222. *amalgamation of metallurgists*
223. *cloud of meteorologists*
    shower of meteorologists [c]
224. junta of military officers
225. fraunch of millers [a]
226. horde of misers [c]
227. slouch of models [c]
228. consternation of mothers [i]
    pride of (stage) mothers
229. mutter of mothers-in-law [c]
230. train of mountebanks
231. cortege of mourners
    pathos of mourners
    ululation of mourners
232. *reflection of narcissists*
233. tribe of natives
234. squad of navvies
235. nerve of neighbours [c]
236. *squeal of nieces*
237. scream of newsboys [i]
238. pallor of nightwatchmen [c]
    patrol of nightwatchmen
239. bunch of no-hopers
240. colony of nudists
    hang-out of nudists
241. slumber of old guard [c]
242. crowd of onlookers
    gallery of onlookers
243. den of opium addicts
244. saturnalia of orgiasts
245. *abandonment of orphans*
246. curse of painters
    illusion of painters [a]

228. *Heep of creeps* [y]
229. helotry of bondsmen
230. herd of harlots [a]

231. *homage of heroes*
232. horde of barbarians
    horde of misers [c]
    horde of savages
    horde of urchins
233. host of men [a]
234. *hostel of backpackers*
    hostel of (homeless) people
235. house of senators
236. huddle of people
237. illusion of painters [a]
238. impatience of wives [a]
239. impertinence of pedlars [a]
240. impi of Bantu warriors
241. *incantation of warlocks*
    incantation of witches
242. incredibility (or incredulity)
    of cuckolds [a]
243. indifference of waiters [c]
244. ingratitude of children [c]
245. institution of people
246. intake of students
247. jam of tarts [f]
248. *jam of W.I. members* [g]
249. jamboree of boy scouts
250. *jerusalem of WIs* [g]
251. junta of military officers

Chapter 5: A Clutch of Characters

madder of painters [c]	252. jury of people
misbelieving of painters [a]	*253. kindness of strangers* [q]
school of painters	254. kitsch of collectors [c]
247. *handful of palmists*	*255. kneeling of parishioners*
248. fall of parachutists	256. knot of astrologers
249. lying of pardoners [a]	knot of knaves
250. persistence of parents [c]	knot of people
251. kneeling of parishioners	*257. knuckle of gangsters*
252. faction of partisans	258. lack of principals [o]
253. promenade of (dance) partners	259. lash of carters [a]
	260. laughter of hostlers
254. body of pathologists	261. league of conspirators
255. impertinence of pedlars [a]	league of friends
malapertness of pedlars [a]	league of gentlemen
256. assembly of people	262. leap of banderilleros [u]
class of people	263. leer of boys [c]
clique of people	264. legion of the damned
cohort of people	legion of fans
colony of people	265. leprosarium (hospital) of lepers
column of people	
concourse of people	266. levee of guests
coterie of people	*267. liaison of lovers*
committee of people	268. line-up of suspects
commune of people	269. livery of tradesmen
community of people	livery of retainers
company of people	270. lodge of freemasons
crocodile of people	*271. lot of auctioneers*
crowd of people	lot of used car dealers [c]
druck of people	272. lying of pardoners [a]
enclave of people	273. madder of painters [c]
family of people	*274. magnum of hitmen*
flock of people	275. malapertness of pedlars [a]
fold of people	276. march of protesters
folkmoot of people	277. Mardi Gras of revellers
gathering of people	278. masquerade of poseurs
generation of people	279. meet of huntsmen

69

Gallimaufry

ghetto of people
group of people
hostel of (homeless) people
huddle of people
institution of people
jury of people
knot of people
mob of people
multitude of people
nation of people
party of people
race of people
queue of people
stable of people (under management)
stream of people
symposium of people
throng of people
257. showcase of performers
258. stampede of philatelists c
259. *ponder of philosophers*
school of philosophers
wrangle of philosophers c
260. click of photographers c
261. *press of photo-journalists*
262. college of physicians
263. nucleus of physicists c
264. *crop of (daffodil) pickers*
265. band of pirates
266. *flood of plumbers*
flush of plumbers c
267. gang of poets
268. cordon of police
division of police
force of police
patrol of police

280. meiny of attendants
281. mêlée of rioters
282. ménage à trois
283. mess of (little) boys
mess of diners (4 at table)
284. misbelieving of painters a
285. mob of people
mob of rioters
286. moiety of aborigines x
287. multiplying of husbands
288. multitude of people
289. mutter of mothers-in-law c
290. nation of people
291. nerve of neighbours c
292. netfull of knaves
293. network of contacts
294. neverthriving of jugglers a
295. nucleus of physicists c

296. obeisance of servants a
297. obscuration of dons
298. observance of hermits a
299. ogle of (office) boys c
300. ohm of electricians c
301. *order of waiters*
302. pack of brownies
pack of cowards
pack of press-men (or

Chapter 5: A Clutch of Characters

precinct of police (USA)	women)
station of police	303. pageant of revellers
269. cell of political activists	304. pallor of nightwatchmen ^c
270. gulag of political prisoners	305. pan of reviewers ^c
271. *whinge of poms*	306. *pander of toadies*
272. grip of porters ^c	307. panel of contestants
safeguard of porters ^a	panel of experts
273. *posse of posers*	panel of speakers
274. masquerade of poseurs	308. parade of mannequins
275. pack of press-men (or	309. parliament of whores
women)	310. party of guests
276. state of princes ^a	party of people
277. lack of principals ^o	party of revellers
278. plagiary of printers ^c	311. passel of brats
279. penitentiary of prisoners	312. *pathos of mourners*
pity of prisoners ^{a d}	313. patrol of nightwatchmen
280. pomposity of professors	patrol of police
281. anthology of (English) pros ^f	314. pavane of matadors ^c
282. stable of prostitutes	315. peal of Jezebels ^f
283. blockade of protesters	316. penitentiary of prisoners
demonstration of protesters	317. persistence of parents ^c
march of protesters	318. phratry of clans ^w
284. complex of psychoanalysts ^c	319. picket-line of strikers
285. twaddle of public speakers ^c	320. pity of prisoners ^{a d}
286. assembly of pupils	321. plagiary of printers ^c
dilation of pupils ^c	322. platform of speakers
287. *blaze of pyromaniacs*	323. *plight of refugees*
conflagration of pyromaniacs	324. plocke (or plucke) of
288. *store of quartermasters*	shoemakers
289. rally of racing drivers	325. pomposity of professors
stable of racing drivers	326. *ponder of philosophers*
290. faction of rebels	327. pool of reporters
291. camp of refugees	pool of typists
flight of refugees	pool of volunteers
plight of refugees	328. posse of deputies
292. board of regents ^t	*posse of posers*

71

293. group of relations
294. descent of relatives [c]
    gossip of relatives
295. truculence of removal men [c]
296. crush of reporters
    pool of reporters
    scoop of reporters [c]
    team of reporters
297. commission of representatives
298. livery of retainers
299. bacchanal of revellers
    Mardi Gras of revellers
    pageant of revellers
    party of revellers

300. pan of reviewers [c]
301. mêlée of rioters
    mob of rioters
302. band of robbers
303. gallery of rogues
304. sample of salesmen [c]
305. band of savages
    horde of savages
    posse of savages
306. disworship of Scots [a]
307. scolding of seamstresses [a]
308. *bond of (British) secret agents*
309. house of senators
    posse of savages
    posse of sheriffs
329. practice of G.P.s
330. prance of equestrians [c]
331. pratfall of clowns [c]
332. precinct of police (USA)
333. *press of photo-journalists*
334. prevarication of bureaucrats
335. *pride of gays*
    pride of (stage) mothers
336. prison of inmates
337. procession of dignitaries
    procession of gladiators
338. promenade of (dance) partners
339. promise of barmen
    promise of tapsters [a]
340. protectory of (destitute) children
341. proud showing of tailors [a]
342. provision of stewards
343. pummel of masseurs [c]
344. *quake of cowards*
345. quest of clerks [v]
346. queue of customers
    queue of people
347. race of people
348. rage of maidens [a]
349. rally of racing drivers
    rally of supporters
350. rangale of camp followers
351. rascal of boys [a]
352. rayful of knaves [a]
353. *reflection of narcissists*
354. regiment of women
355. rendezvous of friends

Chapter 5: A Clutch of Characters

310. obeisance of servants [a]
     retinue of servants
311. colony of settlers
312. credence of sewers (servers) [a]
313. posse of sheriffs
314. blackening of shoemakers
315. plocke (or plucke) of shoemakers
316. *crush of shoppers*
317. *avalanche of skiers*
318. display of skydivers
319. coffle of slaves
     galley of slaves
     gang of slaves
320. harem of slave-girls
321. *billow of smokers*
     hack of smokers [c]
322. panel of speakers
     platform of speakers
323. gallery of spectators
324. complement of staff
325. galaxy of starlets
326. array of stars
327. provision of stewards
328. *kindness of strangers* [q]
329. blockade of strikers
     picket-line of strikers
330. flourish of strumpets [f]
331. academy of students
     assembly of students
     class of students
     intake of students
     union of students
332. transplant of suburbanites [c]
333. *swarm of suitors*
334. untruth of summoners [a]

356. retinue of admirers
     retinue of servants
357. reunion of family members
358. riffraff of knaves [a]
359. ring of jewellers [c]
360. roster of volunteers
     rota of volunteers
361. rout of knights [a]
362. *run of cowards*
363. safeguard of porters [a]
364. salon of hairstylists
365. sample of salesmen [c]
366. saturnalia of orgiasts
367. saunter of cowboys [c]
368. school of artists
     school of clerks [a]
     school of followers
     school of gladiators
     school of painters
     school of philosophers
369. scolding of seamstresses [a]
370. scoop of reporters [c]
371. score of bachelors [c]
372. scream of newsboys [i]
373. seat of ushers
374. seed-bed of (new) talent
375. seraglio of concubines
     seraglio of eunuchs [s]
     seraglio of women
376. *serpent's tooth of teenagers* [m]
377. set of mathematicians
     set of ushers [a]
378. ship of fools
379. showcase of performers
     showcase of talent
380. shower of bastards

73

335. coach-load of supporters
　　 rally of supporters
336. *wave of surfers*
337. *fidget of suspects*
　　 line-up of suspects
338. bleach of sutors (cobblers) ᵃ
339. *swarm of swimmers*
340. claque of sycophants
　　 gush of sycophants ᶜ
　　 stoop of sycophants
341. disguising of tailors
　　 proud showing of tailors ᵃ
342. seed-bed of (new) talent
　　 showcase of talent
　　 'Who's Who' of talent
343. promise of tapsters ᵃ
344. jam of tarts ᶠ
345. cajolery of taverners ᵃ
　　 closing (glozing)of
　　　　taverners ᵃ
346. faculty of teaching staff
347. *attitude of teenagers*
　　 serpent's tooth of teenagers ᵐ
　　 sulk of teenagers
348. *field of theoretical physicists*
349. wandering of tinkers ᵃ
350. den of thieves
　　 gang of thieves
　　 skulk of thieves ᵃ
351. thrave of threshers ᵃ
352. *pander of toadies*
353. *tantrum of toddlers*
354. coachload of tourists
　　 flock of tourists
　　 glaze of tourists ᶜ
355. guild of tradesmen

　　 shower of meteorologists ᶜ
381. shrivel of critics ᶜ
382. shuffle of bureaucrats
383. shush of librarians ᶜ
384. sisterhood of women
385. sitting of diners
386. skulk of thieves ᵃ
387. slant of journalists ᶜ
388. slaver of gluttons ᶜ
389. slew of exterminators ᶜ
390. slouch of models ᶜ
391. slumber of old guard ᶜ
392. smear of curriers ᵃ
393. smelting of whores
394. smere of couriers ᵃ
395. smirk of couriers
396. sneer of butlers ᶜ
397. soiree of guests
398. sorority of women
399. sort of knaves
400. sphere of acquaintances
401. *sprig of vegetarians*
402. sprinkling of gardeners ᶜ
403. squad of beaters (hunting)
　　 squad of navvies
404. *squat of daubers* ᵃ
405. *squeal of nieces*
406. stable of people (under
　　　　management)
　　 stable of prostitutes
　　 stable of racing drivers
407. stack of librarians
408. stalk of foresters
409. stampede of philatelists ᶜ
410. state of princes ᵃ
411. station of firemen

Chapter 5: A Clutch of Characters

livery of tradesmen	station of police
356. *anorak of train-spotters*	412. *stoop of sycophants*
357. *camp of transvestites*	413. *store of quartermasters*
358. graft of tree surgeons c	414. strangle of city-dwellers c
359. tangle of tricksters	415. stream of people
360. ménage à trois	416. *strip of cartoonists*
361. essay of trollops f	417. *sulk of teenagers*
362. bored of trustees c	418. surgery of G.P.s
363. cluster of twitchers	419. *swarm of (literary) drones*
flock of twitchers (bird-watchers) j	swarm of suitors
	swarm of swimmers
364. pool of typists	420. swish of hairdressers c
365. extreme unction of undertakers (an even larger group!) c	421. symposium of people
	422. synod of cooks l
	423. tabernacle of bakers
unction of undertakers c	424. tangle of tricksters
366. galère of undesirables	425. tantrum of decorators c
367. horde of urchins	tantrum of toddlers
368. lot of used car dealers c	426. team of archaeologists
369. seat of ushers	team of experts
set of ushers a	team of reporters
370. *sprig of vegetarians*	team of workmen
371. haggle of vendors c	427. temperance of cooks a
372. audience of viewers	428. *thicket of idiots*
373. army of volunteers	429. think-tank of experts
pool of volunteers	430. thought of barons
roster of volunteers	431. thrave of threshers a
rota of volunteers	432. threatening of courtiers a
374. *desperation of voters*	433. thrill of fans c
375. *absence of waiters*	434. throng of people
indifference of waiters c	435. torque of mechanics c
order of waiters	436. tourney of knights
376. *amble of walkers*	437. train of apothecaries
377. *incantation of warlocks*	train of mountebanks
378. caste of warriors	438. trance of lovers c
379. gam of whalers aa	439. transplant of suburbanites c

Gallimaufry

380. parliament of whores
 smelting of whores
381. ambush of widows [c]
382. *baring of W.I. members* [g]
 jam of W.I. members [g]
383. bouquet of wine-tasters [c]
384. coven of witches
 incantation of witches
385. cloud of witnesses [m]
386. impatience of wives [a]
387. bevy of women
 binder of women [z]
 gaggle of women [a]
 grove of (old) women [n]
 regiment of women
 seraglio of women
 sisterhood of women

 sorority of women
388. *jerusalem of W Is* [g]
389. collective of workers
 co-operative of workers
 union of workers
390. team of workmen
391. grub of (impoverished) writers [r]
 worship of writers [a]
392. fellowship of yeomen
393. crusade of zealots

440. tribe of natives
441. tribulation of children [i]
442. trine of astrologers [c]
443. trinket of cordwainers
444. trip of hippies [c]
445. troop of boy scouts
 troop of brownies
 troop of gypsies
446. troupe of gladiators
447. truculence of removal men [c]
448. truth of barons
449. trynket of cobblers [a]
450. tryst of lovers
451. twaddle of public speakers [c]
452. *ululation of mourners*
453. unction of undertakers
454. unemployment of graduates[b]
455. unhappiness of husbands [b]
456. union of students
 union of workers
457. untruth of summoners [a]
458. vanguard of innovators
459. village of gays
460. wandering of tinkers [a]
461. *wave of surfers*
462. waywardness of haywards
 waywardness of herdsmen
463. *whinge of poms*
464. 'Who's Who' of talent
465. wince of dentists [c]
466. *wisdom of grandparents*
467. workforce of employees
468. worship of writers [a]
469. wrangle of philosophers [c]
470. *wunch of bankers*

Chapter 5: A Clutch of Characters

Notes:

a. Archaic, from one of the 16th century manuscripts (most commonly, The Book of Hawking & Hunting', by Dame Juliana Barnes, 1486).
b. From C E Hare, 'The Language of Field Sports'.
c. From James Lipton, 'An Exaltation of Larks' (1977).
d. From 'Debate between the Hors, Shepe and Ghoos'.
e. From the first 'Harley Manuscript'.
f. From Lipton, 'the dons joke' – see 'The Trouble with Words'.
g. From the suggestion that Women's Institutes are 'all jam and Jerusalem' (which has been given the lie by members of the Burley W.I., who produced a best-selling calendar of their members posing nude).
h. From James Joyce, 'Ulysses'.
i. By Alistair Reed, from 'Voices'.
j. From Jonathon Swift. 'A Confederacy of Dunces' is a tragicomic novel written by John Kennedy Toole. The title is apparently an ironic reference to this saying by the classic master of irony, Jonathan Swift (1667 - 1745), from 'Thoughts on Various Subjects': "When a true genius appears in this world, you may know him by this sign, that the dunces are all in confederacy against him."
k. Shakespeare's 'King Lear'.
l. Boswell's 'Life of Johnson'.
m. Bible: Hebrews 12, 1-3.
n. Reputedly from Dickens.
o. Reputedly from a meeting of ex-prime ministers, looking for a collective name.
p. Shakespeare, 'Henry V', before Agincourt.
q. From Tennessee Williams - 'A Streetcar Named Desire'.
r. Term popularised by Andrew Marvel.
s. Michael Foot, referring to proposed parliamentary reform for an appointed Chamber.
t. A committee of university officers who have general supervision over the welfare and conduct of students.
u. Banderilleros are the bull-fighters who implant decorated darts (banderillos) into the neck or shoulders of the bull during a bullfight. No doubt leaping was essential.
v. From Ivan G Sparkes, 'Dictionary of Collective Nouns & Group Terms'.
w. A phratry is an anthropological term for a kinship division consisting of two or more distinct clans which are considered a single unit, but which retain separate identities within the phratry. (Wikipedia)

x. A moiety is a 'skin group' describing the division of clans within the same language group in Australian Aboriginal culture.
y. From the character Uriah Heep, in Dickens' 'David Copperfield'
z. In October 2012, USA Republican Presidential candidate, Mitt Romney famously used the phrase 'binders full of women', as being brought to him to select female candidates for his administration, at his request – untruthfully, as it turned out. It went viral.
aa. A gam is a social meet of whalers or seaman while at sea.

'an ingratitude of children'

Chapter 5: A Clutch of Characters

'a crocodile of people'

'a gaggle of gossips'

'an avalanche of skiers'

Chapter 5: A Clutch of Characters

'a clamour of cooks'

THE FIRST BIRD OF THE SEASON.

'a blast of hunters'

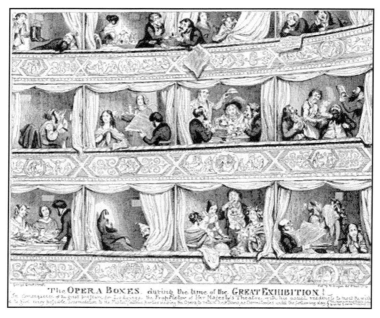

'a gallery of spectators'

'an intrigue of council members'

Chapter 5: A Clutch of Characters

'an illusion of painters'

'a bench of magistrates'

Gallimaufry

'a brigade of firemen'

'an untruth of summoners'

Chapter 5: A Clutch of Characters

'a damning of jurors'

'a wince of dentists'

Gallimaufry

'a tribulation of scholars'

Chapter 5: A Clutch of Characters

'a malapertness of pedlars'

'a bacchanal of revellers'

'an assembly of people'

Chapter Six

A Broadside of Belligerents

a. Military, Naval, Warfare
b. Transport

'a presage of doom'

Gallimaufry

'a bombardment of artillery'

6a. Military, Naval & Warfare

Sorted by noun	Sorted by collective noun
1. bridge of admirals wave of admirals ᵉ	1. argosy of merchant ships
2. flight of aeroplanes	2. armada of ships
3. fleet of aircraft	3. armament of weapons
4. case of ammunition	4. armoury of weapons
5. branch of the armed services	5. army of conscripts army of occupation
	6. army corps of troops
	7. array of troops
	8. arsenal of weapons
	9. avenue of escape
	10. balance of power balance of terror
	11. bandolier of cartridges
	12. barrage of gunfire
6. panoply of armour	13. barrel of gunpowder
suit of armour	14. battalion of soldiers

Chapter 6: A Broadside of Belligerents

7. force of arms
   pile of arms
   stack of arms (3+ or more
      rifles stacked in a
      pyramid)
   stand of arms
8. bundle of arrows
   cloud of arrows
   flight of arrows
   garb of arrows
   quiver of arrows
   sheaf of arrows
   volley of arrows
9. battery of artillery
   cannonade of (heavy)
      artillery
   park of artillery
   rafale of artillery (heavy
      burst)
   rumble of artillery
10. broadside of artillery shells
    salvo of artillery shells

11. field of battle
12. grove of bayonets
13. flotilla of boats
14. squadron of bombers
15. blitz of bombing
    wave of bombing
16. cluster of bomblets
17. blitzkrieg of bombs
18. division of brigades

15. battery of artillery
16. battlefield of combatants
17. belt of cartridges
18. billet of soldiers
19. blast of gunfire
20. blazonry of coats of arms
21. blitz of bombing
22. blitzkrieg of bombs
23. blockade of forces
    blockade of ships
24. boast of soldiers [a]
25. bombardment of gunfire
26. box of dynamite
27. brace of pistols
28. branch of the armed services
29. breach of defences
30. breakdown of negotiations
    breakdown of talks
31. bridge of admirals
32. brigade of soldiers
    brigade of troops
33. broadside of artillery shells
34. bundle of arrows
35. cadre of military personnel
36. caisson of explosives
37. campaign of terror
38. cannonade of (heavy)
    artillery
39. case of ammunition
40. caste of warriors
41. cavalcade of horsemen
42. cavalry of troops
43. cell of terrorists
44. chain of command
45. charge of cavalry
46. circus of fighter aircraft

19. clip of bullets
    hail of bullets
    magazine of bullets
    round of bullets
20. corps of cadets
21. plan of campaign
22. stand of cannon(s)
23. scene of carnage
24. bandolier of cartridges
    belt of cartridges
    round of cartridges
25. charge of cavalry
    squadron of cavalry
    troop of cavalry
26. blazonry of coats of arms
27. trooping of the colours
28. field of combat
29. battlefield of combatants
30. chain of command
31. unit of commandos
32. army of conscripts
    draft of conscripts
33. breach of defences
34. path of destruction
    swathe of destruction
    trail of destruction
35. scene of devastation
36. corps of (military) divisions
37. presage of doom
38. faggot of drummers
39. tour of duty
40. box of dynamite
    shipment of dynamite
    stick of dynamite
41. impedimenta of (army) equipment

47. clank of tanks
48. clatter of tanks
49. clip of bullets
50. cloud of arrows
51. cluster of bomblets
    cluster of mines
52. cohort of troops
53. command of officers
54. company of infantry
    company of ship's crew
    company of soldiers
55. convoy of military vehicles
56. cordage of ropes
57. corps of cadets
    corps of (military) divisions
58. corridor of escape
59. coup d'état
    coup de main
60. crèche of infantry
61. crew of sailors
62. cycle of violence
63. deck of sailors
64. defilade of fortifications
65. deployment of troops
66. detachment of soldiers
    detachment of troops
67. division of brigades
    division of fighter wings
    division of regiments
    division of ships
    division of soldiers
    division of troops
68. draft of conscripts
    draft of soldiers
69. echelon of troops
    echelon of ranks

Chapter 6: A Broadside of Belligerents

42. avenue of escape
    corridor of escape
43. coup d'état
44. pogrom of an ethnic group
45. series of explosions
    volley of explosions
46. caisson of explosives
47. circus of fighter aircraft
    wing of fighter aircraft
48. patrol of fighter planes
49. division of fighter wings
50. show of force
51. blockade of forces
52. defilade of fortifications
53. glitter of generals
54. barrage of gunfire
    blast of gunfire
    bombardment of gunfire
    enfilade of gunfire
    fusillade of gunfire
    salvo of gunfire
    volley of gunfire
55. barrel of gunpowder
    horn of gunpowder
    keg of gunpowder
56. hailstorm of gunships
57. field of honour
58. cavalcade of horsemen
59. escalation of hostilities
    outbreak of hostilities
60. company of infantry
    crèche of infantry
61. field of landmines
62. coup de main
63. morbidity of majors
64. hail of machine gun fire

70. enfilade of gunfire
    enfilade of troops
71. escalation of hostilities
    escalation of violence
72. execution of officers [a]
73. faggot of drummers
74. field of battle
    field of combat
    field of honour
    field of landmines
75. fleet of aircraft

    fleet of ships
76. flight of aeroplanes
    flight of arrows
77. flotilla of boats
    flotilla of ships
78. flurry of skirmishes
79. flush of W.C.s (wing
    commanders)[c]
80. force of arms
    force of military
       organisations
    force of military personnel
81. fusillade of gunfire
    fusillade of shots
82. garb of arrows
83. garrison of soldiers
84. glitter of generals

93

rattle of machine gun fire	85. grove of bayonets
65. hold of machine guns	86. guard of soldiers
nest of machine guns	87. hail of bullets
66. muscle of marines	hail of machine gun fire
67. weapon of mass destruction	hail of missiles
68. hatful of medals	88. hailstorm of gunships
row of medals	89. hatful of medals
69. maniple of men (120)	90. hold of machine guns
70. argosy of merchant ships	91. horn of gunpowder
71. force of military organisations	92. impedimenta of (army) equipment
72. cadre of military personnel	93. keg of gunpowder
force of military personnel	94. legion of soldiers
73. convoy of military vehicles	95. levy of soldiers
74. cluster of mines	96. line of trenches
75. hail of missiles	97. magazine of bullets
volley of missiles	98. maniple of men (120)
76. breakdown of negotiations	99. mess of officers [c]
77. army of occupation	100. mobilisation of troops
78. command of officers	101. morbidity of majors
execution of officers [a]	102. muscle of marines
mess of officers [c]	103. muster of ship's crew
79. theatre of operations	muster of soldiers
80. storm of paratroops	104. navy of ships
81. plug of personnel [d]	105. nest of machine guns
82. brace of pistols	106. ordinance of weapons
83. squadron of planes	107. outbreak of hostilities
84. strake of planks	108. pack of submarines
85. balance of power	109. panoply of armour
86. echelon of ranks	110. parade of troops
87. squad of (new) recruits	111. park of artillery
88. division of regiments	112. path of destruction
89. wave of reinforcements	113. patrol of fighter planes
90. pocket of resistance	patrol of soldiers
91. cordage of ropes	114. payload of weapons
92. rattle of sabres	115. phalanx of troops

Chapter 6: A Broadside of Belligerents

93. crew of sailors
    deck of sailors
    watch of sailors
94. armada of ships
    blockade of ships
    division of ships
    fleet of ships
    flotilla of ships
    navy of ships
95. company of ship's crew
    muster of ship's crew
96. fusillade of shots
97. flurry of skirmishes
98. battalion of soldiers
    billet of soldiers
    boast of soldiers [a]
    brigade of soldiers
    company of soldiers
    detachment of soldiers
    division of soldiers
    draft of soldiers
    garrison of soldiers
    guard of soldiers
    legion of soldiers
    levy of soldiers

    muster of soldiers
    patrol of soldiers
    platoon of soldiers
    regiment of soldiers
    squad of soldiers

116. pile of arms
117. plan of campaign
118. platoon of soldiers
119. plug of personnel [d]
120. pocket of resistance
121. pogrom of an ethnic group
122. presage of doom
123. quiver of arrows
124. rafale of artillery (heavy burst)
125. rally of troops
126. rattle of machine gun fire
     rattle of sabres
127. regiment of soldiers
128. reign of terror
129. ring of steel
130. round of bullets
     round of cartridges
131. row of medals
132. rumble of artillery
133. salvo of artillery shells
     salvo of gunfire
134. scene of carnage
     scene of devastation
135. series of explosions
136. sheaf of arrows
137. shipment of dynamite
138. show of force
     show of strength
139. simplicity of subalterns
140. spearhead of troops
141. spread of torpedoes
142. squad of (new) recruits
     squad of soldiers
143. squadron of bombers
     squadron of cavalry

95

Gallimaufry

    troop of soldiers
99. ring of steel
100. show of strength
101. simplicity of subalterns
102. pack of submarines
    wolfpack of submarines
103. system of systems ᵇ
104. breakdown of talks
105. clank of tanks
    clatter of tanks
106. balance of terror
    campaign of terror
    reign of terror
    state of terror
107. cell of terrorists
108. spread of torpedoes
109. line of trenches
110. army corps of troops
    array of troops
    brigade of troops
    cavalry of troops
    cohort of troops
    deployment of troops
    detachment of troops
    division of troops
    echelon of troops
    enfilade of troops
    mobilisation of troops
    parade of troops
    phalanx of troops
    rally of troops
    spearhead of troops
    unit of troops
    vanguard of troops
111. cycle of violence
    escalation of violence

    squadron of planes
    squadron of warships (<10)
144. stack of arms (3 or more rifles stacked in a pyramid)
145. stand of arms

    stand of cannon
146. state of terror
    state of war
147. stick of dynamite
148. stockade of wooden posts
149. stockpile of weapons
150. storm of paratroops
151. strake of planks
152. suit of armour
153. swathe of destruction
154. system of systems ᵇ
155. theatre of operations
    theatre of war
156. tour of duty
157. trail of destruction
158. troop of cavalry
    troop of soldiers
159. trooping of the colours
160. unit of commandos

Chapter 6: A Broadside of Belligerents

112. state of war	unit of troops
theatre of war	161. vanguard of troops
113. caste of warriors	162. volley of arrows
114. squadron of warships (<10)	volley of explosions
115. flush of W.C.s (wing commanders)[c]	volley of gunfire
	volley of missiles
116. armament of weapons	163. watch of sailors
armoury of weapons	164. wave of admirals [e]
arsenal of weapons	wave of bombings
ordinance of weapons	wave of reinforcements
payload of weapons	165. weapon of mass destruction
stockpile of weapons	166. wing of fighter aircraft
117. stockade of wooden posts	167. wolfpack of submarines

Notes:

a. Archaic, from one of the 16th century manuscripts (most commonly, 'The Book of Hawking & Hunting', by Dame Juliana Barnes, 1486).
b. A grouping of resources, methods and procedures. (US Joint Forces Command).
c. From James Lipton, 'An Exaltation of Larks' (1977).
d. A cell of personnel for a specific mission (US Joint Forces Command).
e. From Ivan G Sparkes, 'Dictionary of Collective Nouns & Group Terms'.

'a balance of power'

Gallimaufry

'a head of steam'

6b. Transport & Vehicles

Sorted by noun	Sorted by collective noun
1. escadrille of aircraft (>6; Fr.)	1. autocade of cars
fleet of aircraft	2. barricade of vehicles
flight of aircraft	3. cancellation of trains c
formation of aircraft	4. cavalcade of riders
2. comedy of airline schedules c	5. charge of taxis c
3. rack of bicycles	6. circle of wagons
wobble of bicycles b	7. *clang of fire engines*
4. fleet of buses	8. column of vehicles
lurch of buses c	column of wagons
5. pageant of carnival floats	9. comedy of airline schedules c
parade of carnival floats	10. *conspiracy of chemtrails*

Chapter 6: A Broadside of Belligerents

6. procession of carriages	11. convoy of lorries
7. autocade of cars	convoy of trucks
fleet of cars	12. cordon of vehicles
gymkhana of (racing) cars	13. corral of wagons
motor-pool of cars	14. cortege of funeral cars
park of cars	15. escadrille of aircraft (>6; Fr.)
pileup of cars	16. fleet of aircraft
pool of cars	fleet of buses
queue of cars	fleet of cars
stable of (luxury) cars	fleet of coaches
8. gang of cartwheels (set) [d]	fleet of lorries
9. fleet of coaches	fleet of narrowboats
10. *conspiracy of chemtrails*	fleet of vans
11. *tangle of contrails*	17. flight of aircraft
12. *clang of fire engines*	18. formation of aircraft
13. cortege of funeral cars	19. gang of cartwheels (set) [d]
14. hover of helicopters [c]	20. gridlock of vehicles
15. motorcade of limousines	21. gymkhana of (racing) cars
16. convoy of lorries	22. hover of helicopters [c]
fleet of lorries	23. laager of weapons
17. fleet of narrowboats	24. lurch of buses [c]
marina of narrowboats	25. marina of narrowboats
18. stack of planes [c]	marina of yachts
19. tragedy of railway schedules [c]	26. mode of transport
	27. motorcade of limousines
20. cavalcade of riders	28. motor-pool of cars
21. charge of taxis [c]	29. pageant of carnival floats
22. rank of taxi cabs	30. parade of carnival floats
23. cancellation of trains [c]	31. park of cars
24. postponement of trains [c]	32. pileup of cars
25. mode of transport	33. pool of cars
26. convoy of trucks	34. postponement of trains [c]
27. fleet of vans	35. procession of carriages
28. barricade of vehicles	36. queue of cars
column of vehicles	37. rack of bicycles
cordon of vehicles	38. rally of vintage cars

gridlock of vehicles	39. rank of taxi cabs
traffic jam of vehicles	40. stable of (luxury) cars
25. rally of vintage cars	41. stack of planes [c]
26. column of wagons	42. traffic jam of vehicles
circle of wagons	43. *tangle of contrails*
corral of wagons	44. tragedy of railway schedules [c]
laager of wagons	
train of wagons	45. train of wagons
31. marina of yachts	46. wobble of bicycles [b]

Notes:

a. Archaic, from one of the 16th century manuscripts (most commonly, The Book of Hawking & Hunting', by Dame Juliana Barnes, 1486).
b. By Alistair Reed, from 'Voices'.
c. From James Lipton, 'An Exaltation of Larks' (1977).
d. From Ivan G Sparkes, 'Dictionary of Collective Nouns & Group Terms'.

'a column of wagons'

Chapter 6: A Broadside of Belligerents

'a procession of carriages'

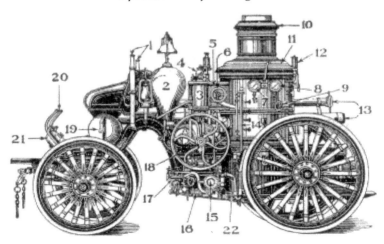

'a clang of fire engines'

101

Gallimaufry

'a drift of balloons'

'a mode of transport'

Chapter Seven

A World of Wonder

a. *Architectural & built landscape*
b. *Astronomical*
c. *Geographical & geological*
d. *Weather, light & colour*

'a Damocles of volcanoes'

Gallimaufry

'a tilt of windmills'

7a. Architectural & built landscape

Sorted by noun	Sorted by collective noun
1. maze of alleyways nest of alleyways	1. acre of land
2. block of apartments	2. alignment of ley-lines
3. arcade of arches	3. allotment of land
4. truss of (supporting) beams	4. aqueduct of water
5. chicane of bends	5. arcade of arches arcade of shops
6. compound of buildings complex of buildings	6. are of land (10m²)

7. row of bungalows	7. avenue of houses
	   avenue of shops
	   avenue of sphinxes

8. network of canals	8. bazaar of shops
9. mews of cathouses [a]	9. bivouac of tents
10. forest of chimneys stack of chimneys	10. blight of urban sprawl
11. cradle of civilisation	11. block of apartments block of flats
12. colonnade of columns	12. bovate of land [c]
13. maze of corridors	13. cairn of stones
14. mews of cottages	

Chapter 7: A World of Wonder

row of cottages	14. canal of water
15. patchwork of fields	15. canton of land
16. block of flats	16. carucate of land [c]
condominium of flats	17. catchment of water
17. network of footpaths	18. cemetery of graves
18. *leer of gargoyles*	19. chain of restaurants or hotels
19. cemetery of graves	chain of supermarkets
20. avenue of houses	20. chicane of bends
crescent of houses	21. circle of huts
estate of houses	circle of stones
street of houses	22. city of tents
terrace of houses	23. cluster of schools
21. circle of huts	
encampment of huts	
kraal of huts	
settlement of huts	
22. acre of land	
allotment of land	
are of land (10m²)	
bovate of land [c]	
canton of land	
carucate of land [c]	
croft of land (5 acres)	24. colonnade of columns
day's work of land (2/3 acre)	25. complex of buildings
demesne of land	26. compound of buildings
domain of land	27. condominium of flats
enclosure of land	28. conurbation of townships
estate of land	29. cradle of civilisation
hectare of land	30. crescent of houses
hide of land (120 acres)	31. croft of land (5 acres)
morgen of land (approx 2 acres) [b]	32. cru of vineyards
	33. day's work of land (2/3 acre)
oxgang of land [c]	34. demesne of land
parcel of land	35. domain of land
patch of land	36. encampment of huts
plot of land	37. enclosure of land

tract of land
virgate of land (¼ of a hide, or 20/30 acres)
23. alignment of ley-lines
24. flight of locks
25. suite of offices
26. honeycomb of passages
network of passages
warren of passages
27. ring of post-holes
28. hall of residence
29. chain of restaurants or hotels
franchise of restaurants
30. junction of roads
network of roads
31. suite of rooms

32. patchwork of rooftops
33. cluster of schools
34. arcade of shops
avenue of shops
bazaar of shops
galleria of shops
mall of shops
35. avenue of sphinxes
36. forest of spires
37. flight of stairs

38. estate of houses
estate of land
39. farm of wind turbines
40. field of tents
41. flight of locks
flight of stairs
flight of steps
42. forest of chimneys
forest of spires
forest of TV aerials
43. franchise of restaurants
44. galleria of shops
45. graveyard of tombs
46. hall of residence
47. hectare of land
48. hide of land (120 acres)
49. hill of windmills
50. honeycomb of passages
51. junction of roads
52. kraal of huts
53. *leer of gargoyles*
54. mall of shops
55. maze of alleyways
maze of corridors
56. mews of cathouses [a]
mews of cottages
57. millrace of water
58. morgen of land (approx 2 acres) [b]
59. necropolis of tombs
60. nest of alleyways
61. network of canals
network of footpaths
network of passages
network of roads
62. oxgang of land [c]

38. palisade of stakes	63. palisade of stakes
39. flight of steps	64. parcel of land
40. cairn of stones	65. patch of land
circle of stones	66. patchwork of fields
41. chain of supermarkets	patchwork of rooftops
42. bivouac of tents	67. plot of land
city of tents	68. reservoir of water
field of tents	69. ring of post-holes
43. graveyard of tombs	70. row of bungalows
necropolis of tombs	row of cottages
44. conurbation of townships	71. settlement of huts
45. forest of TV aerials	72. stack of chimneys
46. blight of urban sprawl	73. street of houses
47. cru of vineyards	74. suite of offices
48. aqueduct of water	suite of rooms
canal of water	75. terrace of houses
catchment of water	76. *tilt of windmills* [d]
millrace of water	77. tract of land
reservoir of water	78. truss of (supporting) beams
49. hill of windmills	79. virgate of land (¼ of a hide,
tilt of windmills [d]	or 20/30 acres)
50. farm of wind turbines	80. warren of passages

Notes:

[a.] From James Lipton, 'An Exaltation of Larks' (1977).

[b.] A South African term.

[c.] A bovate (also known as an oxgang, oxgate, or oxland), was a piece of land, (15-18 acres), that a farmer with one ox could plough in 1 year. A carucate (or ploughland) was land that an 8-ox plough-team could plough in 1 year (120-180 acres).

[d.] The expression 'tilting at windmills' comes from Miguel de Cervantes novel 'Don Quixote'.

'a blight of urban sprawl'

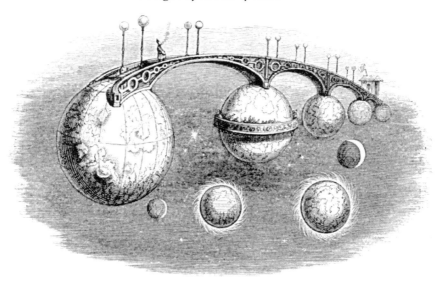

'a syzygy of celestial bodies'

Chapter 7: A World of Wonder

7b. Astronomical

Sorted by noun	Sorted by collective noun
1. belt of asteroids	1. abyss of space
2. ephemeris of celestial bodies	2. alignment of planets
syzygy of celestial bodies	3. array of radio telescopes
3. zodiac of constellations	4. asterism of stars
4. cluster of galaxies	5. belt of asteroids
5. nebula of gas (or dust)	belt of radiation
6. field of gravitation	6. canopy of stars
7. firmament of the heavens	7. *charm of quarks*
8. swarm of meteorites	8. cluster of galaxies
9. shower of meteors	cluster of stars
storm of meteors	9. conjunction of planets
10. planetarium of the night sky	10. constellation of stars
11. alignment of planets	11. continuum of space-time
conjunction of planets	12. crop of sunspots
quincunx of planets [a]	13. ephemeris of celestial bodies
12. *charm of quarks*	14. field of gravitation
13. belt of radiation	15. firmament of the heavens
14. array of radio telescopes	16. galaxy of stars
15. storm of solar particles	17. infinity of space
16. orrery of the solar system	18. nebula of gas (or dust)
17. abyss of space	19. orrery of the solar system
infinity of space	20. panoply of stars
18. continuum of space-time	21. planetarium of the night sky
19. *stare of stargazers*	22. quincunx of planets [a]
20. asterism of stars	23. shower of meteors
canopy of stars	24. *stare of stargazers*
constellation of stars	25. storm of meteors
cluster of stars	storm of solar particles
galaxy of stars	26. swarm of meteorites
panoply of stars	27. syzygy of celestial bodies
21. crop of sunspots	zodiac of constellations

'a stare of stargazers'

Chapter 7: A World of Wonder

'a firmament of heavenly spheres'

'a cluster of crystals'

7c. Geographical & geological

Sorted by noun	Sorted by collective noun
1. series of aftershocks	1. agglomeration of rock
2. meinie of brooks	2. alluvium of sediment
3. rush of bubbles	3. aquifer of water
4. maze of canyons	
5. labyrinth of caves	
6. palisade of cliffs	
7. cluster of crystals	
geode of crystals	
mass of crystal	
8. field of dunes	
train of (underwater) dunes	
9. erg of (sand) dune fields	
10. mound of earth	
11. cluster of earthquakes	4. arc of volcanoes
series of earthquakes	5. archipelago of islands
storm of earthquakes	6. avalanche of mud
12. sequence of earth tremors	7. band of pahas (loess hills)
13. ring of fire (volcanoes)	8. batholith of rock
14. flicker of flame	9. block of stone
gout of flame	10. body of water
inferno of flame	11. cascade of water
jet of flame	12. chain of islands
lick of flame	chain of mountains
spurt of flame	chain of volcanoes
tongue of flame	13. channel of water
tower of flame	14. cluster of crystals
15. spate of flood-water	cluster of earthquakes
16. range of hills	cluster of stalactites
17. pancake of ice	15. colluvium of rock fragments
tongue of ice	16. confluence of rivers
18. *drift of icebergs*	17. conglomerate of rock
flotilla of icebergs	18. cordillera of mountain

Chapter 7: A World of Wonder

19. archipelago of islands
    chain of islands
17. domain of land
    isthmus of land
    neck of land
    peninsula of land
    promontory of land
    spit of land
    strip of land
    tongue of land
    tract of land
18. eruption of lava
    flow of lava
    neck of lava
    plug of lava
    river of lava
    stream of lava
19. vein of minerals
20. chain of mountains

    range of mountains
    ridge of mountains
21. cordillera of mountain
    ranges
22. avalanche of mud
    quagmire of mud
    sea of mud
	ranges
	19. crescent of sand dunes
	20. current of water
	21. *Damocles of volcanoes*
	22. domain of land
	23. dribble of water
	24. *drift of icebergs*
	    drift of sand
	25. dune of sand
	26. eddy of water
	27. eluvium of rock particles
	28. erg of (sand) dune fields
	29. eruption of lava
	30. expanse of ocean
	31. field of dunes
	32. flicker of flame
	33. flood of water
	34. *flotilla of icebergs*
	35. flow of lava
	    flow of water
	36. fountain of water
	37. gangue of (waste) rock
	38. geode of crystals
	39. geyser of water
	40. gout of flame
	41. gyre of ocean currents
	42. head of water
	43. inferno of flame
	44. isthmus of land
	45. jet of flame
	46. labyrinth of caves
	    labyrinth of tunnels
	47. lake of water
	48. layer of permafrost
	49. lick of flame
	50. lode of ore

113

23. expanse of ocean
24. gyre of ocean currents
25. lode of ore
    seam of ore
    vein of ore
26. band of pahas (loess hills)
27. layer of permafrost
28. raft of pumice stone (at sea)
29. confluence of rivers
30. agglomeration of rock
    batholith of rock
    conglomerate of rock
    gangue of rock
    matrix of rock
    moraine of rocks
    outcrop of rock
    strata of rock
31. colluvium of rock fragments
32. eluvium of rock particles
33. drift of sand
    dune of sand
34. crescent of sand dunes
    sea of sand dunes
35. alluvium of sediment
36. shower of sparks
37. cluster of stalactites
38. block of stone
39. scree of (loose) stones
40. labyrinth of tunnels
    warren of tunnels
41. arc of volcanoes
    chain of volcanoes
    Damocles of volcanoes
42. aquifer of water
    body of water
    cascade of water

51. maelstrom of whirlpools
52. mass of crystal
53. matrix of rock
54. maze of canyons
55. meinie of brooks
56. moraine of rocks
57. mound of earth
58. neck of land
    neck of lava
59. outcrop of rock
60. palisade of cliffs
61. pancake of ice
62. peninsula of land
63. plug of lava
64. pool of water
65. promontory of land
66. quagmire of mud
67. raft of pumice stone (at sea)
68. range of hills
    range of mountains
69. ridge of mountains
70. ring of fire (volcanoes)
71. river of lava
72. rivulet of water
73. rush of bubbles
    rush of water
74. scree of (loose) stones
75. sea of mud
    sea of sand dunes
76. seam of ore
77. sequence of earth tremors
78. series of aftershocks
    series of earthquakes
    series of waterfalls
79. set of waves
80. shower of sparks

Chapter 7: A World of Wonder

channel of water	81. spate of flood-water
current of water	82. spit of land
dribble of water	83. splash of water
eddy of water	84. spray of water
flood of water	85. spring of water
flow of water	86. spurt of flame
fountain of water	spurt of water
geyser of water	87. storm of earthquakes
head of water	88. strata of rock
lake of water	89. stream of lava
pool of water	90. strip of land
rivulet of water	91. tongue of flame
rush of water	tongue of ice
splash of water	tongue of land
spray of water	92. torrent of water
spring of water	93. tower of flame
spurt of water	94. tract of land
torrent of water	95. train of (underwater) dunes
trickle of water	96. trickle of water
42. series of waterfalls	97. vein of minerals
43. set of waves	vein of ore
44. maelstrom of whirlpools	98. warren of tunnels

'a palisade of cliffs'

Gallimaufry

'a gust of wind'

7d. Weather, light & colour

Sorted by noun	Sorted by collective noun
1. body of air	1. *array of rainbows*
breath of air	2. avalanche of snow
current of air	3. *awe of aurora*
cushion of air	4. balance of nature
downdraft of air	5. ball of lightning
parcel of air	6. bank of clouds
pocket of air	bank of fog
rush of air	bank of low pressure
stream of air	7. beacon of light
updraft of air	8. blanket of cloud
vortex of air	blanket of fog
2. *awe of aurora*	9. blaze of sunshine
curtain of aurora	10. blazonry of colour
veil of aurora	11. blizzard of snow

Chapter 7: A World of Wonder

3. bank of clouds
   blanket of cloud
   canopy of cloud
   cumulus of cloud
   pillar of cloud
   scud of clouds
   thunderhead of clouds
4. blazonry of colour
   chameleon of colours
   gamut of colours [e]
   kaleidoscope of colours
   palette of colours
   patchwork of colour
   rainbow of colours
   riot of colour
   scheme of colours
   spectrum of colours
   tapestry of colour
   tincture of colour
   triad of colours [b]
5. cloak of darkness
   cover of darkness
6. fall of dew
7. *down of dewdrops*
8. *drear of drizzle*
9. *purgatory of dust devils*
10. bank of fog
    blanket of fog
    patch of fog
11. touch of frost
12. storm of hails
13. ridge of high pressure
    wedge of high pressure
14. *howl of hurricanes*
15. glaze of ice
    pellet of ice

12. body of air
13. breath of air
    breath of wind
14. burst of rain
15. cannonade of thunder
16. canopy of cloud
17. chameleon of colours
18. clap of thunder
19. cloak of darkness

20. cloudburst of rain
21. cluster of tornadoes
    cluster of weather systems
22. congregation of vapours [a]
23. corona of light
24. cover of darkness
25. crack of thunder
26. cumulus of cloud
27. current of air
28. curtain of aurora
29. cushion of air
30. dazzle of sunlight
31. derecho of thunderstorms [c]
32. *down of dewdrops*
33. downdraft of air
34. downpour of rain
35. *drear of drizzle*
36. drift of snow
37. dusting of snow

117

rime of ice	38. eddy of wind
storm of ice	39. fall of dew
16. beacon of light	fall of snow
corona of light	40. flash of lightning
halo of light	41. flicker of sunlight
interplay of light	42. flurry of snowflakes
patchwork of light	43. force of nature
penumbra of light	44. gale of wind
play of light	45. gamut of colours [e]
pool of light	46. glaze of ice
prism of light	47. gust of wind
radiance of light	48. haboob of sandstorms
ray of light	49. halo of light
spectrum of light	50. haze of mist
twinkle of light	51. *howl of hurricanes*
17. ball of lightning	52. interplay of light
flash of lightning	53. kaleidoscope of colours
sheet of lightning	54. knot of wind
storm of lightning	55. *miasma of mist*
streak of lightning	56. monsoon of rain
18. bank of low pressure	57. *murk of mist*
trough of low pressure	58. outbreak of rain
19. haze of mist	outbreak of tornadoes
miasma of mist	59. palette of colours
murk of mist	60. parcel of air
20. shaft of moonlight	61. patch of fog
21. balance of nature	62. patchwork of colour
force of nature	patchwork of light
22. burst of rain	63. peal of thunder
cloudburst of rain	64. pellet of ice
downpour of rain	65. pencil of rays
monsoon of rain	66. penumbra of light
outbreak of rain	67. pillar of cloud
shower of rain	68. pitter-patter of raindrops
spatter of rain	69. play of light
squall of rain	70. pocket of air

tempest of rain
23. *array of rainbows*
    radiance of rainbows
    reassurance of rainbows
24. pitter-patter of raindrops
25. pencil of rays
26. haboob of sandstorms
27. scattering of showers
28. avalanche of snow
    blizzard of snow
    drift of snow
    dusting of snow
    fall of snow
29. flurry of snowflakes
30. dazzle of sunlight
    flicker of sunlight
    shaft of sunlight

31. blaze of sunshine
    ray of sunshine
32. range of temperatures
33. cannonade of thunder
    clap of thunder
    crack of thunder
    peal of thunder
    rumble of thunder
34. derecho of thunderstorms c
    supercell of thunderstorms
35. cluster of tornados

71. pool of light
72. prism of light
73. *purgatory of dust devils*
74. radiance of light
    radiance of rainbows
75. rainbow of colours
76. range of temperatures
77. ray of light
    ray of sunshine
78. *reassurance of rainbows*
79. ridge of high pressure
80. rime of ice
81. riot of colour
82. rumble of thunder
83. rush of air
84. scattering of showers
85. scheme of colours
86. scud of clouds
87. shaft of moonlight
    shaft of sunlight
88. sheet of lightning
89. shower of rain
90. spatter of rain
91. spectrum of colours
    spectrum of light
92. squall of rain
    squall of wind
93. storm of hails
    storm of ice
    storm of lightning
    storm of tornadoes
94. streak of lightning
95. stream of air
96. supercell of thunderstorms
97. tapestry of colours
98. tempest of rain

outbreak of tornadoes	99. thunderhead of clouds
storm of tornadoes	100. tincture of colour
tumult of tornadoes	101. touch of frost
36. *twirl of twisters*	102. triad of colours [b]
37. congregation of vapours [a]	103. trough of low pressure
38. cluster of weather systems	104. *tumult of tornadoes*
39. *whorl of whirlwinds*	105. twinkle of light
40. *wobble of willy willys* [d]	106. *twirl of twisters*
41. breath of wind	107. updraft of air
eddy of wind	108. veil of aurora
gale of wind	109. vortex of air
gust of wind	110. wedge of high pressure
knot of wind	111. *whorl of whirlwinds*
squall of wind	112. *wobble of willy willys* [d]

Notes:

a. Shakespeare, from 'Hamlet'.
b. Any three colours located equidistant from one another on the colour wheel.
c. A line of intense, widespread, and fast-moving thunderstorms that moves across a great distance. They are characterized by damaging straight-line winds over hundreds of miles. Spanish for straight.
d. A willy willy is the Australian aboriginal term for a dust devil.
e. In computer graphics, the gamut, or colour gamut, is a certain complete subset of colours. The most common usage refers to the subset of colours which can be accurately represented in a given circumstance, such as within a given colour space or by a certain output device. (*Wikipedia*)

'a squall of wind'

Gallimaufry

'a downpour of rain'

'a play of sunlight'

Chapter 7: A World of Wonder

THE rain is raining all around,
It falls on field and tree,
It rains on the umbrellas here,
And on the ships at sea.

'*a scattering of showers*'

Chapter Eight

A Banality of Bric-a-Brac

    a. *Domestic Objects*
    b. *Food and Drink*
    c. *Sports, Games and Pastimes*

'a glint of glasses'

Gallimaufry

'an omnium-gatherum of items'

8a. Domestic Objects

Sorted by noun	Sorted by collective noun
1. carboy of acid	1. album of photographs
2. hoarding of advertisements	2. arc of floodlights
3. discography of (recorded) albums	3. atomiser of perfume
	4. bag of goodies
4. museum of antiques	bag of shopping
5. obsolescence of appliances [b]	bag of tricks
6. coat of arms	5. bale of cotton [f]
7. museum of artefacts	bale of dice
8. number of articles	bale of towels
9. portfolio of artwork	6. ball of string
10. bed of ashes	ball of twine
cinerarium of (cremated) ashes	ball of wool
	7. band of gold
11. layette of baby clothes	8. bank of (audio) speakers

Chapter 8: A Banality of Bric-a-Brac

12. festoon of banners
    sheaf of banners
13. barricade of barriers
    line of barriers
14. rosary of beads
    string of beads
    torsade of beads
15. dormitory of beds
16. wad of bills
17. swag of booty
18. nest of bowls
19. barrow-load of bricks
    flat of bricks
    hod of bricks
    ruck of bricks
20. trousseau of bridal wear
21. bavin of brushwood
22. burst of bubbles
23. chain of buckets

24. *stroll of buggies*
25. piece of calico (10 yds)
26. bolt of canvas (40 yds)
    press of canvas (sails)
27. stack of canvases (art)
28. hold of cargo
    jetsam of cargo
    manifest of (ship's) cargo
	9. bar of gold
	10. barrel of oil (35 gallons)
	11. barricade of barriers
	12. barrow-load of bricks
	13. basin of water
	14. basket of laundry
	15. bath of water
	16. batt of wool (wadding, used
	    for spinning or felting)
	17. batterie de cuisine
	18. bavin of brushwood
	19. bed of ashes
	    bed of coal
	20. berry (bury) of (rabbit) holes
	21. blanket of dust
	22. block of wood
	23. bolt of canvas (40 yds)
	    bolt of cloth (40 yds)
	    bolt of material
	24. book of gold leaf [j]
	    book of matches
	    book of stamps
	25. bouquet of fireworks
	    bouquet of rockets
	26. box of cigars
	    box of matches
	27. bracelet of charms
	28. browss of fish bait (dial)
	29. brushful of paint
	30. bucket of cement
	    bucket of manure
	31. budget of papers
	32. bunch of keys
	33. bundle of charms
	    bundle of firewood
	    bundle of sticks

29. collection of CDs	34. bunker of coal
30. bucket of cement	35. burn (burden) of furze (dial)
31. row of chairs	burn (from burden) of turf
set of chairs	36. burst of bubbles
stack of chairs	37. bushel of nuts
32. bracelet of charms	38. butt of water
bundle of charms	39. cabinet of trophies
33. service of china	40. cable of wires
set of china	41. cache of jewels
34. carton of cigarettes	cache of loot
packet of cigarettes	cache of money
35. box of cigars	42. canister of film
humidor of cigars	canister of water
36. bolt of cloth (40 yds)	43. canteen of cutlery
ell of cloth (45")	44. carat of diamonds
piece of cloth (10 yds)	carat of gold
37. closet of clothes	45. carboy of acid
hold-all of clothes	46. card of wool
jumble of clothes	47. carrot of tobacco (US)
outfit of clothes	48. carton of cigarettes
rack of clothes	49. cartridge of film
suit of clothes	50. cascade of fireworks
suitcase of clothes	51. casket of jewellery
wardrobe of clothes	52. caste of flower pots
38. regalia of clothing (Native American)	53. cesspit of sewage
	54. chain of buckets
39. bed of coal	chain of honour
bunker of coal	55. chaldron of coal (London 25.5 cwt)
chaldron of coal (London 25.5 cwt)	chaldron of coal (Newcastle 53 cwt)
chaldron of coal (Newcastle 53 cwt)	56. chatelaine of implements [h]
lump of coal	57. chest of drawers
pack of coal (3 bushels)	58. cinerarium of (cremated) ashes
sack of coal	
scuttle of coal	59. cistern of water

Chapter 8: A Banality of Bric-a-Brac

seam of coal	60. clearance of sale goods
shovelful of coal	61. clew of cords [i]
stock of coal (4 cubic yds)	clew of yarn
40. festoon of cobwebs	62. clod of earth
41. handful of coins	63. closet of clothes
journey of coins (minted tog. 720 oz/2000 gold coins)	64. cloud of dust
	cloud of smoke
roll of coins	65. cluster of diamonds
rouleau of coins	cluster of knots [a]
42. *comfort of cushions*	cluster of scales
43. glut of commercials [b]	66. *clutch of umbrellas*
44. screed of concrete	67. clutter of objects
45. clew of cords [i]	68. coat of arms
raffle of cords [i]	69. coating of plaster
46. coble of corks (dial)	70. coble of corks (dial)
47. stack of correspondence	71. cockade of plumes
48. bale of cotton [f]	72. coffer of money
hank of cotton (7 skeins, 840 yds)	73. coil of rope
	74. collage of photos
reel of cotton	53. collection of CDs
skein of cotton (80 threads)	collection of paintings
spindle of cotton (18 hanks)	collection of records
spool of cotton	collection of stamps
thread of cotton (54 inches)	collection of tapes (cassette)
49. wad of cotton wool	collection of toys
50. pil of crab-buts (dial)	54. column of numbers
51. fleet of crab pots (dial)	column of smoke
52. urn of cremated remains	55. combination of numbers
53. service of crockery	56. *comfort of cushions*
	57. compact of powder
	58. companion set of fire irons
	59. complement of parts
	60. concretion of parts
	61. cord of wood (a stack 4'×4'×8')
54. batterie de cuisine	
55. pair of curtains	62. coven of kettles [e]

56. canteen of cutlery
57. jetsam of debris
58. carat of diamonds
    cluster of diamonds
59. bale of dice
60. service of dinner things
61. rack of dishes
    stack of dishes
62. suit of dittos [d]
63. repository of documents
64. fistful of dollars
65. chest of drawers
66. lifetime of drudgery
67. pile of dung
68. blanket of dust
    cloud of dust
    handful of dust [c]
    speck of dust
69. tincture of dye
    vat of dye
70. clod of earth
71. paraphernalia of equipment
72. fat quarter of fabric (18"x22" approx)
    remnant of fabric
    swatch of fabric (sample)

73. *flirtation of fans*
    flutter of fans
74. panache of feathers

63. cracker of paper
64. crock of gold
65. cruse of oil
66. curriculum of lessons
67. cutch of gold leaf [j]
68. cylinder of gas
69. dab of paint
70. daub of paint
71. delivery of goods
    delivery of stock
72. denier of silk (nylon, rayon) [g]
73. discography of (recorded) albums
74. display of fireworks
    display of merchandise
75. distribution of largesse
76. division of spoils
77. dormitory of beds
78. down of fur
79. drift of fishing nets [i]
80. *eldorado of gold*
81. ell of cloth (45")
82. emporium of goods
83. escalade of ladders
84. etui of (manicure) tools
85. exhibition of paintings
    exhibition of pictures
    exhibition of works of art
86. faggot of sticks
87. fardel of raw or woven silk [k]
88. fascine of wood
89. fat quarter of fabric (18"x22" approx)
90. festoon of banners
    festoon of cobwebs

Chapter 8: A Banality of Bric-a-Brac

plume of feathers	festoon of material
tuft of feathers	91. fichu of lace
75. noil of fibre (left over after carding, as in silk or wool)	92. fid of tobacco [o]
	93. fistful of dollars
76. tow of fibre (coarse broken fibre e.g. flax or jute)	94. fizzle of fireworks
	95. flat of bricks
77. tow of fibres (untwisted bundle of filaments e.g. graphite)	96. fleece of wool (formed from many staples)
	97. fleet of crab pots (dial)
	fleet of fishing nets (dial)
78. canister of film	98. flight of fish-hooks [i]
cartridge of film	*99. flirtation of fans*
reel of film	100. flood of letters
roll of film	101. flotsam of wreckage
79. companion set of fire irons	*102. flounce of petticoats*
80. bundle of firewood	103. flurry of ticker-tape
81. bouquet of fireworks	*104. flutter of fans*
cascade of fireworks	105. froufrou of frills
display of fireworks	106. gallery of paintings
fizzle of fireworks	gallery of pictures
phut of fireworks	gallery of portraits
82. browss of fish bait (dial)	107. gallimaufry (jumble) of objects
lud (lode) of fish bait (dial)	
smack (or smear) of fish bait (dial)	108. gate of takings
	109. gather of glass [l]
83. flight of fish-hooks [i]	*110. glint of glasses*
84. reel of fishing line	111. glut of commercials [b]
85. drift of fishing nets [i]	112. googol of (cardinal) numbers
fleet of fishing nets (dial)	113. googolplex of numbers
shot of fishing nets [i]	114. grid of lines
86. arc of floodlights	115. grimace of masks
87. caste of flower pots	116. halfendale of property [n]
88. trail of footprints	117. handful of coins
89. patter of footsteps	handful of dust [c]
90. froufrou of frills	118. hank of cotton (7 skeins/840yds)
91. down of fur	
92. suite of furniture	

129

Gallimaufry

93. burn (from burden) of furze (dial)	hank of wool
94. cylinder of gas	119. head of steam
95. shower of gifts	120. heap of trash
96. gather of glass ¹	121. hike of rent
pane of glass	hike of taxes
paraison of glass ¹	
shard of glass	
sliver of glass	
splinter of glass	
97. *glint of glasses*	
98. band of gold	122. hoard of gold
bar of gold	hoard of treasure
carat of gold	123. hoarding of advertisements
crock of gold	124. hod of bricks
eldorado of gold	125. hold of cargo
hoard of gold	126. hold-all of clothes
ingot of gold	127. hope chest of linen
nugget of gold	128. hug of teddy bears
99. cutch of gold leaf ʲ	129. humidor of cigars
book of gold leaf ʲ	130. ingot of gold
shoder of gold leaf ʲ	ingot of tin
100. bag of goodies	131. inventory of property
101. delivery of goods	inventory of stock
emporium of goods	132. jetsam of cargo
sale of goods	jetsam of debris
sample of goods	133. journey of coins (minted tog. 720 oz/2000 coins)
shipment of goods	
stock-take of goods	134. jumble of clothes
102. strand of gossamer	135. kit of tools
103. yard of gravel	136. landfill of waste material
104. stock of groceries	137. layer of insulation
trolley of groceries	138. layette of baby clothes
105. rack of hats	139. leer of jack'o'lanterns
106. berry (bury) of (rabbit) holes	140. lick of paint
107. slew of homework	141. lifetime of drudgery

Chapter 8: A Banality of Bric-a-Brac

108. chain of honour
109. mountain of housework
    spot of housework
    stack of housework
110. chatelaine of implements [h]
111. panel of instruments
112. layer of insulation
113. mountain of ironing
    stack of ironing
114. miscellany of items
115. quincunx of (5) items
116. leer of jack'o'lanterns
117. cache of jewels
    regalia of (Crown) jewels
118. casket of jewellery
    parure of jewellery
119. coven of kettles [e]

120. bunch of keys
    rack of keys
    ring of keys
121. reticule of knitting
122. cluster of knots [a]
123. fichu of lace
    ruffle of lace
124. escalade of ladders
125. distribution of largesse
126. basket of laundry
127. curriculum of lessons
    timetable of lessons

142. line of barriers
    line of washing
143. listing of TV/radio
    programmes
144. load of manure
145. lock of wool
146. long hundred of nails (6x20)
    long hundred of quills (6x20)
147. lorry-load of topsoil
148. lud (lode) of fish bait (dial)
149. lump of coal
150. manifest of (ship's) cargo
151. midden of refuse
    midden of shells
152. mint of money
153. miscellany of items
154. moiety of property [n]
155. mosaic of tiles
156. mound of rubble
157. mountain of housework
    mountain of ironing
    mountain of washing-up
158. museum of antiques
    museum of artefacts
    museum of paintings
159. nest of bowls
    nest of suitcases
    nest of tables
160. noil of fibre (left over after
    carding, as in silk or wool)
161. nugget of gold
162. number of articles
163. obsolescence of appliances [b]
164. omnium-gatherum of
    miscellaneous items
165. outfit of clothes

128. flood of letters
129. hope chest of linen
130. grid of lines
131. pencil of lines
    tracery of lines
132. string of lobster pots
133. trawl of lobster traps
134. pile of logs
    sack of logs
135. cache of loot
136. bucket of manure
    load of manure

137. grimace of masks
138. book of matches
    box of matches
139. bolt of material
    festoon of material
    swag of material
    swathe of material
140. scrapbook of mementoes
141. display of merchandise
142. omnium-gatherum of
    miscellaneous items
    ragbag of miscellaneous
    items
143. cache of money
    coffer of money
    mint of money
    tribute of money
    wad of money
144. long hundred of nails (6x20)
145. pile of newspapers

outfit of sails
166. pack of coal (3 bushels)
167. packet of cigarettes
    packet of seeds
168. pad of (sheets of) paper
169. pair of curtains
    pair of panniers

pair of shoes/boots/trousers
pair of spectacles
170. pall of smoke
171. panache of feathers
172. pane of glass
173. panel of instruments
174. paper of pins
175. paraison of glass ¹
176. paraphernalia of equipment
177. parure of jewellery
178. patter of footsteps
179. pencil of lines
180. phut of fireworks
181. piece of calico (10 yds)
    piece of cloth (10 yds)
182. pil of crab-buts (dial)
183. pile of dung
    pile of logs
    pile of newspapers
    pile of rubbish
184. pinch of snuff
185. pipeline of oil
186. plank of wood

Chapter 8: A Banality of Bric-a-Brac

146. wad of notes	187. plug of tobacco
147. column of numbers	
combination of numbers	
googol of (cardinal) numbers	
googolplex of numbers	
148. string of numerals	
149. bushel of nuts	
150. clutter of objects	
gallimaufry (jumble) of objects	
151. barrel of oil (35 gallons)	
cruse of oil	188. plume of feathers
pipeline of oil	plume of smoke
spill of oil	189. *plump of pillows*
tanker of oil	190. pomade of ointment
152. pomade of ointment	191. pomander of perfume
153. brushful of paint	192. pool of slurry
dab of paint	193. portfolio of artwork
daub of paint	194. pot of paint
lick of paint	195. potpourri of scents
pot of paint	196. press of canvas (sails)
tin of paint	197. puff of smoke
tube of paint	198. purse of winnings
154. collection of paintings	199. quid of tobacco [o]
exhibition of paintings	200. quincunx of (5) items
gallery of paintings	201. quiver of surf boards
museum of paintings	202. quiz of questions
155. pair of panniers	203. rack of clothes
156. cracker of paper	rack of dishes
pad of (sheets of) paper	rack of hats
scrap of paper	rack of keys
screw of paper	rack of ties
sheet of paper	rack of tools
spill of paper	204. raffle of cords [i]
twist of paper	205. ragbag of miscellaneous items
157. budget of papers	

158. stack of paperwork
    welter of paperwork
159. *twirl of parasols*
160. complement of parts
    concretion of parts
161. rope of pearls
    string of pearls
    torsade of pearls
162. atomiser of perfume
    pomander of perfume
    vial of perfume
163. tanker of petrol
164. *flounce of petticoats*
165. album of photographs
166. collage of photos
167. exhibition of pictures
    gallery of pictures
168. trough of pig-swill
169. *plump of pillows*
170. paper of pins
171. coating of plaster
172. stack of plates
173. cockade of plumes
174. gallery of portraits
175. compact of powder
176. tariff of prices
177. tithe of produce
178. range of products
179. halfendale of property [n]
    inventory of property
    moiety of property [n]
180. quiz of questions
181. long hundred of quills (6x20)
182. collection of records
183. midden of refuse
184. hike of rent

206. range of products
207. reel of cotton
    reel of film
    reel of fishing line
208. regalia of clothing (Native American)
    regalia of (Crown) jewels
209. remnant of fabric
210. repository of documents
211. reticule of knitting
212. ring of keys
213. rolag of wool (made by rolling fibre off the cards)
214. roll of coins
    roll of film
    roll of tape
    roll of wallpaper
215. rope of pearls
216. rosary of beads
217. rouleau of coins
218. roving of wool (a pulled & twisted sliver)
219. row of chairs
    row of tables
220. ruck of bricks
    ruck of stones
221. ruffle of lace
222. sachet of shampoo
223. sack of coal
    sack of logs
224. sale of goods
225. sample of goods
226. satchel of schoolbooks
227. scrap of paper
228. scrapbook of mementoes
229. screed of concrete

Chapter 8: A Banality of Bric-a-Brac

185. bouquet of rockets
186. coil of rope
187. pile of rubbish
    skipful of rubbish
188. mound of rubble
189. outfit of sails
    suit of sails
190. clearance of sale goods
191. set of saucepans
192. cluster of scales
193. potpourri of scents
194. satchel of schoolbooks
195. *shear of scissors*
196. packet of seeds
197. cesspit of sewage
198. sachet of shampoo
199. midden of shells
200. pair of shoes/boots/ trousers
201. bag of shopping
202. denier of silk (nylon, rayon) g
    fardel of raw or woven silk k
    skein of silk
    strand of silk
203. pool of slurry
204. cloud of smoke
    column of smoke
    pall of smoke
    plume of smoke
    puff of smoke
    wisp of smoke
205. pinch of snuff
206. bank of (audio) speakers
207. pair of spectacles
208. splurge of spending
    spree of spending

230. screw of paper
231. scuttle of coal
232. seam of coal
233. series of TV programmes
234. service of china
    service of crockery
    service of dinner things
235. set of chairs
    set of china
    set of saucepans
    set of spoons
236. shag of tobacco
237. shard of glass
238. sheaf of banners

239. *shear of scissors*
240. sheet of paper
241. shipment of goods
242. shoder of gold leaf j
243. shot of fishing nets i
244. shovelful of coal
245. shower of gifts
246. skein of cotton (80 threads)
    skein of silk
    skein of wool
247. skipful of rubbish
248. slew of homework
249. sliver of glass
    sliver of wool (long bundle of fibre)

Gallimaufry

209. division of spoils

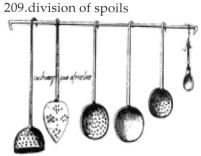

210. set of spoons
211. book of stamps
     collection of stamps
212. head of steam
213. bundle of sticks
     faggot of sticks
214. delivery of stock
     inventory of stock
215. ruck of stones
216. thatch of straw
217. ball of string
     tangle of string
218. nest of suitcases
219. stock of supplies
220. quiver of surf boards
221. nest of tables
     row of tables
222. gate of takings
223. roll of tape
224. collection of tapes (cassette)
225. hike of taxes
226. hug of teddy bears
227. flurry of ticker-tape
228. rack of ties
229. mosaic of tiles
230. ingot of tin

250. smack (smear) of fish bait (dial)
251. speck of dust
252. spill of oil
     spill of paper
253. spindle of cotton (18 hanks)
254. splinter of glass
     splinter of wood
255. splurge of spending
256. spool of cotton
257. spot of housework
258. spree of spending
259. stack of canvases (art)
     stack of chairs
     stack of correspondence

     stack of dishes
     stack of housework
     stack of ironing
     stack of paperwork
     stack of plates
260. staple of wool (naturally formed cluster or lock)
261. stock of coal (4 cubic yds)
     stock of groceries
     stock of supplies
262. stock-take of goods
263. strand of gossamer
     strand of silk
264. string of beads

Chapter 8: A Banality of Bric-a-Brac

231.carrot of tobacco (US)	string of lobster pots
fid of tobacco ᵒ	string of numerals
plug of tobacco	string of pearls
quid of tobacco ᵒ	265.*stroll of buggies*
shag of tobacco	266.suit of clothes
tin of tobacco	suit of dittos ᵈ
232.etui of (manicure) tools	suit of sails
kit of tools	suit of tools
rack of tools	267.suitcase of clothes
suit of tools	268.suite of furniture
233.tube of toothpaste	269.swag of booty
234.lorry-load of topsoil	swag of material
235.bale of towels	270.swatch of fabric (sample)
236.collection of toys	271.swathe of material
237.heap of trash	272.tangle of string
238.hoard of treasure	273.tank of water
239.bag of tricks	274.tanker of oil
240.cabinet of trophies	tanker of petrol
241.ball of twine	275.tariff of prices
242.burn (burden) of turf (dial)	276.thatch of straw
243.listing of TV/radio programmes	277.thread of cotton (54 inches)
series of TV programmes	278.timetable of lessons
244.*clutch of umbrellas*	279.tin of paint
245.roll of wallpaper	tin of tobacco
246.line of washing	280.tincture of dye
247.mountain of washing-up	281.tithe of produce
248.landfill of waste material	282.tod of wool (28 lbs)
249.basin of water	283.top of wool (semi-processed)
bath of water	284.torsade of beads
butt of water	torsade of pearls
canister of water	285.tow of fibre (coarse broken fibre, e.g. flax or jute)
cistern of water	tow of fibres (untwisted bundle of filaments e.g. graphite)
tank of water	
250.purse of winnings	
251.cable of wires	286.tracery of lines

Gallimaufry

252. block of wood
    cord of wood (a stack 4'×4'×8')
    fascine of wood
    plank of wood
    splinter of wood
253. ball of wool
    batt of wool (wadding, used for felting or spinning)
    card of wool
    fleece of wool (formed from many staples)
    hank of wool
    lock of wool
    rolag of wool (made by rolling fibre off the cards)
    roving of wool (a pulled & twisted sliver)
    skein of wool
    sliver of wool (long bundle of fibre)
    staple of wool (naturally formed cluster or lock)
    tod of wool (28 lbs)
    top of wool (semi-processed)
254. exhibition of works of art
255. flotsam of wreckage
256. clew of yarn
	287. trail of footprints
	288. trawl of lobster traps
	289. tribute of money
	290. trolley of groceries
	291. trough of pig-swill
	292. trousseau of bridal wear
	293. tube of paint
	    tube of toothpaste
	294. tuft of feathers
	295. *twirl of parasols*
	296. twist of paper
	297. urn of cremated remains
	298. vat of dye

	299. vial of perfume
	300. wad of bills
	    wad of cotton wool
	    wad of money
	    wad of notes
	301. wardrobe of clothes
	302. welter of paperwork
	303. wisp of smoke
	304. yard of gravel

Notes:

a. Archaic, from one of the 16th century manuscripts (most commonly, The Book of Hawking & Hunting', by Dame Juliana Barnes, 1486).
b. From James Lipton, 'An Exaltation of Larks' (1977).
c. 'A Handful of Dust' is a novel by Evelyn Waugh.
d. A suit of dittoes is a suit in which coat, waistcoat, and trousers are all of one cloth.

Chapter 8: A Banality of Bric-a-Brac

e. From 'Under Milkwood' by Dylan Thomas.
f. A bundle of compressed raw cotton. Typically, for American cotton a bale weighs about 500 lbs, for Egyptian about 700 lbs, Brasilian about 250 lbs, and Indian about 400 lbs.
g. A denier is the weight in grammes of 9000 metres of a yarn.
h. A chatelaine is an ornamental chain or pin usually worn at a woman's waist to which keys, trinkets, scissors and purse are attached.
i. From Ivan G. Sparkes, 'Dictionary of Collective Nouns & Group Terms'.
j. Cutch and Shoder are bookbinding terms: A packet of leaves in which thinly rolled and cut gold is first beaten in the manufacture of gold leaf. After the gold is rolled to a thickness of 0.001 inch and 1¼ inches wide, it is then cut into 1¼ inch squares. 290 of these sheets are interleaved with 4 ½ inch squares of vellum/paper, forming the "cutch," which is secured with heavy bands of parchment. Derives from the Latin calcare, to tread. A shoder is another 'mould' stage in the process of producing gold leaf in its final 'book' form.
k. A fardel is a canvas-covered bale of raw or woven silk such as might be carried on the back of donkey; hence, also a term meaning 'a burden which must be borne". Dorothy Parker says "I took them ... as part of the fardels to which we all are heir'.
l. A paraison of glass is a 'gather' of molten glass at the end of the blow pipe when it is first inflated into a small bubble.
m. A torsade is a multiple string of pearls/beads/chains forming 1 necklace.
n. A moiety or halfendale both mean a small part, or a half; an archaic term often used in wills and leases to distribute owned goods.
o. A fid or a quid is the amount of tobacco chewed in the mouth at one time. A quid, from the small pieces of tow with which the vent or touch hole of a cannon is stopped. (Grosse 1811 Dictionary).

'a collection of toys'

'an affectation of accoutrements'

'a coven of kettles'

Chapter 8: A Banality of Bric-a-Brac

'a vernissage of brushes'

'a line of washing'

Gallimaufry

'a superfluity of cooks'

8b. Food & Drink

Sorted by noun	Sorted by collective noun
1. chopin of ale (Scots, 2 mutchkins) firkin of ale (9 gall) flagon of ale flask of ale jug of ale kilderkin of ale (18 gall) mutchkin of ale (Scots, 4 gills) noggin of ale (¼ pint) pitcher of ale toby of ale yard of ale 2. basket of apples bushel of apples	1. amphora of wine 2. ampulla of wine 3. bag of potatoes bag of sugar, flour etc. bag of sweets 4. balloon of brandy 5. balthazar of Bordeaux (16b) balthazar of champagne (16 b) 6. banquet of food 7. bar of chocolate 8. baron of beef 9. barrel of beer (36 gall) barrel of biscuits

Chapter 8: A Banality of Bric-a-Brac

    newton of apples
    peck of apples (2 gall)
    pomace of apples
    pot of apples (5 pecks)
    pyrus of apples
    seam of apples (9 pecks)
3. bundle of asparagus
4. flitch of bacon
    gammon of bacon
    rasher of bacon
    side of bacon
5. bunch of bananas
    hand of bananas
    stalk of bananas
6. boll of barley (Scots) g

    chalder of barley (Scots) g
    firlot of barley (Scots) g
    forpet of barley (Scots) g
    lippie of barley (Scots) g
    peck of barley (Scots) g
7. mess of beans
    sheaf of (green) beans
8. baron of beef
    carbonade of beef
    sirloin of beef
9. barrel of beer (36 gall)
    bottle of beer

    barrel of pilchards
    barrel of wine
10. basket of apples
    basket of eggs
    basket of fruit
    basket of strawberries

11. batch of bread
    batch of cakes
12. bellyful of food
13. binge of drinking
14. block of butter
    block of cheese
    block of margarine
    block of salt
15. boll of barley (Scots) g
16. bottle of beer
    bottle of milk
    bottle of wine
17. bout of drinking
18. bowl of fruit
    bowl of punch
    bowl of soup
    bowl of sugar
19. box of chocolates
20. brew of beer

Gallimaufry

brew of beer
can of beer
crate of beer
gut-full of beer
hogshead of beer (54 gall)
keg of beer (5-10 gall)

schooner of beer
six-pack of beer
stein of beer
10. barrel of biscuits
11. balthazar of Bordeaux (16 b)
chopine of Bordeaux (1/3 b)
demi of Bordeaux (½ b)
double magnum of Bordeaux (4b)
filette of Bordeaux (½ b)
imperial of Bordeaux (8 b)
jeroboam of Bordeaux (6 b)
magnum of Bordeaux (2 b)
Marie Jeanne of Bordeaux(3b)
melchior of Bordeaux (24 b)
nebuchadnezzar of Bordeaux (20b)
12. balloon of brandy

21. brood of eggs [h]
22. bulb of garlic
23. bulk of pilchards (layers in salt)
24. bunch of bananas
bunch of carrots
bunch of coconuts
bunch of grapes
25. bundle of asparagus
26. burn of hake (21, dial)
burn of pollack (21, dial)
27. burst of bubbles
28. bushel of apples
bushel of fruit
bushel of grain
29. butt of malmsey [d]
butt of sack
30. cabinet of drinks
31. cade of herrings (dial)
cade of sprats (dial)
32. caddy of tea
33. cafetiere of coffee
34. can of beer
can of lager
can of sardines
35. canteen of water
36. carbonade of beef
37. carton of eggs
38. case of champagne (12 b)
case of whisky
case of wine
39. cask of pilchards
cask of whisky
40. cast of fish (3, dial)
cast of haddocks (4)
cast of herrings (4)

Chapter 8: A Banality of Bric-a-Brac

13. batch of bread
    caste of bread
    crumb of bread
    crust of bread
    loaf of bread
    slice of bread
14. burst of bubbles
    fizz of bubbles
15. tray of buns
16. demi of burgundy (½ b)
    filette of burgundy (½ b)
    jeroboam of burgundy (6 b)
    magnum of burgundy (2 b)
    melchior of burgundy (24 b)
    methusaleh of burgundy(8b)
    nebuchadnezzar of
       burgundy (20b)
    rehoboam of burgundy (6b)
    salmanazar of burgundy
       (12b)
17. block of butter

    churn of butter
    mountain of butter (glut)
    pat of butter
18. crate of cabbages
    head of cabbage

    cast of oysters (4)
41. caste of bread
42. cellar of salt
    cellar of wine
43. chalder of barley (Scots) ᵍ
44. chopin of ale (Scots, 2
       mutchkins)
45. chopine of Bordeaux (1/3 b)
46. chub of pepperoni
47. churn of butter
    churn of milk
48. cloth of congers (dial)
49. clove of garlic
50. cluster of grapes ᶜ
51. clutch of eggs
52. cocktail of drinks
53. comb of honey
54. concoction of ingredients
55. cookbook of recipes

56. cornucopia of food
57. cowel of fish (dial)
58. cran of herrings (800, dial)
59. crate of beer
    crate of cabbages
60. cruet of condiments
    cruet of wine ᵇ
61. crumb of bread

145

Gallimaufry

19. batch of cakes
    portion of cake
    slice of cake
    tier of cakes
20. pipe of Canary (wine, 477 lt)
21. bunch of carrots
22. head of cauliflower
23. head of celery
24. balthazar of champagne (16b)
    case of champagne (12 b)
    demi of champagne (½ b)
    filette of champagne (½ b)
    jeroboam of champagne (4 b)
    magnum of champagne (2 b)
    melchior of champagne (24b)
    methusaleh of champagne (8b)
    nebuchadnezzar of champagne (20 b)
    picolo of champagne (¼ b)
    rehoboam of champagne (6b)
    salmanazar of champagne (12b)
25. block of cheese
    selection of cheeses
    wedge of cheese
26. bar of chocolate
    box of chocolates
    selection of chocolates
27. quill of cinnamon
28. riddle of claret [a]
29. bunch of coconuts
30. cafetiere of coffee
    flask of coffee
    jar of coffee

62. crust of bread
63. cube of ice
    cube of sugar
64. cup of tea
65. cut of meat
66. demi of Bordeaux (½ b)
    demi of burgundy (½ b)
    demi of champagne (½ b)
67. demijohn of wine (3-10 gall)
68. double magnum of Bordeaux (4b)
69. dram of whisky
70. ewer of water
71. feast of oysters
72. filette of Bordeaux (½ b.)
    filette of burgundy (½ b.)
    filette of champagne (½ b.)
73. fillet of fish

74. firkin of ale (9 gall)
75. firlot of barley (Scots) [g]
    firlot of wheat (Scots) [g]
76. fizz of bubbles
77. flagon of ale
    flagon of wine

Chapter 8: A Banality of Bric-a-Brac

    mug of coffee
    thermos of coffee
31. cruet of condiments
    tray of condiments
32. cloth of congers (dial)
33. *superfluity of cooks*
34. hully (pot) of crabs (dial)
35. menu of dishes
    serving of dishes
36. binge of drinking
    bout of drinking
    spell of drinking
37. cabinet of drinks
    cocktail of drinks
    round of drinks
38. weel (pot) of eels (dial)
39. basket of eggs
    brood of eggs [h]
    carton of eggs
    clutch of eggs
    laughter of eggs [h]
    long hundred of eggs (6x20)
    sitting of eggs [h]
    tray of eggs
40. glut of farm produce
    surplus of farm produce
41. pot au feu
42. frail of figs (50-75 lbs)
    sort of figs [h]
43. cast of fish (3, dial)
    cowel of fish (dial)
    fillet of fish
    sebbard of fish (dial)
    warp of fish (dial)
44. gowpenful (2 handfuls) of flour [i]

78. flask of ale
    flask of coffee
    flask of wine
79. flitch of bacon
80. forpet of barley (Scots) [g]

81. frail of figs (50-75 (lbs)
    frail of raisins (50-75 lbs)
82. gammon of bacon
    gammon of ham
83. *gargantua of greed*
84. garner of grain
85. glut of farm produce
86. gowpenful (2 handfuls) of flour [i]
87. grain of salt
88. grinder of pepper
89. gun of salt (56 lbs, dial)
90. gut-full of beer
91. hamper of food
92. hand of bananas
93. haunch of venison
94. head of cabbage
    head of cauliflower
    head of celery
    head of garlic
95. hogshead of beer (54 gall)
    hogshead of pilchards (in

sack of flour	salt)
45. banquet of food	hogshead of wine (52½ gall)
bellyful of food	96. hopper of grain
cornucopia of food	97. hully (pot) of crabs (dial)
hamper of food	98. imperial of Bordeaux (8 b)
larder of food	99. jar of coffee
morsel of food	jar of honey
pantry of food	100. jeroboam of Bordeaux (6 b)
ration of food	jeroboam of burgundy (6 b)
46. basket of fruit	jeroboam of champagne (4b)
bowl of fruit	101. joint of meat
bushel of fruit	102. jorum of punch
47. trug of garden produce	103. jug of ale
48. bulb of garlic	jug of water
clove of garlic	104. keg of beer (5-10 gall)
head of garlic	105. kilderkin of ale (18 gall)
49. bushel of grain	106. lake of wine (as in glut)
garner of grain	107. larder of food
hopper of grain	108. laughter of eggs [h]
mountain of grain	109. leg of mutton (pork, lamb)
silo of grain	110. lippie of barley (Scots) [g]
store of grain	111. live tuck of pilchards (dial)
50. bunch of grapes	112. loaf of bread
cluster of grapes [c]	113. long hundred of eggs (6x20)
51. *gargantua of greed*	114. macedoine of vegetables
52. mess of grits	115. magnum of Bordeaux (2 b)
53. cast of haddock (4)	magnum of burgundy (2 b)
54. burn of hake (21, dial)	magnum of champagne (2 b)
55. gammon of ham	116. Marie Jeanne of Bordeaux
56. cade of herrings (500, dial)	(3b)
cast of herrings (4)	117. marinade of ingredients
cran of herrings (800, dial)	118. mawn of potatoes (dial)
mease of herrings (5/600 dial)	119. mease of herrings (5/600 dial)
wisket of herring (100, dial)	120. melchior of Bordeaux (24 b)
57. comb of honey	melchior of burgundy (24 b)

jar of honey
spoonful of honey
58. cube of ice
59. concoction of ingredients
marinade of ingredients
mixture of ingredients
recipe of ingredients
60. can of lager
61. rack of lamb
62. slice of lemon
squeeze of lemon
63. team of links (sausages)
64. pipe of Malaga (wine, 477 lt)
65. butt of malmsey [d]
penny-pot of malmsey [e]
pipe of malmsey (477 lt)
66. block of margarine
tub of margarine
67. cut of meat
joint of meat
slice of meat
68. bottle of milk
churn of milk
pail of milk
saucer of milk
tanker of milk
69. leg of mutton (pork, lamb)
70. rope of onions
string of onions
71. cast of oysters (4)
feast of oysters
72. terrine of pâté
73. pack of peas
pod of peas
74. grinder of pepper
shaker of pepper

melchior of champagne (24b)
121. menu of dishes
122. mess of beans
mess of grits
mess of potage
123. methusaleh of burgundy (8b)
methusaleh of champagne (8b)
124. mixture of ingredients
125. mob of tucker (Austr)
126. morsel of food
127. mountain of butter (glut)
mountain of grain
128. mug of coffee

129. mutchkin of ale (Scots, 4 gills)
130. nebuchadnezzar of Bordeaux (20b)
nebuchadnezzar of burgundy (20b)
nebuchadnezzar of champagne (20b)
131. newton of apples
132. noggin of ale (¼ pint)
133. olio of stewed meats
134. pack of peas
135. packet of tea
136. pail of milk

75. chub of pepperoni
76. peck of peppers
77. salmagundi of pickled meats
78. barrel of pilchards
    bulk of pilchards (layers in salt)
    cask of pilchards
    hogshead of pilchards (in salt)
    live tuck of pilchards (dial)

    rose of pilchards (dial)
79. prunus of plums
80. burn of pollack (21, dial)
81. porringer of porridge
82. mess of potage
83. bag of potatoes
    mawn of potatoes (dial)
    sack of potatoes
84. bowl of punch
    jorum of punch
85. frail of raisins (50-75 lbs)
86. cookbook of recipes
87. tot of rum
88. butt of sack
89. block of salt

137. pantry of food
138. pat of butter
139. peck of apples (2 gall)
     peck of barley (Scots) [g]
     peck of peppers
140. penny-pot of malmsey [e]
141. picolo of champagne (¼ b)
142. pinch of salt
143. pipe of Canary (wine 477 lt)
     pipe of Malaga (wine 477 lt)
     pipe of malmsey (wine 477 lt)
144. pitcher of ale
     pitcher of water
145. pod of peas
146. pomace of apples
147. porringer of porridge
148. portion of cake
149. pot of apples (5 pecks)
     pot au feu
     pot of tea
150. prunus of plums
151. punnet of strawberries
152. pyrus of apples
153. quill of cinnamon
154. rack of lamb
155. rasher of bacon
156. ration of food
157. recipe of ingredients
158. rehoboam of burgundy(6b)
     rehoboam of champagne(6b)
159. riddle of claret [a]
160. rope of onions
161. rose of pilchards (dial)
162. round of drinks
163. sack of flour

Chapter 8: A Banality of Bric-a-Brac

cellar of salt	sack of potatoes
grain of salt	164. saddle of venison
gun of salt (56 lbs, dial)	165. salmagundi of pickled meats
pinch of salt	166. salmanazar of burgundy
90. can of sardines	(12b)
91. string of sausages	salmanazar of champagne
92. schooner of sherry	(12b)
93. bowl of soup	167. samovar of tea
tureen of soup	168. *saturnalia of wee bevies* ᶠ
94. cade of sprats (dial)	169. saucer of milk
95. olio of stewed meats	170. schooner of beer
96. basket of strawberries	schooner of sherry
	171. seam of apples (9 pecks)
	172. sebbard of fish (dial)
	173. selection of cheeses
	selection of chocolates
	174. serving of dishes
	175. shaker of pepper
	176. sheaf of (green) beans
	177. side of bacon
	178. silo of grain
	179. sirloin of beef
punnet of strawberries	180. sitting of eggs ʰ
97. bag of sugar, flour etc.	181. six-pack of beer
bowl of sugar	182. slice of bread
cube of sugar	slice of cake
spoonful of sugar	slice of lemon
98. bag of sweets	slice of meat
99. caddy of tea	183. sort of figs ʰ
cup of tea	184. spell of drinking
packet of tea	185. spoonful of honey
pot of tea	spoonful of sugar
samovar of tea	186. sprig of thyme (or other
urn of tea	herbs)
100. sprig of thyme (or other	187. squeeze of lemon
herbs)	188. stalk of bananas

101. mob of tucker (Austr)	189. stein of beer
102. macedoine of vegetables	190. store of grain
103. haunch of venison	191. string of onions
saddle of venison	string of sausages
104. canteen of water	*192. superfluity of cooks*
ewer of water	193. surplus of farm produce
jug of water	194. tanker of milk
pitcher of water	195. team of links (sausages)
105. *saturnalia of wee bevies* [f]	196. terrine of pâté
106. firlot of wheat [g]	197. thermos of coffee
107. case of whisky	198. tier of cakes
cask of whisky	199. tierce of wine (42 gall)
dram of whisky	200. toby of ale
108. amphora of wine	201. tot of rum
ampulla of wine	202. tray of buns
barrel of wine	tray of condiments
bottle of wine	tray of eggs
case of wine	203. trug of garden produce
cellar of wine	204. tub of margarine
cruet of wine [b]	205. tun of wine (252 gall)
demijohn of wine (3-10 gall)	206. tureen of soup
flagon of wine	207. urn of tea
flask of wine	208. vat of wine
hogshead of wine (52½ gall)	209. vintage of wine
lake of wine (as in glut)	210. warp of fish (dial)
tierce of wine (42 gall)	211. wedge of cheese
tun of wine (252 gall)	212. weel (pot) of eels (dial)
vat of wine	213. wisket of herring (100, dial)
vintage of wine	214. yard of ale

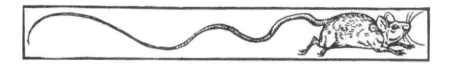

Chapter 8: A Banality of Bric-a-Brac

Notes:

a. Riddle of Claret: thirteen bottles, a magnum and twelve quarts – so called because in golf matches the magistrates invited to the celebration dinner presented to the club a "riddle of claret," sending it in a riddle or sieve; Brewers' Dictionary of Phrase and Fable.
b. A cruet is used for the water or wine for the Eucharist.
c. Archaic, from one of the 16th century manuscripts (most commonly, The Book of Hawking & Hunting', by Dame Juliana Barnes, 1486).
d. George, Duke of Clarence, third son of Richard, Duke of York, and brother of King Edward IV, reputedly drowned in 'a butt of malmsey' – as described in Shakespeare's 'Richard III'.
e. Penny-pot of malmsey from 'The Fortunes of Nigel' by Sir Walter Scott.
f. Billy Connolly, from wife Pamela Stephenson's biography 'Bravemouth'.
g. A firlot was a dry measure used in Scotland between 1500 and 1900; the 4th part of a boll of grain or meal. The Linlithgow wheat firlot was to the imperial bushel as 998 to 1000; the barley firlot as 1456 to 1000. The firlot was equal to about 36 litres (in the case of certain crops, such as wheat, peas, beans and meal), and about 53 litres (in the case of barley, oats and malt). 1 chalder = 16 bolls; 1 boll = 4 firlots; 1 firlot = 4 pecks; 1 peck = 4 lippies or forpets.
h. From Ivan G Sparkes, 'Dictionary of Collective Nouns & Group Terms'. A 'laughter' (or lafter) was the number of eggs laid by a fowl before she sits. From old Scandinavian 'lay' –a place where animals lay their young.
i. A gowpenful (2 handfuls) of flour, was a measure used by the Miller to count out his toll (in flour) for his services of grinding the flour.

'a joint of meat'

'a cast of oysters'

'a burst of bubbles'

Chapter 8: A Banality of Bric-a-Brac

'*a newton of apples*'

Gallimaufry

'a gargantua of greed'

'a line of dominoes'

Chapter 8: A Banality of Bric-a-Brac

'a den of gamblers'

8c. Sports, Games & Pastimes

Sorted by noun	Sorted by collective noun
1. arcade of amusements	1. arcade of amusements
2. quiver of arrows	arcade of games machines
3. team of athletes	2. arsenal of bowling balls
4. *blazon of balloons (advertising)*	3. association of (football) clubs
drift of balloons	4. bench of substitutes (football)
montgolfier of balloons (large meet)	5. blast of hunters
5. nine of basketball	6. *blazon of balloons (advertising)*
6. squad of beaters	7. book of wagers
7. chicane of bends (racing)	8. bout of sumo
8. parlay of bets (cards)	9. bowl of keglers (or vice versa) [a]
9. game of billiards/pool	10. box of tricks
10. rain of blows (boxing)	11. brood of chess-players [a]
11. arsenal of bowling balls	12. casino of games machines
12. four of bridge/polo team	13. century of runs (cricket)
rubber of bridge	

table of bridge
13. deck of cards
    flush of cards
    game of cards
    hand of cards
    meld of cards
    pack of cards
    sequence of cards
    suit of cards
    tableau of cards (Solitaire)
    tierce of cards [c]
    trick of cards
14. game of chance

15. brood of chess-players [a]
16. meiny of chessmen
17. stack of (gambling) chips
18. association of (football) clubs
    league of clubs
19. line-up of competitors
    team of competitors
20. field of contenders
21. slate of credit
22. six of cub scouts
23. core of curling players [b]
24. line of dominoes
    nieveful (handful) of
        dominoes [b]

14. chicane of bends (racing)

15. *chimera of kites*
16. cluster of sprockets (cycling)
17. *clutch of wrestlers*
18. combination of moves
    combination of punches
19. compendium of games
20. core of curling players [b]
21. *crescendo of kites*
22. crew of oarsmen
23. crunch of wrestlers [a]
24. *dabble of paddlers*
25. deck of cards
    deck of tarot cards
26. den of gamblers
27. down of plays (Amer. Football)
28. *drift of balloons*
29. eight of oarsmen
30. field of contenders
    field of hunters
    field of runners
31. fifteen at rugby
32. flight of fences (horse-racing)
    flight of hurdles (on a racetrack)

Chapter 8: A Banality of Bric-a-Brac

      topple of dominoes
25. gang of fencers
26. flight of fences (horse-racing)
27. net of footballs
28. ruck of footballers (3 Austr)
      squad of footballers
29. den of gamblers
      talent of gamblers
30. compendium of games
      tournament of games
31. arcade of games machines
      casino of games machines
32. hat-trick of goals (3)
      tally of goals
33. round of golf
34. lie of golfers [a]
      tedium of golfers [a]
35. tumble of gymnasts [a]
36. blast of hunters
      field of hunters
      meet of hunters
37. flight of hurdles (on a racetrack)
38. race of jockeys [a]
39. wheeze of joggers [a]
40. bowl of keglers (or vice versa) [c]
41. *chimera of kites*
      crescendo of kites
42. twelve of lacrosse
43. piece of meld (in Pinochle)
44. pool of money (gambling)
45. combination of moves
46. crew of oarsmen
      eight of oarsmen

33. flush of cards
34. four of bridge/polo team
35. gala of sports
36. gambit of play (cards, chess)
37. game of billiards/pool
      game of cards
      game of chance
      game of skill
38. gang of fencers
39. hand of cards
40. hat-trick of goals (3)
41. league of clubs
42. lie of golfers [a]
43. line of dominoes
44. line-up of competitors
45. measure of umpires
46. meet of hunters
47. meiny of chessmen
48. meld of cards
      meld of (mah-jong) tiles
49. *montgolfier of balloons (large meet)*
50. net of footballs
51. nieveful (handful) of dominoes [b]
52. nine of basketball
53. pack of cards
54. parlay of bets (cards)
55. piece of meld (in Pinochle)
56. pool of money (gambling)
57. quiver of arrows
      quiver of surfboards
      quiver of (windsurfing) sails
58. race of jockeys [a]
59. raft of swimmers [a]
60. rain of blows (boxing)

row of oarsmen [a]
47. *dabble of paddlers*
48. gambit of play (cards, chess)
49. team of players
50. down of plays (Amer. Football)
51. school of poker players
    stud of poker players [a]
52. combination of punches
53. fifteen at rugby
54. ruck of rugby-players
    scrum of rugby-players
55. field of runners
56. century of runs (cricket)
57. quiver of (windsurfing) sails
58. *squeal of skaters*
59. game of skill
60. gala of sports
61. cluster of sprockets (cycling)
62. bench of substitutes (football)
63. bout of sumo
64. quiver of surfboards
65. raft of swimmers [a]
66. deck of tarot cards
67. round robin of tennis matches
    set of tennis matches
68. rally of tennis strokes
69. meld of (mah-jong) tiles
70. box of tricks
71. measure of umpires
72. book of wagers
73. table of whist
74. *clutch of wrestlers*
    crunch of wrestlers [a]

61. rally of tennis strokes
62. round of golf
63. round robin of tennis matches
64. row of oarsmen [a]
65. rubber of bridge
66. ruck of footballers (3 Austr)
    ruck of rugby-players
67. school of poker players
68. scrum of rugby-players
69. sequence of cards
70. set of tennis matches
71. six of cub scouts
72. slate of credit
73. squad of beaters
    squad of footballers
74. *squeal of skaters*
75. stack of (gambling) chips
76. stud of poker players [a]
77. suit of cards
78. table of bridge
    table of whist
79. tableau of cards (Solitaire)
80. talent of gamblers
81. tally of goals
82. team of athletes
    team of competitors
    team of players
83. tedium of golfers [a]
84. tierce of cards [c]
85. topple of dominoes
86. tournament of games
87. trick of cards
88. tumble of gymnasts [a]
89. twelve of lacrosse
90. wheeze of joggers [a]

Chapter 8: A Banality of Bric-a-Brac

Notes:

a. From James Lipton, 'An Exaltation of Larks' (1977)
b. From Ivan G Sparkes, 'Dictionary of Collective Nouns & Group Terms'
c. Tierce is a sequence of 3 playing cards of the same suit.

'a deck of cards'

'a dabble of paddlers'

'a tumble of gymnasts'

Chapter Nine

A Play of Words

a. *Theatrical & Dance*
b. *Musical & Sounds*
c. *Literary & Printing*
d. *Popular Culture*
e. *Religion*
f. *Myth & Magic*

'a harlequinade of clowns'

Gallimaufry

'a show of hands'

9a. Theatrical & Dance

Sorted by noun	Sorted by collective noun
1. theatre of the absurd	1. array of loudspeakers
2. troupe of acrobats	array of talent
3. cast of actors	2. assemblé of choreographers [b]
company of actors	3. audience of people
condescension of actors [a]	4. audition of hopefuls

	5. badinage of jokes
	6. balcony of seats
	7. bank of spotlights
	8. batten of lights
	9. box of greasepaint
tableau of actors	box of props
troupe of actors	10. brace of stagehands [b]
4. entrance of actresses [b]	11. burst of applause

Chapter 9: A Play of Words

5. wave of adulation
6. burst of applause
   ripple of applause
   roar of applause
   round of applause
   smattering of applause
   thunder of applause
7. corps de ballet

8. salvo of bravos ᶜ
9. cast of characters
10. assemblé of choreographersᵇ
11. circus of clowns
    harlequinade of clowns
12. riot of comedians ᵇ
13. change of costume
    panoply of costumes
    wardrobe of costumes
14. float of dancers (female) ᵇ
    flight of dancers (male) ᵇ
    troupe of dancers
15. set of designers ᵇ
16. gild of directors ᵇ
17. concert party of entertainers
18. programme of entertainment
19. masquerade of fools
20. list of functions
21. box of greasepaint
22. show of hands

12. cast of actors

    cast of characters
    cast of thousands
13. chamber of horrors
14. change of costume
    change of scenery
15. chorus of numbers
16. circus of clowns
17. company of actors
    company of performers
18. concert party of entertainers
19. condescension of actors ᵃ
20. corps de ballet
21. coup de theatre
22. crew of stagehands
23. cry of players/actors
24. entrance of actresses ᵇ
25. flight of dancers (male) ᵇ
26. float of dancers (female) ᵇ
27. gild of directors ᵇ
28. grimace of masks
29. group of players
30. harlequinade of clowns
31. *hug of lovies*
32. line-up of stage acts
33. list of functions
    list of venues
34. masquerade of fools
35. measure of wardrobe ladies ᵇ
36. museum of waxworks
37. *ogle of spectators*

165

Gallimaufry

23. audition of hopefuls	38. panic of producers ᵇ
24. chamber of horrors	39. panoply of costumes
25. badinage of jokes	40. plot of playwrights ᵇ
26. batten of lights	41. programme of entertainment
27. range of locations	42. range of locations
28. array of loudspeakers	43. riot of comedians ᵇ
29. *hug of lovies*	44. ripple of applause
30. grimace of masks	45. roar of applause
31. chorus of numbers	46. round of applause
32. audience of people	47. run of performances
33. run of performances	48. salvo of bravos ᶜ
34. company of performers	49. series of (drama) workshops
35. cry of players/actors	50. set of designers ᵇ
group of players	
36. plot of playwrights ᵇ	
37. spite of prima donnas ᵇ	
38. panic of producers ᵇ	
39. box of props	
40. timetable of rehearsals	
41. change of scenery	
set of scenery	
42. tier of seating	set of scenery
43. balcony of seats	51. show of hands
44. *ogle of spectators*	52. smattering of applause
45. bank of spotlights	53. spite of prima donnas ᵇ
46. line-up of stage acts	54. tableau of actors
47. brace of stagehands ᵇ	55. theatre of the absurd
crew of stagehands	56. thunder of applause
48. array of talent	57. tier of seating
wave of talent	58. timetable of rehearsals
49. coup de theatre	59. troupe of acrobats
50. cast of thousands	troupe of actors
51. list of venues	troupe of dancers
52. measure of wardrobe ladiesᵇ	60. wardrobe of costumes
53. museum of waxworks	61. wave of adulation
54. series of (drama) workshops	wave of talent

Notes:

a. Archaic, from one of the 16th century manuscripts (most commonly, The Book of Hawking & Hunting', by Dame Juliana Barnes, 1486).
b. From James Lipton, 'An Exaltation of Larks' (1977).
c. Applause given by French 'claqueurs' (hired applauders) in the theatre.

'an ogle of spectators'

'a quadrille of dancers'

Gallimaufry

'an ensemble of musicians'

9b. Musical & Sounds

Sorted by noun	Sorted by collective noun
1. set of bagpipes	1. album of songs
2. congeries of ballads	2. amplification of sound
garland of ballads	3. antiphony of performers
3. furore of bandsmen	
4. rumble of basses ᵇ	
5. carillon of bells	
change of bells	
chime of bells	
peal of bells	4. arpeggio of notes
ring of bells	5. array of instruments
tintinnabulation of bells	6. babble of voices
tolling of bells	7. band of musicians
6. parenthesis of cellists ᵇ	8. bar of music
7. cadence of chords	9. battery of percussion
progression of chords	instruments

168

8. whine of clarinettists [b]
9. quaver of coloraturas [b]
10. clash of cymbals
11. rafale of drum rolls
12. choir of echoes [e]
   diminution of echoes
   reverberation of echoes
13. consort of fiddlers [e]
   covey of fiddlers [e]
   gang of fiddlers
14. circle of fifths [c]
15. cadence of harmonies
16. melody of harpers/harpists [a]
17. string of hits/hit records
18. cadence of horse's hooves

19. array of instruments
20. tattoo of military bands
21. troupe of minstrels
22. bar of music
   canto of music
   collection of music
   library of music
   manuscript of music
   recital of music
   rhapsody of music
   score of music
   symphony of music
23. olio of musical
   entertainment [d]
24. band of musicians
   ceilidh of musicians

10. blast of trumpets
11. burden of syllables
12. cacophony of noise
13. cadence of chords
   cadence of harmonies
   cadence of horse's hooves
14. cadenza of notes
15. canto of music
16. carillon of bells
17. ceilidh of musicians
18. change of bells
19. chime of bells
20. choir of echoes [e]
   choir of singers
   choir of voices
21. chorale of singers
22. chorus of voices
23. circle of fifths [c]
24. clash of cymbals
25. cluster of notes
26. collection of music
27. concertino of soloists
28. concerto of voices
29. concord of sounds
30. congeries of ballads
31. consonance of sounds
32. consort of fiddlers [e]
   consort of musicians
33. cord of woodwinds [b]
34. corps of woodwinds
35. covey of fiddlers [e]
36. crescendo of voices
37. diminution of echoes
38. division of organ stops
39. duo of musicians (2)
40. duplet of notes

consort of musicians	41. eisteddfod of performers
duo of musicians (2)	42. ensemble of musicians
ensemble of musicians	43. euphony of sounds
nonet of musicians (9)	44. fanfare of trumpets
octet of musicians (8)	45. flourish of trumpets
orchestra of musicians	46. furore of bandsmen
quartet of musicians (4)	47. gang of fiddlers
quintet of musicians (5)	48. garland of ballads
septet of musicians (7)	49. library of music
sextet of musicians (6)	50. manuscript of music
trio of musicians (3)	51. medley of tunes
25. cacophony of noise	52. melody of harpers/harpists [a]
26. arpeggio of notes	53. minstrelsy of songs
cadenza of notes	54. nonet of musicians (9)
cluster of notes	55. octet of musicians (8)
duplet of notes	56. olio of musical entertainment [d]
scale of notes	
triad of (musical) notes	57. opus of (musical) work
trill of notes	58. orchestra of musicians
triplet of notes	59. parenthesis of cellists [b]
27. division of organ stops	60. peal of bells
28. battery of percussion instruments	61. pound of pianists [b]
	62. poverty of pipers
29. antiphony of performers	63. programme of songs
eisteddfod of performers	64. progression of chords
30. pound of pianists [b]	65. quartet of musicians (4)
31. poverty of pipers	66. quaver of coloraturas [b]
skirl of pipers [b]	67. quintet of musicians (5)
32. choir of singers	68. rafale of drum rolls
chorale of singers	69. recital of music
33. concertino of soloists	70. repertoire of songs
34. album of songs	71. reverberation of echoes
minstrelsy of songs	72. rhapsody of music
programme of songs	73. ring of bells
repertoire of songs	74. rumble of basses [b]
35. amplification of sound	75. scale of notes

Chapter 9: A Play of Words

concord of sounds	76. score of music
consonance of sounds	77. septet of musicians (7)
euphony of sounds	78. set of bagpipes
36. set of strings	set of strings
37. burden of syllables	79. sextet of musicians (6)
38. medley of tunes	80. skirl of pipers [b]
39. blast of trumpets	81. string of hits/hit records
fanfare of trumpets	string of violinists [b]
flourish of trumpets	82. suite of (instrumental) works
40. tumult of tubas	83. symphony of music
41. string of violinists [b]	84. tattoo of military bands
42. babble of voices	85. tintinnabulation of bells
choir of voices	86. tolling of bells
chorus of voices	87. triad of (musical) notes
concerto of voices	88. trill of notes
crescendo of voices	89. trio of musicians (3)
43. cord of woodwinds [b]	90. triplet of notes
corps of woodwinds	91. troupe of minstrels
44. opus of (musical) work	92. tumult of tubas
suite of (instrumental) works	93. whine of clarinettists [b]

Notes:

a. Archaic, from one of the 16th century manuscripts (most commonly, The Book of Hawking & Hunting', by Dame Juliana Barnes, 1486).
b. From James Lipton, 'An Exaltation of Larks' (1977)
c. The succession of keys or chords proceeding by fifths.
d. Vaudeville or musical entertainment presented between the acts of a burlesque or minstrel show.
e. From Ivan G Sparkes, 'Dictionary of Collective Nouns & Group Terms'.

'a band of musicians'

'a tintinnabulation of bells'

'a consort of musicians'

Chapter 9: A Play of Words

'an alphabet of letters'

9c. Literary & Printing

Sorted by noun	Sorted by collective noun
1. forest of apostrophes ʲ	1. almanac of information
2. consort of authors ⁱ	2. alphabet of letters
fry of authors ⁱ	3. anthology of poems
3. edition of books	anthology of prose
library of books	4. archive of documents
	archive of scrolls
	5. athenaeum of learning
	athenaeum of reading material
	6. atlas of maps
	7. bale of paper (5000 sheets)
	8. bibliography of reference works
	9. bind of signatures ᶠ
	10. body of work
	11. book of rules
	book of verse
stack of books	12. bundle of paper (1000 shts.)
4. cipher of codes	13. cacography of words
5. *quiddity of collective nouns*	14. canon of work (artistic)
6. crowd of commas ʲ	15. canto of poetry
7. cluster of consonants	16. cartouche of hieroglyphs
8. table of contents	
9. rash of correspondence	
10. flourish of curlicues	
11. archive of documents	

12. symposium of essays
13. pitfall of fine print [c]
14. rash of graffiti
15. cartouche of hieroglyphs
16. almanac of information
    directory of information
    dossier of information
    encyclopaedia of information
    fount (or fountain) of information
    wealth of information
17. manual of instructions
18. athenaeum of learning
19. signature of leaves [e]
20. alphabet of letters
    jumble of letters
21. chrestomathy of literary passages
22. cycle of literary works
    varia of literary works
23. compendium of literature
24. atlas of maps
25. wealth of material

26. olio of miscellaneous pieces
27. collective of nouns
28. collection of novellas
29. collation of pages
30. spread of pages (2)

17. chapbook of poems
18. chapel of printers [d]
19. chase of printers' blocks
20. chrestomathy of literary passages
21. chronicle of stories
22. cipher of codes
23. classification of words
24. *cliterati of feminist writers* [c]
25. cluster of consonants
26. collation of pages
27. collection of novellas
    collection of short stories
28. collective of nouns
29. compendium of literature
    compendium of stories
30. compilation of poems
31. concordance of words
32. conjugation of verbs
33. consort of authors [i]
34. construction of words
35. corpus of work
36. crowd of commas [j]
37. cycle of literary works
38. dictionary of words
39. directory of information
40. divan of poems (Persian) [h]
41. dossier of information
42. edition of books
43. encyclopaedia of information
44. fascicle of a printed work [b]
45. festschrift of (celebratory) writings
46. flourish of curlicues
47. forest of apostrophes [j]

31. bale of paper (5000 sheets)
    bundle of paper (1000 shts.)
    quire of paper (25 sheets)
    ream of paper (500 sheets)
    sea of paper
    web of paper (printing roll)
32. scroll of papyrus
33. scroll of parchment
34. gazetteer of place-names
35. anthology of poems
    chapbook of poems
    compilation of poems
    divan of poems (Persian) h
36. canto of poetry
    nonet of poetry (9 lines)
    quatrain of poetry (4 lines)
    quintet of poetry (5 lines)
    reading of poetry
    recital of poetry
    school of poetry
    sestet of poetry (6 lines)
    sonnet of poetry (14 lines)
    stanza of poetry
    triolet of poetry (8 lines)
    verse of poetry
37. fascicle of a printed work b
38. chapel of printers d
39. chase of printers' blocks
40. galley of printers' type
    pi of printers' type
41. anthology of prose
    purple passage of prose g
42. athenaeum of reading material
43. selection of readings
44. work of reference

48. fount (or fountain) of information
49. fry of authors i
50. galley of printers' type
51. garble of words
52. gathering of signatures f
53. gazetteer of place-names
54. glossary of words
55. index of words
56. jumble of letters
    jumble of words
57. lacuna of space
58. lexicon of words

59. library of books
60. manual of instructions
61. *muse of wordsmiths*
62. nonet of poetry (9 lines)
63. œuvre of work
64. olio of miscellaneous pieces
65. omnibus of stories
66. paideia of spellings

45. bibliography of reference works
46. book of rules
47. archive of scrolls
48. collection of short stories
49. round robin of signatories
50. bind of signatures ᶠ
    gathering of signatures ᶠ
51. *paper-trail of snail mail*
52. lacuna of space
53. paideia of spellings
54. chronicle of stories
    compendium of stories
    omnibus of stories
    saga of stories
55. syllabary of symbols
56. conjugation of verbs
57. book of verse
53. cacography of words
    classification of words
    concordance of words
    construction of words
    dictionary of words
    garble of words
    glossary of words
    index of words
    jumble of words
    lexicon of words
    paradigm of words
    prolixity of words
    spew of words
    thesaurus of words
    vocabulary of words
54. *muse of wordsmiths*
55. body of work
    canon of work (artistic)

67. *paper-trail of snail mail*
68. paradigm of words
69. pi of printers' type
70. pitfall of fine print ᶜ
71. prolixity of words
72. purple passage of prose ᵍ
73. quatrain of poetry (4 lines)
74. *quiddity of collective nouns*
75. quintet of poetry (5 lines)
76. quire of paper (25 sheets)
77. rash of correspondence
    rash of graffiti
78. reading of poetry
79. ream of paper (500 sheets)
80. recital of poetry
81. round robin of signatories
82. saga of stories
83. school of poetry
84. screed of writing
85. scroll of papyrus

    scroll of parchment
86. sea of paper
87. selection of readings
88. sestet of poetry (6 lines)
89. signature of leaves ᵉ
90. sonnet of poetry (14 lines)
91. spew of words
92. spread of pages (2)
93. stack of books

corpus of work	94. stanza of poetry
œuvre of work	95. syllabary of symbols
56. *cliterati of (feminist) writers* c	96. symposium of essays
57. worship of writers a	97. table of contents
58. festschrift of (celebratory) writings	98. thesaurus of words
	99. triolet of poetry (8 lines)
	100. varia of literary works
	101. verse of poetry
	102. vocabulary of words
	103. wealth of information
	wealth of material
	104. web of paper (printing roll)
	105. work of reference
screed of writing	106. worship of writers a

Notes:

a. From James Lipton, 'An Exaltation of Larks' (1977).
b. One of the temporary divisions of a printed item that, for convenience in printing or publication, is issued in small instalments, usually incomplete in themselves (e.g. the OED).
c. The American Dialect Society recently awarded its prize for 'Most Outrageous (new) Word of the Year' to this phrase.
d. The correct term for an association of employees in a printer's office.
e. A 'signature' has 16 leaves (of paper), each side of a leaf is one page.
f. Almost every book is constructed using 'a gathering (or a 'bind') of signatures', which can be seen and counted by looking at the upper edge of the spine, as a series of small 'booklets'.
g. A passage full of ornate and flowery language.
h. From the Turkish habit of piling rugs & cushions for reclining while reading.
i. From Ivan G Sparkes, Dictionary of Collective Nouns & Group Terms.
j. From Lynne Truss, 'Eats, Shoots and Leaves'.

"The Age of Intellect"

'an invasion of aliens'

9d. Popular Culture

Sorted by noun	Sorted by collective noun
1. civilisation of aliens invasion of aliens	1. chart of hit songs
2. race of beings	2. civilisation of aliens
3. invasion of body-snatchers	3. collective of the Borg
4. collective of the Borg hive of the Borg	4. convention of trekkies [a] convention of x-philes
5. cult of celebrity	5. *corpus of zombies*
6. *Ibiza of clubbers*	6. cult of celebrity
7. line of cocaine	7. *deck of D.J.s*
8. *doom of conspiracy theorists*	8. *descent of drop-outs*
9. *deck of D.J.s*	9. *doom of conspiracy theorists*
10. *descent of drop-outs*	10. enterprise of trekkies [a]
11. overdose of drugs	11. festival of films
12. festival of films	12. *google of geeks*
13. *google of geeks*	13. fix of heroin
14. *pride of girl power*	14. gang of hooligans gang of yobs gang of youths
15. fix of heroin wrap of heroin	15. genre of horror movies
16. trip of hippies	16. hive of the Borg
17. chart of hit songs	17. hood of street gangs
18. *hope of hitch-hikers*	18. *hope of hitch-hikers*
19. gang of hooligans	19. *Ibiza of clubbers*
20. genre of horror movies	20. invasion of aliens invasion of body-snatchers
21. shop of horrors	21. library of videos
22. *prey of paparazzi*	22. line of cocaine
23. shit-load of problems	23. orgy of swingers
24. *rant of rap artists*	24. overdose of drugs
25. hood of street gangs	25. *prey of paparazzi*
26. orgy of swingers	26. *pride of girl power*
27. convention of trekkies [a] enterprise of trekkies [a]	27. race of beings
28. library of videos	28. *rant of rap artists*

Gallimaufry

29. stash of weed	29. shit-load of problems
30. convention of x-philes	30. shop of horrors
31. gang of yobs	31. stash of weed
32. gang of youths	32. trip of hippies
corpus of zombies	33. wrap of heroin

Notes

a. trekkies: fans of Star Trek

'a cult of celebrity'

Chapter 9: A Play of Words

'an army of angels'

Gallimaufry

9e. Religion

Sorted by noun	Sorted by collective noun
1. fidget of altarboys	1. abominable sight of monks [a]
2. army of angels	
chorus of angels	
flock of angels	
host of angels	
3. fellowship of apostles	
4. immersion of baptists	
5. doctrine of belief	
6. cult of believers	
sect of believers	
7. antiphonary of biblical passages	
	abomination of monks [e]
8. bench of bishops	2. act of faith
bully of bishops	3. antiphonary of biblical passages
consistory of bishops	
multiplying of bishops	4. army of angels
psalter of bishops	army of martyrs
sea of bishops	5. assemblage of the clergy
9. chapter of canons	6. assembly of ministers
dignity of canons [a]	assembly of churches
10. body of cardinals	7. band of pilgrims
college of cardinals [c]	8. bench of bishops
conclave of cardinals	9. body of cardinals
11. evensong of choirboys	10. bully of bishops
12. confraternity of Christians	11. calendar of saints
13. lectionary of church readings	12. canon of saints
	canon of scripture
14. assembly of churches	13. caste of priests
conference of churches	14. cenoby of monks
15. assemblage of the clergy	15. chantry of priests
college of clergy	16. chapter of canons
convocation of clergy	chapter of monks

182

Chapter 9: A Play of Words

16. charge of curates [a]
17. decanter of deans
    decorum of deans
18. ennead of (9) deities
    trinity of (3) deities
19. pilgrimage of devotion
20. doctrine of doctors (of divinity) [a]
21. government of episcopalians
22. act of faith
    tenet of faith

23. skulk of friars [a]
24. society of friends (Quakers)
25. pantheon of gods
26. multitude of heavenly host
27. phylactery of Hebrew texts
28. vision of hell
29. observance of hermits [a]
30. minyan of Jews (quorum for a congregation)
31. fall of manna
32. army of martyrs
33. assembly of ministers
    convocation of ministers
    council of ministers
    synod of ministers

17. charge of curates [a]
18. chartulary of monastic documents
19. chorus of angels
20. college of cardinals [c]
    college of clergy
21. communion of religious groups
22. community of saints
23. concelebration of priests
24. conclave of cardinals
25. concordance of words (bible)
26. conference of churches
27. confraternity of Christians
28. congregation of worshippers
29. consistory of bishops
30. convent of nuns
31. conventicle of religious dissenters
32. converting of preachers [a]
33. convocation of clergy
    convocation of ministers
34. council of ministers
35. cult of believers
36. decanter of deans
37. decorum of deans
38. devoutness of monks [d]
39. dignity of canons [a]
40. discretion of priests [a]
41. doctrine of belief
    doctrine of doctors (of divinity) [a]
42. ennead of (9) deities
43. evensong of choirboys
44. fall of manna
45. fellowship of apostles

Gallimaufry

34. party of missionaries	46. fidget of altarboys
35. laura of monastic cells	47. flap of nuns [b]
36. lavra of monastic cells	48. flock of angels
37. chartulary of monastic documents	flock of worshippers
	49. government of episcopalians
38. abominable sight of monks [a]	50. hagiography of sacred writings
abomination of monks [e]	
cenoby of monks	51. hagiology of saints
chapter of monks	52. harvest of souls
devoutness of monks [d]	53. holiness of nuns [d]
monastery of monks	54. host of angels
swarm of monks	55. immersion of baptists
39. convent of nuns	56. laura of monastic cells
flap of nuns [b]	57. lavra of monastic cells
holiness of nuns [d]	58. lectionary of church readings
pray of nuns	
superfluity of nuns [a]	59. litany of prayers
40. band of pilgrims	60. liturgy of worship
41. pæan of praise	61. mass of priests [b]
42. litany of prayers	62. meeting of quakers
43. converting of preachers [a]	63. membership of presbyterians
pontification of preachers	
44. pontificality of prelates [a]	64. minyan of Jews (quorum for a congregation)
45. membership of presbyterians	
	65. monastery of monks
46. caste of priests	66. multiplying of bishops
chantry of priests	67. multitude of heavenly host
concelebration of priests	68. observance of hermits [a]
discretion of priests [a]	69. *odium of sanctity*
mass of priests [b]	70. odour of sanctity
47. meeting of quakers	71. pæan of praise
48. conventicle of religious dissenters	72. pantheon of gods
	73. party of missionaries
49. tenet of religious doctrine	74. phylactery of Hebrew texts
50. communion of religious groups	75. pilgrimage of devotion
	76. pontificality of prelates [a]

Chapter 9: A Play of Words

51. hagiography of sacred writings	77. pontification of preachers
52. calendar of saints	78. pray of nuns
canon of saints	79. prudence of vicars [a]
community of saints	80. psalter of bishops
hagiology of saints	81. pyx of (Communion) wafers
53. *odium of sanctity*	82. sea of bishops
odour of sanctity	sea of souls
54. canon of scripture	83. sect of believers
55. harvest of souls	84. skulk of friars [a]
sea of souls	85. society of friends (Quakers)
56. prudence of vicars [a]	86. superfluity of nuns [a]
57. pyx of (Communion) wafers	87. swarm of monks
58. concordance of words (bible)	88. synod of ministers
59. liturgy of worship	89. tenet of faith
60. congregation of worshippers	tenet of religious doctrine
flock of worshippers	90. trinity of (3) deities
	91. vision of hell

Notes:

a. Archaic, from one of the 16th century manuscripts (most commonly, The Book of Hawking & Hunting', by Dame Juliana Barnes, 1486).
b. From James Lipton, 'An Exaltation of Larks' (1977).
c. Shakespeare, 'Henry VI Part II'.
d. Earlier than the derogatory 'an abominable sight of monks', or 'a superfluity of nuns'.
e. The phrase "An abomination of monks" is frequently cited as a legitimate collective noun for monks. It is actually a misinterpretation of the title of a protestant treatise written by Jan Hus around 1400.

'a congregation of worshippers'

Gallimaufry

'a pantheon of gods'

'an enchantment of fairies'

9f. Myth & Magic

Sorted by noun	Sorted by collective noun
1. tribe of Amazons	1. army of ghosts
2. chorus of angels	2. bestiary of mythological creatures
flock of angels	3. blessing of unicorns
host of angels	4. bridge of trolls [a]
3. *wail of banshees*	5. charm of fairies
4. horde of demons	6. chorus of angels
5. dignity of dragons	7. coven of witches (13+)
doom of dragons	8. *delving of dwarves*
	9. dignity of dragons
	10. *doom of dragons*
	11. *enchantment of fairies*
	12. flight of dragons
	flight of witches
	13. flock of angels
	14. *gabble of goblins*
flight of dragons	15. *garboil of goblins*
weyr of dragons	16. *glitch of gremlins*
wing of dragons	17. grace of unicorns
6. *delving of dwarves*	18. grimoire (book) of magical spells
shortage of dwarves	
7. *mischief of elves*	19. herd of fairies
8. charm of fairies	20. horde of demons
enchantment of fairies	horde of orcs
herd of fairies	21. host of angels
9. army of ghosts	22. incantation of magical spells
10. *gabble of goblins*	23. knot of witches [a]
garboil of goblins	24. *limerick of leprechauns*
11. *glitch of gremlins*	25. *mischief of elves*
12. *pryde of griffins*	26. *pryde of griffins*
13. *limerick of leprechauns*	27. race of Titans
14. grimoire (book) of magical	28. riddle of sphinx

spells	29. sabbat of witches
incantation of magical spells	30. *shortage of dwarves*
15. bestiary of mythological creatures	
16. horde of orcs	
17. riddle of sphinx	
18. swarm of sprites	
19. race of Titans	
20. bridge of trolls ᵃ	
21. blessing of unicorns	
grace of unicorns	31. swarm of sprites
22. coven of witches (13+)	32. tribe of Amazons
flight of witches	33. *wail of banshees*
knot of witches ᵃ	34. weyr of dragons
sabbat of witches	35. wing of dragons

Notes:

a. From Kipling West's book "A Rattle of Bones: A Halloween Book of Collective Nouns".

'a mischief of elves'

Chapter 9: A Play of Words

'a charm of fairies'

'a flight of witches'

'a horde of demons'

Chapter Ten

A Comedy of Errors

a. *Intangibles (Ideas, Idioms, Clichés & Abstract Concepts)*
b. *Communication & Language*
c. *Emotions & Characteristics*
d. *Time*

'a montage of images'

Gallimaufry

'a distribution of largesse'

10a. Intangibles
(Ideas, Idioms, Clichés & Abstract Concepts)

Sorted by noun	Sorted by collective noun
1. period of abstinence	1. abundance of options
2. tirade of abuse	abundance of plentifulness
torrent of abuse	2. acceleration of speed
3. burst of acceleration	3. act of faith
4. chapter of accidents	4. agenda of tasks
5. pinnacle of achievement	5. allocation of duties
record of achievements	6. annal of events
6. hive of activity	7. arena of public awareness
7. series of adventures	8. *argosy of plenty* g
8. state of affairs	9. armoury of skills
9. token of affection	10. array of talents
10. crucible of affliction	11. assessment of risk

11. patina of age	12. assignment of tasks
12. camp of allegations ⁱ	13. assimilation of knowledge
13. crib-list of answers	14. atmosphere of gloom
14. string of attacks	15. attraction of opposites
15. focus of attention	16. auction of promises
shower of attention	17. aura of mystery
span of attention	18. avalanche of work
16. commonality of attributes	19. axis of evil ʲ
herd of attributes	20. backlog of work
17. degree of autonomy	21. ball of fire
18. pile of baloney	22. bank of images
19. hill of beans ᵏ	23. baptism of fire
20. vision of beauty	24. barrel-full of monkeys
21. shower of blessings	25. bastion of support
22. spot of bother	26. battle of wills
23. oasis of calm	27. benchmark of quality
24. house of cards	28. biosphere of life
25. cycle of changes	29. blaze of glory
wind of change	30. blur of images
26. state of chaos	31. body of evidence
27. bowl of cherries	32. bonanza of good luck
28. plethora of choices	bonanza of wealth
29. veneer of civilisation	33. bone of contention
30. trail of clues	34. bowl of cherries
31. load of cobblers	35. branch of knowledge
32. modicum of common sense	branch of learning
smattering of common sense	36. breach of faith
33. unease of compromises	breach of premises ᵈ
34. list of concerns	breach of promise
modicum of concern	37. burden of proof
35. code of conduct	burden of responsibility
36. deal of confusion	38. burgeoning of interest
huggermugger of confusion	39. burst of acceleration
state of confusion	40. cabinet of curiosities
welter of confusion	41. call of nature
37. stream of consciousness	42. camp of allegations ⁱ

38. bone of contention
39. mass of contradictions
40. welter of controversies
41. hotbed of corruption
42. catalogue of crime
    life of crime
    lifetime of crime
    spate of crime
43. melting pot of cultures
44. cabinet of curiosities

45. dance of death
    kiss of death
46. catalogue of debts
47. cloak of deceit
    web of deceit
48. ounce of decency
49. process of deduction
50. stand of defiance
51. garden of delights
    cornucopia of delights
    smorgasbord of (culinary) delights
52. list of demands
53. culture of dependency
54. vision of destiny
55. minutiæ of details
56. jot of difference
    world of difference

43. can of worms
44. canon of rules
45. caravan of dreams
46. catalogue of crime
    catalogue of debts
    catalogue of disasters
    catalogue of errors
    catalogue of misfortune
    catalogue of problems
47. centre of excellence
48. chain of events
    chain of supply
49. chapter of accidents
    chapter of possibilities
50. chimera of imagination
51. chronicle of events
52. chronology of events
53. city of dreams
54. clash of events
55. cloak of deceit
    cloak of secrecy
56. coagulum of matter
57. code of conduct
    code of honour
    code of practice
58. coign of vantage [f]
59. combination of factors
60. commonality of attributes
61. composite of images
62. concentration of effort
63. cone of silence
64. consolidation of material
65. conspiracy of silence
66. cornucopia of delights
67. coup de grace
    coup de foudre

Chapter 10: A Comedy of Errors

57. catalogue of disasters
58. regime of discipline
59. voyage of discovery
60. scintilla of doubt (L 'spark') [1]
    shadow of doubt
61. caravan of dreams
    city of dreams
62. allocation of duties
63. concentration of effort
    diminution of effort
    redoubling of effort
64. process of elimination
65. field of endeavour
66. overload of energy
    powerhouse of energy
67. hint of equivocation [1]
68. catalogue of errors
    litany of errors
    margin of error
69. token of esteem
70. annal of events
    chain of events
    chronicle of events
    chronology of events
    clash of events
    diary of events
    journal of events
    log of events
    logbook of events
    panorama of events
    profile of events
    programme of events
    record of events
    roller coaster of events
    testimony of events
    timetable of events

coup d'œil
68. crib-list of answers
69. crock of shite
70. crucible of affliction
71. culture of dependency
72. cycle of changes [i]
73. dance of death
74. day of judgement
75. deal of confusion
76. decline of standards
77. degree of autonomy
78. den of iniquity
79. diary of events
80. diminution of effort
81. dossier of secrets

82. drift of shadows
83. element of risk
84. embarras de richesses
85. embarrassment of riches
86. embodiment of evil
87. *enigma of variations*
88. error of judgement
89. *eureka of inventions*
90. field of endeavour
91. figment of imagination
92. figure of fun

195

Gallimaufry

turn of events	93. finger of fate
71. body of evidence	finger of suspicion
scintilla of evidence (legal)	94. flicker of life
shred of evidence	95. flight of fancy
trace of evidence	flight of imagination
trail of evidence	96. flurry of interest
72. axis of evil ʲ	97. focus of attention
embodiment of evil	98. fount of knowledge
73. centre of excellence	99. frame of reference
74. monotony of existence	100. fusion of material
75. wealth of experience	101. garden of delights
76. sea of faces	102. glow of satisfaction
77. combination of factors	103. gnome of truth
78. litany of failures	104. goldmine of information
79. act of faith	105. grain of salt
breach of faith	106. guarantee of success
leap of faith	107. herd of attributes
80. flight of fancy	108. hill of beans ᵏ
	109. hint of equivocation ˡ
	hint of suspicion
	110. hive of activity
	111. horn of plenty
	112. hotbed of corruption
	113. house of cards
	house of straw
	114. huggermugger of confusion
	115. imbroglio of intrigue
81. finger of fate	116. iota of sense
82. ball of fire	117. itinerary of places
baptism of fire	118. jot of difference
83. kettle of fish	119. journal of events
84. regime of fitness	120. kernel of truth
85. series of flaws	121. kettle of fish
86. tour de force	122. kiss of death
87. symmetry of forms	kiss of life
88. wheel of fortune	123. land of plenty

89. coup de foudre
90. suggestion of foul play
91. taste of freedom
92. figure of fun
93. atmosphere of gloom
    miasma of gloom
94. blaze of glory
95. bonanza of good luck
    run of good luck
96. coup de grace
97. spurt of growth
98. minefield of hazards
99. taste of honey
100. code of honour
101. Pandora's box of ills
102. bank of images
    blur of images
    composite of images
    montage of images
    phantasmagoria of images
103. chimera of imagination
    figment of imagination
    flight of imagination
104. vagary of impediments
105. sphere of influence
106. goldmine of information
    mine of information
    treasure trove of information
    wealth of information
107. den of iniquity
108. burgeoning of interest
    flurry of interest
    rally of interest
109. imbroglio of intrigue
    web of intrigue
110. eureka of inventions

124. leap of faith
125. life of crime
126. lifetime of crime
127. list of concerns
    list of demands
128. litany of errors
    litany of failures
129. load of cobblers
    load of kinnocks [e]
    load of tripe
130. log of events
131. logbook of events
132. maelstrom of motherhood [h]
133. march of progress
134. margin of error
135. mass of contradictions
136. measure of security
137. meeting of minds
138. meld of minds
139. melting pot of cultures
140. miasma of gloom
141. mine of information
142. minefield of hazards
143. minutiæ of details
144. mob of metaphors [d]
145. modicum of common sense
    modicum of concern

197

Gallimaufry

111. morass of issues	modicum of morals
112. day of judgement	modicum of respect
error of judgement	146. monotony of existence
113. travesty of justice	147. montage of images
114. load of kinnocks [e]	148. morass of issues
115. assimilation of knowledge	149. multitude of sins
branch of knowledge	150. oasis of calm
fount of knowledge	151. orgy of violence
repository of knowledge	152. ounce of decency
reservoir of knowledge	153. overload of energy
sum of knowledge	154. pall of silence
treasure trove of knowledge	155. Pandora's box of ills
116. branch of learning	156. panorama of events
117. biosphere of life	panorama of scenes
flicker of life	panorama of views
kiss of life	157. patina of age
quality of life	patina of respectability
tree of life	158. period of abstinence
walk of life	period of reflection
way of life	159. phantasmagoria of images
118. vision of loveliness	160. piece of work [a]
119. stroke of luck	161. pile of baloney
120. consolidation of material	pile of nonsense
121. fusion of material	pile of shit
122. coagulum of matter	162. pinch of salt
123. mob of metaphors [d]	163. pinnacle of achievement
124. meeting of minds	164. plethora of choices
meld of minds	165. policy of non-intervention
125. catalogue of misfortune	166. pool of resources
126. barrel-full of monkeys	167. powerhouse of energy
127. modicum of morals	powerhouse of strength
128. maelstrom of motherhood [h]	168. process of deduction
129. aura of mystery	process of elimination
130. call of nature	169. profile of events
131. policy of non-intervention	170. programme of events
132. pile of nonsense	171. quagmire of problems

Chapter 10: A Comedy of Errors

133. coup d'œil
134. string of offences
135. range of opportunities
136. window of opportunity
137. attraction of opposites
138. abundance of options
    range of options
139. scenario of (possible)
    outcomes
140. rite of passage
141. itinerary of places
142. abundance of plentifulness
143. *argosy of plenty* g
    horn of plenty
    land of plenty
144. chapter of possibilities
145. code of practice
146. breach of premises d
147. set of priorities
148. catalogue of problems
    quagmire of problems

149. march of progress
    tide of progress
150. auction of promises

172. quality of life
173. rally of interest
174. range of opportunities
    range of options
    range of talents
    range of values
175. record of achievements
    record of events
176. redoubling of effort
177. regime of discipline
    regime of fitness
    regime of secrecy
178. reign of terror
179. renaissance of thought
180. repository of knowledge
181. reservoir of knowledge
182. rite of passage
183. roller coaster of events
184. rule of thumb
185. rumpus of shapes c
186. run of good luck
    run of success
187. scenario of (possible)
    outcomes
188. school of thought
189. scintilla of doubt 1
    scintilla of evidence
    scintilla of truth
190. sea of faces
    sea of red ink
    sea of troubles b
191. sense of proportion
192. series of adventures
    series of flaws
193. set of priorities
194. shadow of doubt

199

breach of promise	195. shower of attention
151. burden of proof	shower of blessings
152. sense of proportion	196. shred of evidence
153. slew of proposals	197. sign of the times
154. arena of public awareness	198. slew of proposals
155. tide of publicity	199. smattering of common sense
156. benchmark of quality	200. smorgasbord of (culinary)
157. variety of reasons	delights
158. sea of red ink	201. span of attention
159. mountain of red tape	202. spate of crime
tangle of red tape	spate of vandalism
160. frame of reference	spate of violence
161. period of reflection	203. sphere of influence
162. pool of resources	204. spot of bother
163. modicum of respect	205. spurt of growth
164. patina of respectability	206. stand of defiance
veneer of respectability	207. state of affairs
165. burden of responsibility	state of chaos
weight of responsibility	state of confusion
166. embarrassment of riches	208. stratum of society
167. embarras de richesses	209. stream of consciousness
168. assessment of risk	210. string of attacks
element of risk	string of offences
169. canon of rules	211. stroke of luck
170. grain of salt	212. suggestion of foul play
pinch of salt	213. sum of knowledge
171. glow of satisfaction	214. superfluity of toasts
172. panorama of scenes	(speeches)
173. cloak of secrecy	215. sweet smell of success
regime of secrecy	216. syllabus of study
174. dossier of secrets	217. symmetry of forms
175. measure of security	218. tangle of red tape
176. iota of sense	219. taste of freedom
177. drift of shadows	taste of honey
178. rumpus of shapes c	220. testimony of events
179. pile of shit	221. tide of progress

Chapter 10: A Comedy of Errors

180. crock of shite
181. cone of silence
    conspiracy of silence
    pall of silence
182. multitude of sins
183. armoury of skills
184. whirl of social engagements
185. stratum of society
186. acceleration of speed
187. decline of standards
188. wall of steel
189. house of straw
190. powerhouse of strength
    tower of strength
191. syllabus of study
192. guarantee of success
    run of success
    sweet smell of success
193. chain of supply
194. bastion of support
195. finger of suspicion
    hint of suspicion
196. array of talents
    range of talents
197. agenda of tasks
    assignment of tasks
198. variety of techniques
199. reign of terror
200. renaissance of thought
    school of thought
201. rule of thumb
202. sign of the times
203. superfluity of toasts
    (speeches)
204. load of tripe
205. sea of troubles ᵇ

    tide of publicity
222. timetable of events
223. tirade of abuse
224. token of affection
    token of esteem
225. torrent of abuse
226. tour de force
227. tower of strength
228. trace of evidence
229. trail of clues
    trail of evidence
230. travesty of justice
231. treasure trove of information
    treasure trove of knowledge

232. tree of life
233. turn of events
234. unease of compromises
235. vagary of impediments
236. variety of reasons
    variety of techniques
237. veneer of civilisation
    veneer of respectability
238. vision of beauty
    vision of destiny
    vision of loveliness

206. gnome of truth	239. vista of views
kernel of truth	240. voyage of discovery
scintilla of truth	241. walk of life
207. range of values	242. wall of steel
208. spate of vandalism	243. way of life
209. coign of vantage f	244. wealth of experience
210. enigma of variations	wealth of information
211. panorama of views	245. web of deceit
vista of views	web of intrigue
212. orgy of violence	246. weight of responsibility
spate of violence	247. welter of confusion
213. bonanza of wealth	welter of controversies
214. battle of wills	248. wheel of fortune
215. avalanche of work	249. whirl of social engagements
backlog of work	250. wind of change
piece of work a	251. window of opportunity
216. can of worms	252. world of difference

Notes:

a. In Shakespeare's Hamlet: 'What a piece of work is man'; and also in Macbeth: '… this most bloody piece of work'.
b. In Shakespeare's Hamlet, the soliloquy: '… to take arms against a sea of troubles …'.
c. From Dylan Thomas' Prologue … 'This rumpus of shapes…'.
d. From James Lipton, An Exaltation of Larks (1977).
e. From a speech by Michael Heseltine, in April 1992 (meaning 'a load of cobblers').
f. A Coign of Vantage, is a painting by Sir Lawrence Alma-Tadema (1895).
g. Joseph Heller, in Catch 22, describes Milo Minderbender's 'argosies of plenty'.
h. 'From the Foreword to ; The Writers' and Artists' Yearbook 2002, by Deborah Moggach.
i. From Ivan G Sparkes, Dictionary of Collective Nouns & Group Terms.
j. From US President George Bush, a description of the countries reputedly supporting terrorist organisations.
k. Famously, from Humphrey Bogart's final speech to Ingrid Bergman in the film Casablanca: 'the problems of three little people don't amount to a hill of beans in this crazy world".

1. "There was never a scintilla of doubt, or a hint of equivocation, in Michael about his commitment to the party". - "Ferris's decency and sense of fun recalled", Irish Times, March 23, 2000.

'a sense of proportion'

'a web of intrigue'

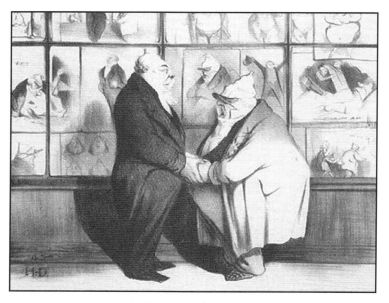

'a bastion of support'

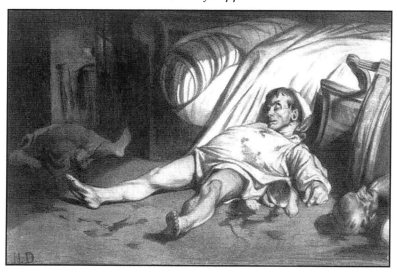

'an orgy of violence'

Chapter 10: A Comedy of Errors

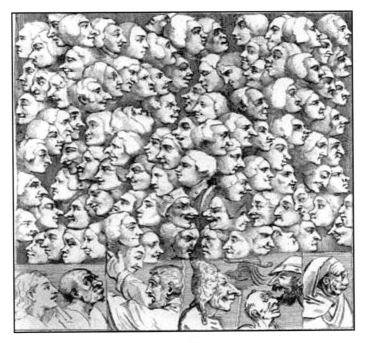

'a sea of faces'

'a tirade of abuse'

10b. Communication & Language

Sorted by noun	Sorted by collective noun
1. harangue of abuse	1. accolade of praise
tirade of abuse	2. acknowledgement of thanks
torrent of abuse	3. ambiguity of expression
2. bit of advice	4. ambivalence of meaning
word of advice	5. Babel of tongues
3. chorus of approval	6. barrage of criticism
4. murmur of assent	barrage of questions
5. salvo of bravos [a]	7. battle of wits
6. stream of calls	8. bit of advice
7. chorus of complaint	9. body of opinion
diatribe of complaints	10. brouhaha of noise
flood of complaints	11. burst of invective
litany of complaints	burst of polemic
slew of complaints	burst of rhetoric
trickle of complaints	12. campaign of objection
8. mass of contradictions	13. cannonade of criticism
9. storm of controversy	cannonade of reproach
10. thread of conversation	14. carp of criticism
wisp of conversation	15. catch-all of meaning
11. barrage of criticism	16. chain of logic
cannonade of criticism	17. chorus of approval
carp of criticism	chorus of complaint
12. volley of curses	chorus of disapproval
13. imbroglio of disagreement	18. clash of opinions
14. chorus of disapproval	19. climate of opinion
15. torrent of eloquence	20. cobweb of lies
16. ambiguity of expression	21. cocktail of lies
freedom of expression	22. concentration of ideas
17. gift of the gab	23. consensus of ideas (taut)
18. grapevine of gossip	24. consolidation of ideas
hotbed of gossip	25. construct of ideas
snippet of gossip	26. convergence of ideas

titbit of gossip
19. concentration of ideas
consensus of ideas (taut)
consolidation of ideas
construct of ideas
convergence of ideas
fusion of ideas
hotchpotch of ideas
interplay of ideas
melting pot of ideas
paradigm of ideas
ragbag of ideas
synergy of ideas
synthesis of ideas
20. whisper of impropriety
21. hail of insults
rain of insults
22. burst of invective
flood of invective
stream of invective
23. macaroni of languages
phylum of languages
polyglot of languages

rosetta stone of languages
24. cobweb of lies

27. declaration of love
28. diatribe of complaints

29. eulogy of praise
30. faculty of speech
31. farrago of lies
farrago of nonsense
32. figure of speech
33. flood of complaints
flood of invective
34. flow of rhetoric
35. freedom of expression
36. fusion of ideas
37. galimatias of nonsense [b]
38. gift of the gab
gift of speech
39. grapevine of gossip
40. hail of insults
41. harangue of abuse
42. hotbed of gossip
43. hotchpotch of ideas
44. howl of protest
45. imbroglio of disagreement
46. interplay of ideas
47. layer of meaning
48. litany of complaints

cocktail of lies
farrago of lies
pack of lies
tissue of lies
25. chain of logic
string of logic
26. declaration of love
27. ambivalence of meaning
catch-all of meaning
layer of meaning
nuance of meaning
portmanteau of meanings
28. relay of messages
29. meeting of minds
30. brouhaha of noise
31. farrago of nonsense
galimatias of nonsense ᵇ
32. volley of oaths
33. campaign of objection
34. body of opinion
clash of opinions
climate of opinion
polarity of opinion
referendum of opinion
spectrum of opinion
survey of opinions
tide of opinion
unanimity of opinion
35. turn of phrase
36. burst of polemic
37. accolade of praise
eulogy of praise
panegyric of praise
shower of praise
38. *quiddity of profundities*
39. howl of protest

49. macaroni of languages
50. manner of speaking
51. mass of contradictions
52. meeting of minds
53. melting pot of ideas
54. murmur of assent
55. nuance of meaning
56. pack of lies
57. panegyric of praise
58. paradigm of ideas
59. pearl of wisdom
60. peep of protest
61. phylum of languages
62. polarity of opinion
63. polyglot of languages
64. portmanteau of meanings
65. *quiddity of profundities*
66. ragbag of ideas
67. rain of insults
68. range of topics
69. referendum of opinion
70. relay of messages
71. *rosetta stone of languages*
72. salvo of bravos ᵃ
73. shower of praise
74. slew of complaints

75. snippet of gossip

Chapter 10: A Comedy of Errors

peep of protest	76. spate of words
volley of protest	77. spectrum of opinion
wave of protest	78. storm of controversy
40. barrage of questions	79. stream of calls
41. string of reasoning	stream of invective
thread of reasoning	80. string of logic
42. cannonade of reproach	string of reasoning
43. burst of rhetoric	81. survey of opinions
flow of rhetoric	82. synergy of ideas
44. whiff of scandal	83. synthesis of ideas
45. manner of speaking	84. thread of conversation
46. faculty of speech	thread of reasoning
figure of speech	85. tide of opinion
gift of speech	86. tirade of abuse
47. acknowledgement of thanks	87. tissue of lies
	88. titbit of gossip
	89. torrent of abuse
	torrent of eloquence
	90. trickle of complaints
	91. turn of phrase
	92. unanimity of opinion
	93. volley of curses
	volley of oaths
	volley of protest
48. Babel of tongues	94. war of words
49. range of topics	95. wave of protest
50. pearl of wisdom	96. whiff of scandal
51. battle of wits	97. whisper of impropriety
52. spate of words	98. wisp of conversation
war of words	99. word of advice

Notes:

a. Applause given by French 'claqueurs' (hired applauders) in the theatre.
b. 'Her dress, like her talk, is a galimatias of several countries.' - Walpole.

'a declaration of love'

'a barrage of criticism'

Chapter 10: A Comedy of Errors

'a stroke of genius'

'an ambiguity of expression'

Gallimaufry

'a well of despair'

10c. Emotions & Characteristics

Sorted by noun	Sorted by collective noun
1. wave of adulation	1. abundance of feeling
2. spirit of adventure	2. agenbite of inwit ᵉ
3. eruption of anger	3. agony of indecision
outburst of anger	agony of waiting
stirring of anger	4. air of complacency
4. spasm of anxiety	air of despondency
5. lightness of being	air of disdain
6. gasconade of bravado	air of gloom
7. intake of breath	air of melancholy
8. aura of calm	air of menace
haven of calm	air of mystery
9. feeling of camaraderie	5. ardour of love
10. multitude of cares	6. attack of conscience
11. air of complacency	attack of nerves
12. crisis of confidence	7. aura of calm
13. attack of conscience	aura of sanctity

Chapter 10: A Comedy of Errors

prick of conscience	8. barrel of laughs
14. lack of consideration	9. bellyful of laughs
15. ounce of courage	10. bout of depression
16. streak of cowardice	11. bray of laughter
17. bout of depression	12. cackle of laughter
spell of depression	13. catharsis of emotions
18. snort of derision	14. cauldron of desire
19. cauldron of desire	15. clash of personalities
20. well of despair	clash of temperaments
21. slough of despond [c]	16. climate of fear
22. air of despondency	17. clutch of second thoughts [a]
23. foreboding of disaster	
24. hotbed of discontent	
murmur of discontent	
25. air of disdain	
26. wave of disgust	
27. presage of doom	
28. sense of dread	
29. dash of élan	
30. soar of elation	
31. catharsis of emotions	18. cocoon of love
conflict of emotions	19. conflict of emotions
display of emotions	20. crisis of confidence
flood of emotions	21. cup of sorrow
floodgate of emotion	22. dash of élan
gamut of emotions [b]	23. display of emotions
jumble of emotions	24. eruption of anger
rollercoaster of emotions	25. expression of goodwill
stirring of emotion	expression of sentiment
tide of emotions	expression of sorrow
whirl of emotions	26. feeling of camaraderie
32. spirit of endeavour	feeling of pressure
33. wave of ennui	27. fire of passion
34. frisson of excitement	28. fit of giggles
35. climate of fear	fit of jealousy
36. abundance of feeling	fit of pique
	29. flash of inspiration

intensity of feeling
mishmash of feelings
37. stroke of genius
touch of genius
38. fit of giggles
39. air of gloom
40. expression of goodwill
41. outpouring of grief

threnody of grief
42. pang of guilt
spasm of guilt
twinge of guilt
43. glimmer of hope
ray of hope
spirit of hope
44. scintilla of humility [d]
45. welter of ignorance
46. agony of indecision
47. host of inhibitions
48. picture of innocence
protestation of innocence
49. flash of inspiration
50. agenbite of inwit [e]
51. fit of jealousy
52. radiance of joy
53. barrel of laughs
bellyful of laughs
54. bray of laughter

flash of temper
30. flood of emotions
flood of tears
31. floodgate of emotion
32. foreboding of disaster
33. frame of mind
34. frisson of excitement
35. gale of laughter
36. gamut of emotions [b]
37. gasconade of bravado
38. glimmer of hope
39. grip of terror
40. guffaw of laughter
41. haven of calm
42. host of inhibitions
43. hotbed of discontent
hotbed of vice
44. intake of breath
45. intensity of feeling
46. joie de vivre
47. jumble of emotions
48. lack of consideration
49. lifetime of sorrow
50. lightness of being
51. loss of nerve
52. maelstrom of vice
53. mishmash of feelings
54. model of propriety
55. moment of madness
56. multitude of cares
57. murmur of discontent
58. ocean of tears
59. odour of sanctity
60. ounce of courage
61. outburst of anger
outburst of laughter

cackle of laughter
gale of laughter
guffaw of laughter
outburst of laughter
paroxysm of laughter
peal of laughter
ripple of laughter
roar of laughter
snicker of laughter
snigger of laughter
tinkle of laughter
55. sea of loneliness
well of loneliness
56. ardour of love
cocoon of love
57. moment of madness
58. air of melancholy
59. air of menace
60. frame of mind
state of mind
61. air of mystery
62. surge of nationalism
63. wave of nausea
64. attack of nerves
loss of nerve
65. spirit of optimism
66. fire of passion
67. surge of patriotism
68. clash of personalities
69. fit of pique
70. ripple of pleasure
71. feeling of pressure
72. model of propriety
73. storm of protest
74. sigh of relief
surge of relief

62. outpouring of grief
63. pang of guilt
64. paragon of virtue
65. paroxysm of laughter
66. peal of laughter
67. picture of innocence
68. pool of resentment
69. presage of doom

70. prick of conscience
71. profundity of thought
72. protestation of innocence
73. radiance of joy
74. ray of hope
75. ripple of laughter
ripple of pleasure
76. roar of laughter
77. rollercoaster of emotions
78. rush of tenderness
79. school of thought
80. scintilla of humility [d]
scintilla of remorse
81. sea of loneliness
sea of resentment
82. sense of dread
83. sigh of relief

75. scintilla of remorse
76. pool of resentment
    sea of resentment
    wave of resentment
77. wave of revulsion
78. aura of sanctity
    odour of sanctity
    whiff of sanctity
79. clutch of second thoughts [a]
80. expression of sentiment
81. cup of sorrow
    expression of sorrow
    lifetime of sorrow
82. wave of sympathy
83. spark of talent
84. flood of tears
    ocean of tears
    smattering of tears

    vale of tears
    veil of tears
85. flash of temper
86. clash of temperaments
87. rush of tenderness
88. grip of terror
    soupcon of terror

84. slough of despond [c]
85. smattering of tears
86. snicker of laughter
87. snigger of laughter
88. snort of derision
89. soar of elation
90. soupcon of terror
91. spark of talent
92. spasm of anxiety
    spasm of guilt
93. spell of depression
94. spirit of adventure
    spirit of endeavour
    spirit of hope
    spirit of optimism
95. state of mind
96. stirring of anger
    stirring of emotion
97. storm of protest
98. streak of cowardice
99. stroke of genius
100. surge of nationalism
    surge of patriotism
    surge of relief
101. threnody of grief
102. tide of emotions
103. tinkle of laughter
104. touch of genius
105. train of thought
106. twinge of guilt
107. vale of tears
108. veil of tears
109. wave of adulation
    wave of disgust
    wave of ennui
    wave of nausea

Chapter 10: A Comedy of Errors

89. profundity of thought	wave of resentment
school of thought	wave of revulsion
train of thought	wave of sympathy
well of thought	110. well of despair
90. hotbed of vice	well of loneliness
maelstrom of vice	well of thought
91. paragon of virtue	111. welter of ignorance
92. joie de vivre	112. whiff of sanctity
93. agony of waiting	113. whirl of emotions

Notes:

a. From James Lipton, 'An Exaltation of Larks' (1977).
b. Dorothy Parker, in a 1933 review of 'The Lake', starring Katherine Hepburn, witheringly wrote 'Miss Hepburn ... runs the whole gamut of emotions from A to B'.
c. From John Bunyan's 'The Pilgrim's Progress'.
d. "In victory, they must hold on to at least a scintilla of humility..." Bill Breen, Fast Company magazine, May 2000
e. From James Joyce 'Ulysses', meaning a prick of remorse or conscience.

'a feeling of pressure'

217

'a wave of ennui'

'an air of disdain'

Chapter 10: A Comedy of Errors

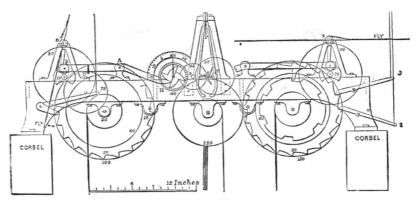

'a test of time'

10d. Time

Sorted by noun	Sorted by collective noun
1. leash of days (3)	1. aeon of time
2. span of history	2. age of time
timeline of history	3. brace of shakes [a]
3. calendar of months	4. calendar of months
4. brace of shakes [a]	5. centenary of years (100)
5. month of Sundays	6. chiliad of years (1000)
6. aeon of time	7. decade of years (10)
age of time	8. epoch of time
epoch of time	9. eternity of time
eternity of time	10. flight of yesterdays [b]
fullness of time	11. fullness of time
interval of time	12. interval of time
passage of time	13. jubilee of years (50)
tenor of time [c]	14. leash of days (3)
test of time	15. matter of weeks (months etc)
whale of a time	16. millennium of years (1000)
7. twinkling of todays [b]	17. month of Sundays
8. promise of tomorrows [b]	18. passage of time
9. matter of weeks (months etc)	19. pentad of years (5)
10. centenary of years (100)	20. promise of tomorrows [b]

219

chiliad of years (1000)	21. span of history
decade of years (10)	span of years
jubilee of years (50)	22. tenor of time ^c
millennium of years (1000)	23. test of time
pentad of years (5)	24. timeline of history
span of years	25. twinkling of todays ^b
11. flight of yesterdays ^b	26. whale of a time

Notes:

a. Reputedly from the shaking of dice.
b. From James Lipton, 'An Exaltation of Larks' (1977).
c. The length of time until a loan is due.

'an eternity of time'

Chapter Eleven

A Compound of Collectives

a. *Anatomical*
b. *Computing, Scientific, Technical*
c. *Medical*
d. *Legal, Business, Economic, Political*

'a head of hair'

'a phalanx of noses'

11a. Anatomical

Sorted by noun	Sorted by collective noun
1. expanse of belly	
2. crop of blackheads	
3. clot of blood	
pool of blood	
river of blood	
4. headcount of bodies	
tally of bodies	
5. assemblage of bones	1. assemblage of bones
charnel-house of bones	2. braid of hair
ossuary of bones	3. bunch of fives (fist)
rattle of bones	4. carnage of carcasses
skeleton of bones	5. charnel-house of bones
6. mass of bruises	6. *closet of skeletons*
7. carnage of carcasses	7. clot of blood
	8. clutch of penises
	clutch of phalluses
	9. crop of blackheads
	10. dusting of freckles [c]
	11. embarrassment of twitches [a]
	12. eruption of spots
	13. expanse of belly
	14. fascicle of nerve fibres
8. *flounce of curls*	15. *flounce of curls*
hurly-burly of curls [b]	16. ganglion of nerve cells
ringlet of curls	

Chapter 11: A Compound of Collectives

9. set of dentures	17. gob of phlegm
10. bunch of fives (fist)	18. hank of hair
11. dusting of freckles [c]	19. head of hair
12. braid of hair	20. headcount of bodies
hank of hair	21. hurly-burly of curls [b]
head of hair	22. lock of hair
lock of hair	23. mass of bruises
plait of hair	24. ossuary of bones
shock of hair	25. *phalanx of noses*
tangle of hair	26. plait of hair
thatch of hair	27. pool of blood
tress of hair	28. rack of ribs
13. tangle of limbs	29. rash of spots
14. six-pack of (pectoral)	30. rattle of bones
muscles	31. ringlet of curls
15. ganglion of nerve cells	32. river of blood
16. fascicle of nerve fibres	33. set of dentures
17. *phalanx of noses*	34. shock of hair
18. clutch of penises	35. six-pack of (pectoral)
19. clutch of phalluses	muscles
20. gob of phlegm	36. skeleton of bones
21. rack of ribs	37. tally of bodies
22. *closet of skeletons*	38. tangle of hair
23. eruption of spots	tangle of limbs
rash of spots	39. thatch of hair
24. web of skin	40. tracery of veins
25. embarrassment of twitches [a]	41. tress of hair
26. tracery of veins	42. web of skin

Notes:

a. From James Lipton, 'An Exaltation of Larks' (1977).
b. Hurly burly comes from 'hurluberlu', a female hairstyle appearing about 1670, in which short curls covered the entire head.
c. From Lynne Truss, 'Eats, Shoots and Leaves'; describing her pen-friend, 'Kerry-Anne'.

Gallimaufry

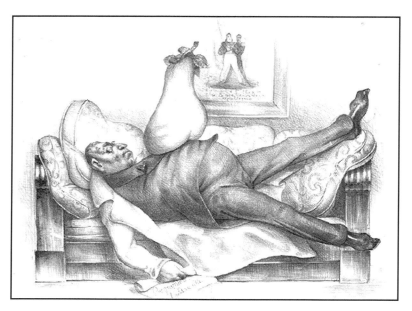

'an expanse of belly'

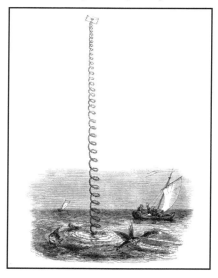

'a helix of springs'

11b. Computing, scientific & electrical

Sorted by noun	Sorted by collective noun
1. array of aerials	1. address book of contacts
2. triad of assemblages	address book of e-mail contacts
3. concatenation of characters	
keyboard of characters	
4. cascade of chemical reactions	
5. compound of chemicals	
6. bank of circuits	
7. matrix of circuit elements	
8. menu of commands	
9. network of communications	
10. assembly of computer code	
11. archive of computer files	
12. *click of computer mice*	2. alloy of metals
13. Beowolf cluster of (old) computers [e]	alloy of substances
botnet of (hijacked) computers [f]	3. amalgam of substances
	4. amount of substance
	5. *annoyance of mobile phones*
cluster of (small) computers	6. archive of computer files
network of computers	7. array of aerials
	array of data
	array of databases
14. battery of condensers	
15. assemblage of conductors	8. assemblage of conductors
triplex of conductors	9. assembly of computer code
16. address book of contacts	10. backup of data
17. array of data	11. bank of circuits
backup of data	bank of monitors
bit of data	12. battery of condensers
byte of data	battery of dynamos
cache of data	battery of tests
donut of data	13. benchmark of tests
spool of data	14. Beowolf cluster of (old)
18. array of databases	

19. group of digits
20. compass rose of directions
21. nest of directories
22. double helix of DNA
    strand of DNA
23. battery of dynamos
24. echelon of eavesdropping [b]
25. cascade of electrical relays
26. mole of elementary entities
27. compound of elements
28. address book of e-mail contacts
29. erg of energy
    grid of energy
30. directory of files
31. newton of force
32. *gaggle of geeks*
33. force of gravity
34. *cruft of hackers*
35. database of information
36. elint of information [d]
37. suite of integrated software
38. *browse of kindlers*
39. alloy of metals
40. *annoyance of mobile phones*
41. whistle of modems [a]

computers [e]
15. bit of data
16. botnet of (hijacked) computers [f]
17. bottle of source code
18. bouquet of multimedia services [c]
19. branch of science
20. *browse of kindlers*
21. byte of data
22. cache of data
23. cascade of chemical reactions
    cascade of electrical relays
    cascade of (computer) windows
24. charlotte of web-pages
25. *click of computer mice*
26. cluster of (small) computers
27. compass rose of directions
28. compound of chemicals
    compound of elements
29. concatenation of characters
30. crucible of molten metal
31. *cruft of hackers*
32. curie of radioactivity
33. database of information
34. directory of files
    directory of phone numbers
35. donut of data
36. double helix of DNA
37. echelon of eavesdropping [b]
38. elint of information [d]
39. erg of energy
40. force of gravity
41. *gaggle of geeks*

42. mole of molecules
43. crucible of molten metal
44. bank of monitors
45. bouquet of multimedia services [c]
46. sequence of numbers
47. directory of phone numbers
48. grid of power lines
49. pascal of pressure
50. patch of program code
51. curie of radioactivity
52. branch of science
53. laboratory of scientific instruments
54. repository of software packages
55. bottle of source code
56. *python of spam*
    splurge of spam
57. helix of springs
58. network of subscribers
59. alloy of substances
    amalgam of substances
    amount of substance
60. gang of switches
61. battery of tests
    benchmark of tests
62. *twitch of tweeters*
63. set of vectors
64. *spider of web-masters*
65. charlotte of web-pages
    web-site of web-pages
66. trawl of web-sites
    web-ring of web-sites
64. cascade of (computer) windows

42. gang of switches
43. grid of energy
    grid of power lines
44. group of digits
45. helix of springs
46. keyboard of characters
47. laboratory of scientific instruments
48. matrix of circuit elements
49. menu of commands
50. mole of elementary entities
    mole of molecules
51. nest of directories
52. network of communications
    network of computers
    network of subscribers
53. newton of force
54. pascal of pressure
55. patch of program code
56. *python of spam*
57. repository of software packages
58. sequence of numbers
59. set of vectors
60. *spider of web-masters*
61. *splurge of spam*
62. spool of data
63. strand of DNA
64. suite of integrated software
65. trawl of web-sites
66. triad of assemblages
67. triplex of conductors
68. *twitch of tweeters*
69. web-ring of web-sites
70. web-site of web-pages
71. whistle of modems [a]

Gallimaufry

Notes:

a. Reported from an article in the computer magazine 'Byte'.
b. The current electronic surveillance system used by the United States. This complex system can monitor any electronic communication in the world.
c. A collection of digital multimedia services marketed as a single package, often transmitted in a single data stream.
d. ELINT is short for 'electronic information', i.e. information gathered by electronic means from aircraft or ships.
e. A Beowolf cluster is a collection of old 486-style computers wired up in an Ethernet and set up with a special Linux system which allows computer programs to be run on the network of computers as if it was one supercomputer.
f. A botnet is a global network of hijacked computers used for purposes of fraud, identified on the BBC News website 30.11.07.

'a bouquet of multimedia services'

Chapter 11: A Compound of Collectives

'an epidemic of disease'

11c. Medical

Sorted by noun	Sorted by collective noun
1. corps of anatomists [a]	1. ampoule of drugs
2. *gallipot of apothecaries*	2. armamentarium of doctors' equipment
3. attack of asthma	
bout of asthma	3. attack of asthma
4. cluster of cancer cases	4. blister pack of pills
5. flutter of cardiologists [a]	5. bottle of medicine
6. epidemic of cholera	6. bout of asthma
7. gallipot of compounds	bout of diarrhoea
8. rash of dermatologists [a]	bout of sickness
9. guess of diagnosticians [a]	7. brace of orthodontists [a]
10. bout of diarrhoea	8. branch of medicine
11. contagion of disease	9. cabinet of drugs

229

epidemic of disease
outbreak of disease
pandemic of disease
12. team of doctors
13. armamentarium of doctors' equipment
14. ampoule of drugs
    cabinet of drugs

cocktail of drugs
codex of drugs (list of receipts)
pharmacopœia of drugs
15. series of experiments
16. dose of flu
17. practice of G.P.s
    surgery of G.P.s
18. smear of gynaecologists [a]
19. cocktail of injections
20. tincture of iodine
21. bottle of medicine
    branch of medicine
    cabinet of medicines
    dose of medicine
    overdose of medicine
    shot of medicine
    spoonful of medicine

cabinet of medicines
10. caseload of (doctor's) work
11. cluster of cancer cases
12. cocktail of drugs
    cocktail of injections
13. codex of drugs (list of receipts)
14. contagion of disease
15. corps of anatomists [a]
16. course of tablets
    course of treatment
17. dose of flu
    dose of medicine
18. epidemic of cholera
    epidemic of disease
19. flutter of cardiologists [a]
20. gallipot of compounds
    gallipot of apothecaries
21. guess of diagnosticians [a]
22. joint of osteopaths [a]
23. outbreak of disease
24. overdose of medicine
    overdose of radiation
25. pandemic of disease
26. pharmacopeia of drugs
27. phial of poison
28. pile of proctologists [a]
29. practice of G.P.s
30. rash of dermatologists [a]
31. sample of sperm
32. sanatorium of patients
33. series of experiments
34. shot of medicine
35. smear of gynaecologists [a]
36. specimen of urine
37. spoonful of medicine

Chapter 11: A Compound of Collectives

vial of medicine	38. surgery of G.P.s
22. team of nurses	39. team of doctors
23. tube of ointment	team of nurses
24. brace of orthodontists [a]	40. tincture of iodine
25. joint of osteopaths [a]	41. tube of ointment
26. sanatorium of patients	
ward of patients	
27. blister pack of pills	
28. phial of poison	
29. pile of proctologists [a]	
30. overdose of radiation	
31. bout of sickness	
32. sample of sperm	
33. course of tablets	
34. course of treatment	
35. specimen of urine	
36. caseload of (doctor's) work	42. vial of medicine
	43. ward of patients

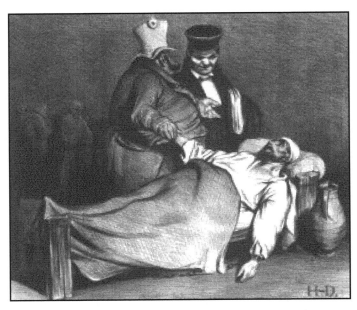

'a bout of sickness'

Gallimaufry

'a team of doctors'

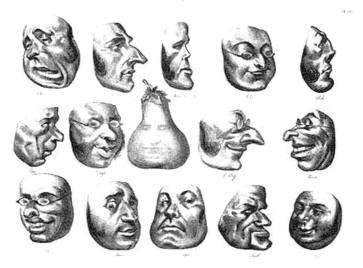

'an odium of politicians'

Chapter 11: A Compound of Collectives

11d. Legal, business, economic & political

Sorted by noun	Sorted by collective noun
1. brain drain of academics / flight of academics ᵉ	1. accumulation of funds
2. balance of accountants / column of accountants ᵇ	2. affiliation of groups
	3. alignment of political parties
	4. allocation of funds
3. statement of accounts	5. allotment of shares
4. campaign of action / plan of action	6. allowance of expenses
	7. amalgamation of businesses
5. campaign of advertising	8. arm of government
6. council of advisors	9. array of attorneys
7. bench of aldermen / guzzle of aldermen ᵉ	10. audit of bookkeepers
	11. balance of accountants / balance of payments / balance of power / balance of trade
8. delegation of ambassadors / embassy of ambassadors	12. ballot of voters' preferences
9. court of appeal	13. barratry of lawsuits
10. array of attorneys	14. basket of currencies
11. revolt of back-benchers	15. bench of aldermen / bench of magistrates
12. inn of barristers / mess of barristers	16. bill of particulars
13. block of bonds	17. blacklist of union members
14. audit of bookkeepers	18. block of bonds / block of shares
15. boredom of briefs (legal)	19. board of directors
16. portfolio of brokers ᵇ	20. body of evidence
17. tide of bureaucracy	21. boredom of briefs (legal)
18. consortium of business partners	22. brain drain of academics
19. amalgamation of businesses / cartel of businesses / federation of businesses	23. breakdown of plans ᵇ
	24. budget of tax measures
	25. cabinet of M.P.s / cabinet of ministers
20. lobby of campaigners	26. campaign of action
21. field of candidates / shortlist of candidates / slate of candidates	

233

Gallimaufry

22. company of capitalists / syndicate of capitalists	campaign of advertising / campaign of political activities
23. levy of charges	27. cartel of businesses / cartel of nations
24. tidal wave of colonialism	
25. chamber of commerce	28. cartulary of legal records
26. quorum of committee members	29. caucus of legislators
27. network of companies (e.g. phone)	30. chamber of commerce
	31. coalition of political parties
28. package of compensation	32. college of electors
29. troop of congressmen	33. column of accountants [b] / column of figures
30. merger of corporations	
31. spiral of costs	34. commonwealth of states
32. intrigue of council members	35. community of nations
33. divan of (Muslim) councillors [f]	36. company of capitalists
	37. compurgation of oaths
34. nest of cuckoos (spies)	38. concert party of share buyers
35. basket of currencies	39. confederacy of states
36. sea of debts / spiral of debts	40. conference of delegates
	41. congress of representatives
37. quango of (non-elected) decision-makers	42. consortium of business partners / consortium of organisations / consortium of property developers
38. conference of delegates	
39. kettle of demonstrators g	
40. board of directors	
41. college of electors	43. constabulary of police
42. staff of employees	44. constituency of voters
43. period of employment / term of employment	45. cordon of police
	46. council of advisors / council of ministers
44. panel of enquiry	
45. body of evidence / scintilla of evidence	47. course of lectures
	48. court of appeal
46. allowance of expenses	49. damning of jurors [a]
47. column of figures / tally of figures	50. delegation of ambassadors
	51. detachment of police
48. field of front-runners	52. disagreement of statesmen [b]

Chapter 11: A Compound of Collectives

49. accumulation of funds
   allocation of funds
   injection of funds
   withdrawal of funds
50. arm of government
   division of government
51. affiliation of groups
52. pair of handcuffs
53. posse of head-hunters
54. hive of industry
55. team of inspectors
56. series of investigations
57. pool of investments
58. panel of judges
   sentence of judges [a]
59. damning of jurors [a]
   panel of jurors
60. division of labour
   pool of labour
   stint of labour
   withdrawal of labour
61. pandect of laws
62. barratry of lawsuits
63. eloquence of lawyers [a]
   escheat of lawyers [b]
   huddle of lawyers
64. quadrumvirate of (4) leaders
65. course of lectures
66. cartulary of legal records
67. caucus of legislators
68. cabinet of M.P.s
   division of M.P.s
69. bench of magistrates
70. package of measures
   raft of measures
71. register of members'
	53. divan of (Muslim)
	   councillors [f]
	54. division of government
	   division of labour
	   division of M.P.s
	55. draft of police
	56. electoral roll of voters

	57. eloquence of lawyers [a]
	58. embargo of trade
	59. embassy of ambassadors
	60. equivocation of politicians
	61. escheat of lawyers [b]
	62. federation of businesses
	63. field of candidates
	   field of front-runners
	64. firm of solicitors
	65. flight of academics [e]
	66. flurry of phone calls
	67. force of police officers
	68. government of ministers
	69. group of sponsors
	70. guzzle of aldermen [e]
	71. hive of industry
	72. house of representatives
	   house of senators

interests	73. huddle of lawyers
72. cabinet of ministers	74. index of share prices
council of ministers	75. inheritance of property or money
government of ministers	76. injection of funds
73. spate of murders	77. inn of barristers
string of murders	78. intrigue of council members
74. cartel of nations	79. kettle of demonstrators [g]
community of nations	80. kitchen cabinet of political advisers
75. lavender list of nominations [d]	81. lavender list of nominations [d]
76. compurgation of oaths	82. legacy of property or money
77. term of office	83. levy of charges
78. consortium of organisations	levy of taxes
79. bill of particulars	84. lie of politicians
80. balance of payments	85. line-up of suspects
81. flurry of phone calls	86. lobby of campaigners
82. breakdown of plans [b]	87. merger of corporations
83. constabulary of police	88. mess of barristers
cordon of police	89. monopoly of share holders
detachment of police	90. nest of cuckoos (spies)
draft of police	91. network of companies (e.g. phone)
posse of police	92. odium of politicians [b]
squad of police	93. oligarchy of Republicans
84. force of police officers	94. package of compensation
85. campaign of political activities	package of measures
86. kitchen cabinet of political advisers	package of proposals
87. alignment of political parties	95. pair of handcuffs
coalition of political parties	96. pandect of laws
88. equivocation of politicians	97. panel of enquiry
lie of politicians	panel of judges
odium of politicians [b]	panel of jurors
platform of politicians	98. period of employment
89. stock of portfolio managers	period of unrest
90. balance of power	

Chapter 11: A Compound of Collectives

91. series of programmes	99. petition of signatures
92. inheritance of property or money	100. picket line of strikers
legacy of property or money	101. plan of action
93. consortium of property developers	102. platform of politicians
	103. pomposity of senators
94. package of proposals	104. pool of investments
95. quiver of rebuttals	pool of labour
96. congress of representatives	105. portfolio of brokers [b]
house of representatives	portfolio of shares
97. oligarchy of Republicans	106. posse of head-hunters
98. house of senators	posse of police
pomposity of senators	107. quadrumvirate of (4) leaders
99. subtiltie of sergeants [a c]	108. quango of (non-elected) decision-makers
100. concert party of share buyers	109. quiver of rebuttals
101. monopoly of share holders	110. quorum of committee members
102. allotment of shares	111. raft of measures
block of shares	112. register of members' interests
portfolio of shares	register of voters
103. index of share prices	113. revolt of back-benchers
104. petition of signatures	114. scintilla of evidence
105. firm of solicitors	115. sea of debts
106. group of sponsors	116. sentence of judges [a]
	117. series of investigations
	118. series of programmes
	119. ship of state
	120. shortlist of candidates
	121. slate of candidates
	122. spate of murders
	123. spiral of costs
	spiral of debts
	124. squad of police
107. ship of state	125. staff of employees
108. disagreement of statesmen [b]	126. statement of accounts

109. line-up of suspects	127. stint of labour
110. commonwealth of states	128. stock of portfolio managers
confederacy of states	129. string of murders
111. picket line of strikers	130. subtiltie of sergeants [a c]
112. budget of tax measures	131. syndicate of capitalists
113. levy of taxes	132. tally of figures
114. balance of trade	133. team of inspectors
embargo of trade	134. term of employment
115. blacklist of union members	term of office
116. period of unrest	106. tidal wave of colonialism
117. constituency of voters	107. tide of bureaucracy
electoral roll of voters	108. troop of congressmen
register of voters	109. withdrawal of funds
118. ballot of voters' preferences	withdrawal of labour

Note:

a. Archaic, from one of the 16th century manuscripts (most commonly, 'The Book of Hawking & Hunting', by Dame Juliana Barnes, 1486)
b. From James Lipton, 'An Exaltation of Larks' (1968 & 1977)
c. 'Sergeant' was on old term for a lawyer – 'subtlety' is probably sardonic, as I doubt that sergeants were ever that subtle.
d. Reputedly from the colour of the paper used by Harold Wilson to draw up his nominations for the honours list on leaving office.
e. From Ivan G Sparkes, 'Dictionary of Collective Nouns & Group Terms''.
f. Probably from the Turkish habit of piling rugs and cushions for reclining while doing business.
g. Kettling is a police tactic to contain demonstrators in a confined area.

Chapter 11: A Compound of Collectives

'an array of attorneys'

Gallimaufry

'a line-up of suspects'

A word is dead
When it is said,
Some say.
I say it just
Begins to live
That day.

Emily Dickinson 1830-1886

Part Three

A Ragbag of References

Bibliography, Notes on images, Index of Collective Nouns

'a drunkship of collective noun collectors'

Gallimaufry

Part Three: A Ragbag of References

Bibliography

Collections of Collective Nouns

- **An Exaltation Of Larks: The Ultimate Edition**
  James Lipton; Paperback; 324 pages (1993 – 4th Edition); Publisher: Penguin Books, New York ISBN: 0140170960
- **Dictionary Of Collective Nouns And Group Terms**
  Ivan G. Sparkes (Editor) Hardcover 283 pages (1 September, 1985); Publisher: Gale Research Company; ISBN: 0810321882
- **An Exaltation Of Business And Finance**
  James Lipton; Hardcover; 64 pages (1993); Publisher: Villard Books, New York (Random House)
- **An Exaltation Of Romance And Revelry**
  James Lipton; Hardcover; 64 pages 1993; Publisher: Villard Books, New York ISBN: 0679418725
- **An Exaltation Of Home And Family**
  James Lipton; Hardcover; 1993; Publisher: Villard Books, New York. ISBN:0679418717
- **A Menagerie Of Animals: Illustrated Collective Nouns Of Animals**
  Steve Palin (Illustrator) Paperback 56 pages (January 2000); Publisher: Taghan Press, Norfolk; ISBN: 1871482194
- **A Dissimulation Of Birds: Illustrated Collective Nouns Of Birds**
  Steve Palin Paperback (March 1998); Publisher: Minerva Press, London; ISBN: 0754102904
- **The Language Of Sport**
  C E Hare; Country Life, 1939
- **A Guide To Collective Nouns**
  Christine Towndrow; Paperback; Grammar Gamecards; Revised Ed edition (Feb 2004); ISBN: 0954685911
- **Agreement With Collective Nouns In English (Lund Studies In English, 103)**
  Magnus Levin; Paperback, 180 pages; Lund Univ Pr (Dec 2001); ISBN-10: 919740232X
- **A Mess of Iguanas, A Whoop of Gorillas**
  Alon Shulman; Hardcover; 229 pages; Publisher: Particular Books, 2009; ISBN: 978-1-846-14255-0

Other useful sources

- The Book of Hawking and Hunting (also known as The Book of St. Albans) 1486, by Dame Juliana Barnes, ISBN 9-022-10151-7. (Many of these are fanciful or humorous terms which probably never had any real currency, but have been taken up by Joseph Strutt in 'Sports and Pastimes of England' (1801) and by other antiquarian writers.)
- Debate between the Hors, Ghoos, and Shepe, by John Lydgate, printed by Caxton in 1476.
- Rural Sports, Reverend W B Daniel, 1801.
- The Trivia Encyclopedia, by Fred L. Worth, published by Berkley Pub Group, 1984. ISBN 0-441-82412-9.
- Merriam Webster's Collegiate Dictionary (10th Edition), published by Merriam Webster, 1996. ISBN 0-877-79709-9.
- Schott's Original Miscellany, by Ben Schott, published by Bloomsbury Publishing Plc, 2002; ISBN 0-7475-6320-9
- Schott's Food & Drink Miscellany, by Ben Schott, published by Bloomsbury Publishing Plc, 2003, ISBN 0-7475-6654-2
- Shite's Unoriginal Miscellany, published by Michael O'Mara Books Ltd, 2003, ISBN 1-84317-064-7
- Some terms for groups of animals, birds, etc., in The Oxford Reference Dictionary
- Distinctive Group Phraseology, in The Quickway Crossword Dictionary (H W Hill, for Warne)
- Collective Names, in Crossword Lists & Solver (Blitz Editions, for Bloomsbury Publishing)
- Group Terms, in The Complete Crossword Companion (Chancellor Press)
- Usage and Abusage: A Guide to Good English. Partridge, Eric (1973) First published 1942. London: Penguin Books. ISBN 0140510249.

Part Three: A Ragbag of References

Useful web-sites

- http://all-sorts.org/ for a Collective noun free-for-all, and follow #collectivenouns on Twitter for updates or to add your own
- The Collective Noun Page by Ojophoyimbo http://www.ojohaven.com/collectives/
- Fun with words: http://rinkworks.com/words/collective.shtml
- Animal Congregations from the USGS NPWRC (new) http://www.npwrc.usgs.gov/help/faq/animals/names.htm
- Enchanted learning – (US site for kids) http://www.enchantedlearning.com/subjects/animals/Animalbabies.shtml
- http://www.encyclopedia4u.com/l/list-of-collective-nouns-by-collective-term.html
- http://www.sanjeev.net/collective-nouns/index.html
- http://encycl.opentopia.com/term/List_of_collective_nouns_by_subject
- For an interpretation of The Book of St Albans: http://en.wikipedia.org/wiki/Book_of_St._Albans
- For an exhaustive list of New Zealand bird groups: http://www.nzbirds.com/more/nouns.html
- Wikipedia's scholarly explanation: http://en.wikipedia.org/wiki/List_of_collective_nouns
- http://adfos.com/collective-nouns.nsf
- http://collectivenoun.co.uk/
- An interesting selection of animal & bird collectives with pictures and associated articles: http://www.perlgurl.org/archives/2007/03/critter_collectives_crazy_terms_for_animal_groups_1.html
- For a detailed explanation of Scottish Weights and Measures: http://www.scan.org.uk/measures/capacity.asp

All images are understood to be in the Public Domain...

	My Title	Source	Page
1.	A Torrent of Eloquence	*Front cover*: Louis-Léopold Boilly (French, 1824). 'Le Pouvoir de l'Eloquence' (The Power of Eloquence). Colored lithograph.	Fr.
2.	Happy Thought	*Frontispiece*: from 'A Child's Garden of Verses', Robert Louis Stevenson, illust. Charles Robinson, 1895. Library of Congress Rare Books Digital Edition.	
3.	Contents	From 'A Child's Garden of Verses', Robert Louis Stevenson, illust. Myrtle Sheldon, 1916, Project Gutenberg.	
4.	A Flock of Sheep	Tailpiece, from 'Household Stories' by Brothers Grimm, illust. Walter Crane 1886 Project Gutenberg.	

Chapter 1: A Nobility of Beasts - Animals

5.	A Panoply of Elephants	Mongolia – The Yuan Dynasty. Elephants carrying Khubilai Khan's command post in battle. Unattributed.	1
6.	A Mischief of Rats	Illustration by Gustav Dore (1868) for 'The Combat of the Weasels & the Rats' from the Fables of Jean de La Fontaine, 1600s.	2
7.	A Singularity of Boars	Unattributed. From 'Medieval Life Illustrations'.	3
8.	A Train of Camels	From Beeswax Rubber Stamping.	4
9.	A Crash of Hippopotami	From Webster's New International Dictionary of the English Language, 1911.	4

10.	A Doylt of Tame Swine	From 'Medieval Life Illustrations'.	5
11.	A Fez of Armadillos	From Webster's New International Dictionary of the English Language, 1911	6
12.	A Tower of Giraffes	From Beeswax Rubber Stamping.	7
13.	A Span of Horses	Unattributed.	8
14.	A Little Herd of Deer	From 'Medieval Life Illustrations'.	9
15.	A Plague of Rats	From 'Medieval Life Illustrations'.	11
16.	A Round-up of Sheep	Unattributed. From 'Medieval Life Illustrations'.	13
17.	A Boogle of Weasels	Attrib. G Mutzel.	14
18.	A Stubbornness of Rhinoceros	By Albrecht Durer	15
19.	A Mission of Monkeys	Unattributed.	16
20.	A Ring of Bulls	'Bull Ring' – by Francisco de Goya, Spanish, 1746 – 1828 Dibersion de España (Spanish Entertainment), 1825.	16

Chapter 2: A Flight of Fancy - Birds

21.	A Battery of Quails	Game birds of America. California or Valley Quail (Laphortyx Californicus); Library of Congress, Washington.	17
22.	A Cast of Hawks	'Hawking of Herons', early 1670s, by Wenceslaus Hollar, English.	18
23.	A Flight of Cormorants	From Clip-Art Etc (see links following).	19
24.	A Flamboyance of Flamingos	Adapted, from Beeswax Rubber Stamping.	21
25.	A Gaggle of Geese	From Beeswax Rubber Stamping.	22
26.	A Gatling of Woodpeckers	Black-backed woodpecker - Unattributed.	23
27.	A Company of Parrots	From Beeswax Rubber Stamping.	24
28.	An Ostentation of Peacocks	From Beeswax Rubber Stamping.	25

29.	A Conspiracy of Ravens	Tailpiece, from 'Household Stories' by Brothers Grimm, illust. Walter Crane 1886 Project Gutenberg.	26
30.	A Scamper of Sanderlings	Unattributed.	27
31.	A Whiteness of Swans	Unattributed.	28
32.	A Chime of Wrens	British Birds and Their Haunts. Rev. C.A. Johns, publ 1862 Society for Promoting Christian Knowledge.	29
33.	A True Love of Turtle Doves	From Beeswax Rubber Stamping.	29
34.	A Dissimulation of Birds	'Curiosities of Ornithology', by George Cruikshank (1792-1878).	30
35.	A Regatta of Swans	By George Cruikshank.	31
36.	A Sedge of Cranes	Three Fighting Cranes in the nest, Library of Congress.	31
37.	A Brood of Chickens	From Clip-Art Etc (see sources p266).	32
38.	Zoology	by Charles Keene – an illustration for Punch.	32

Chapter 3: A Congregation of Creatures - Insects, Fish, Reptiles

39.	A Fraid of Sea Monsters	By Grandville, title unknown.	33
40.	An Army of Wasps	"Deux guêpes en guerries" (Two Wasps at War), by Grandville, 1842.	34
41.	A Skep of Bees	From 'Medieval Life Illustrations'.	35
42.	A Walk of Snails	'Six Little Snails' by Dalziel Brothers Studio, one of the most successful studios providing illustrations for Victorian children's books.	37
43.	A Rabble of Bees	From 'Medieval Life Illustrations'.	37
44.	A Swarm of Midges	'Les moucherons politiques' ('Political Midges'), by Honoré Daumier, 1808-1879.	38
45.	A Garden of Sea Anemones	19th century scientific illustration. Unattrib.	39
46.	A Shoal of Bass	Adapted from Centropristis striata by Linnaeus (1758).	39
47.	A Bush of Pilchards	From 'Medieval Life Illustrations'	40

Part Three: A Ragbag of References

48.	A Tally of Fish	From 'Medieval Life Illustrations'.	41
49.	A Run of Fish	From 'Medieval Life Illustrations'.	43
50.	A Scabbard of Swordfish	Unattributed.	44
51.	A Tangle of Octopuses	From Webster's New International Dictionary of the English Language, 1911.	44
52.	A Chorus of Frogs	Illustration by Gustav Dore (1868) for 'The Sun & the Frogs', from the Fables of Jean de la Fontaine, 1600s.	45
53.	A Bale of Turtles	From Webster's New International Dictionary of the English Language, 1911.	46
54.	A Float of Crocodiles	From Webster's New International Dictionary of the English Language, 1911.	46
55.	A Camouflage of Chameleons	From Webster's New International Dictionary of the English Language, 1911.	47
56.	A Lounge of Lizards	A Basilisk Lizard, from Webster's New International Dictionary of the English Language, 1911.	47
57.	A Quiver of Cobras	Cobra di Capello (Hooded Snake) Illustrated London Reading Book 1851, Project Gutenberg.	48
58.	A Rhumba of Rattlesnakes	Illustrated London Reading Book 1851, Project Gutenberg.	48

Chapter 4: A Grotto of Greenery – Plants, Trees, Agriculture

59.	A Tussock of Turf	By Albrecht Durer, 'The Large Turf' (1503).	49
60.	A Chain of Daisies	'Marguerite', from 'Les Fleurs Animee', by Grandville (1847).	50
61.	A Stand of Bamboo	From Beeswax Rubber Stamping.	50
62.	A Pride of Dandelions	From Clip-Art Etc (see Sources, p265).	51
63.	A Garland of Flowers	Unattributed.	52
64.	A Host of Daffodils	From Clip-Art Etc (see Sources, p265).	53
65.	A Hang of Plums	From Clip-Art Etc (see Sources, p265).	54
66.	A Ring of Toadstools	From Clip-Art Etc (see Sources, p265).	54

67.	A Vineyard of Grape Vines	From 'Medieval Life Illustrations'.	55
68.	A Stook of Corn Sheaves	From 'Childland' by Oscar Petch & M Rictor, Project Gutenberg.	56
69.	A Bank of Violets	'Violette', from 'Les Fleurs Animee', by Grandville (1847).	56

Chapter 5: A Clutch of Characters - People

70.	A Catch of Anglers	By Grandville, Les Poissons d'Avril' from 'Un Autre Monde', Paris (1844). 'The Fish of April', or April Fools' Day. In France, tricks are played by secretly sticking a paper fish on someone on April 1st. Here the fish are angling for the anglers by using wealth, titles and honours as bait.	57
71.	A Heep of Creeps	Honoré Daumier: 'Tres humbles, tres soumis, tres obeissans...'. ('Very humble, very submissive, very obedient... and especially voracious.'). Publ. in La Caricature, 1832.	58
72.	A Rascal of Boys	From Beeswax Rubber Stamping.	60
73.	A Credence of Servers	From 'Medieval Life Illustrations'.	63
74.	A Faith of Merchants	From 'Medieval Life Illustrations'.	65
75.	A Tryst of Lovers	From Beeswax Rubber Stamping.	67
76.	An Homage of Heroes	From Beeswax Rubber Stamping.	68
77.	A Obeisance of Servants	From 'The Book of St Albans' itself – by Dame Juliana Barnes. Westminster 1496.	70
78.	A Pan of Reviewers	By Daumier, Three amateurs in front of the night review of Raffet.	72
79.	A Sorority of Women	Game of Blind Man's Bluff, from 'Le Bon Genre' (Paris), ca. (1803).	76
80.	An Ingratitude of Children	Believed to be by one of the Breugels – title unknown.	78

81.	A Crocodile of People	By Daumier, 'Panthéon Nadar' (1854). Nadar, journalist, photographer, aeronaut; 1st Impressionist show was in his studio.	79
82.	A Gaggle of Gossips	By Daumier: 'Types Parisiens'.	79
83.	An Avalanche of Skiers	Unattributed. Possibly Punch.	80
84.	A Clamour of Cooks	By Daumier: 'Une mauvaise cuisine'. Published in: Le Charivari, June 6, 1850.	81
85.	A Blast of Hunters	'The First Bird of the Season', Library of Congress.	81
86.	A Gallery of Spectators	By Cruikshank, 'The Opera Boxes, during the Great Exhibition,' India proof etching for Henry Mayhew, 1851. Visitors to the Great Exhibition discovered that London was very short of lodgings, just like any overcrowded city during a World Fair. Cruikshank takes a whimsical route to solving the problem by turning theatre boxes into hotel rooms.	82
87.	An Intrigue of Council Members	By Daumier – 'The Legislative Belly'. 1834 Perspective View of the Ministers' Seats.	82
88.	An Illusion of Painters	By Daumier – 'Les illusions d'artistes' (1842).	83
89.	A Bench of Magistrates	By Hogarth, 'The Bench' Etching and engraving, September 1758.	83
90.	A Brigade of Firemen	By Grandville – Les Metamorphoses du Jour (Today's Metamorphoses). 'La mienne est assuree aussi; ... j'm'en moque'.('Mine is insured as well...I could really give a damn.') Publisher: Garnier Freres, Paris 1829.	84
91.	An Untruth of Summoners	By Daumier – from the series 'Law and Justice' 1840-1848.	84
92.	A Damning of Jurors	By Daumier – from the series 'Law and Justice' 1840-1848.	85
93.	A Wince of Dentists	By Daumier, 'Elle tenait ferme!', 1839. Images from the History of Medicine.	85
94.	A Tribulation of Scholars	By William Hogarth, 'Scholars at a Lecture, or Daur Vaccum' (1737).	86

Gallimaufry

95. A Malapertness of Pedlars	By Daumier, 'To Anyone With Capital To Lose'.	87
96. A Bacchanal of Revellers	By Daumier: 'Fête du 4 Mai'.	88
97. An Assembly of People	By Daumier, the audience at the theatre, title unknown.	88

Chapter 6: A Broadside of Belligerents – Warfare, Naval, Transport

98. A Presage of Doom	By Albrecht Durer, 'The Four Horsemen of the Apocalypse', 1498.	89
99. A Bombardment of Artillery	By Leonhard Zubler, Nova geometrica pyrobolia. Neuwe geometrische Büchsenmeisterery (first edition, 1608; this edition, Zurich 1614).	90
100. A Panoply of Armour	Knight on horseback; from Fierabras, Lyon, about 1485.	90
101. A Field of Battle	From 'Medieval Life Illustrations'.	91
102. A Fleet of Ships	Unattributed. From Medieval Life Illustrations.	93
103. A Muster of Soldiers	Battle scene; from Johannes de Thwrocz, Chronica Hungarorum, Augsburg (Ratdolt) 1488.	95
104. A Stand of Cannon	By Leonhard Zubler, Nova geometrica pyrobolia. Neuwe geometrische Büchsenmeisterery (first edition, 1608; this edition, Zurich 1614).	96
105. A Balance of Power	By Grandville. 'Un Grand et Un Petit...'; From 'Un Autre Monde'.	97
106. A Head of Steam	Satire on the coming age of steam: "A View in Whitechapel Road", after H. T. Alken, 1831. The two large steam coaches are "The Infernal Defiance -- From Yarmouth to London" and "The Dreadful Vengeance -- Colchester, London". On the rear of the front coach is a banner proclaiming "Warranted free from Damp", the small delivery wagon has "Bread served Hot" on its side, and the service station offers "Coals Sold Here: only	98

Part Three: A Ragbag of References

	4s. 6d. per Pound". As Paul Johnson says in his book The Birth of the Modern, the early British railroad companies were at pains to preclude any possible competition from free-running steam coaches.	
107. A Column of Wagons	'Pilgrims of the Plains' from USA Library of Congress Prints and Photographs Division Washington, D.C.	100
108. A Procession of Carriages	By Grandville, racing traffic seen from above, from 'A vol et la vue d'oiseau' (A flight and a bird's-eye view), Un Autre Monde.	101
109. A Clang of Fire Engines	From Webster's New International Dictionary of the English Language, 1911.	101
110. A Drift of Balloons	By H. Daumier. 'Nadar élevant la photographie à la hauteur de l'Art', 1862. 'Nadar Elevating Photography to the Height of Art'. 1st published in Le Boulevard 1862.	102
111. A Mode of Transport	1820's satire on the coming of the Age of Steam. The inventions to be expected in the wake of the new-fangled steam railroad are, from left to right: a steam walker, a steam carriage, and a steam ornithopter.	102

Chapter 7: A World of Wonder - The Natural World

112. A Damocles of Volcanoes	By Grandville – 'La Montagne qui accouche' 1837. ('The mountain which sleeps').	103
113. A Tilt of Windmills	From 'The History of the Most Renown'd Don Quixote of Mancha', by Miguel de Cervantes. London, 1687.	104
114. A Colonnade of Columns	From Medieval Life Illustrations.	105
115. A Patchwork of Rooftops	View of a town, from Gringore, Castell of Laboure, London, about 1505.	106
116. Landscape tailpiece	From 'All Round the Year', Edith & Saretta Nesbit, Project Gutenberg.	107
117. A Blight of Urban Sprawl	By George Cruikshank – 'London Going Out of Town - On the March of Bricks & Mortar'	108

253

	(1829). Unhappy about the changes resulting from the Industrial Revolution, Cruikshank was attacking the building of houses on the green fields of Islington.	
118. A Syzygy of Celestial Bodies	By Grandville, 'A Bridge Between the Worlds', from "Un Autre Monde" ('Another World') 1844.	108
119. A Stare of Stargazers	By Daumier, title unknown.	110
120. A Firmament of the Heavenly Spheres	An astronomer peers into the celestial heavens; from Maurice Hussey's Chaucer's World: A Pictorial Companion, Cambridge 1968.	111
121. A Cluster of Crystals	By Grandville, rock crystals masquerading as obelisks, dice, dominoes & medals. Title unknown.	111
122. An Arc of Volcanoes	The volcano Cotopaxi in eruption, 1743.	112
123. A Range of Mountains	By Bartholomaeus Anglicus, from 'All the Proprytees of Thynges', Westminster 1495.	113
124. A Palisade of Cliffs	By Joseph Mallord William Turner R. A. – 'Land's End'.	115
125. A Gust of Wind	Detail from "The Three Graces in A High Wind", satirical engraving by Gillray (1810).	116
126. A Cloudburst of Rain	From 'Childland' by Oscar Petch & M Rictor, Project Gutenberg.	117
127. A Blaze of Sunshine	The sun of Ethiopia; from Dover Coloring Book: The Middle Ages, 1971.	119
128. A Squall of Wind	'The Wind', by R L Stevenson from 'A Child's Garden of Verses, taken from Library of Congress Rare Book & Special Collections Digital Editions	120
129. A Scattering of Showers	'Rain' by R L Stevenson from 'A Child's Garden of Verses, taken from Library of Congress Rare Book & Special Collections Digital Editions	121
130. A Downpour of Rain	By Daumier, 'Le Ravageur'.	122

Part Three: A Ragbag of References

131. A Play of Sunlight	By Daumier, 'Ils voudraient eteindre jusqu'a soleil' (They would like to extinguish the sun'). Le Charivari 15.8.1851	122

Chapter 8: A Banality of Bric-a-Brac – Things, Edibles, Sports

132. A Glint of Glasses	By Louis-Léopold Boilly, 'Les Lunettes'. (1761-1845).	123
133. An Omnium-Gatherum of Items	Relics from Franklin's ill-fated expedition to find the North-West passage – 19th century drawing. Unattributed.	124
134. A Stroll of Buggies	Courtesy of Rattlesnake Jack's Old West Clipart Parlour.	125
135. A Batterie de Cuisine	From 'Il Cuoco Segreto Di Papa Pio V' (The Private Chef of Pope Pius V), by Bartolomeo Scappi, Venice, 1570.	127
136. A Flirtation of Fans	Adapted from an image from Beeswax Rubber Stamping.	128
137. A Hoard of Gold	From Beeswax Rubber Stamping.	130
138. A Bunch of Keys	From Beeswax Rubber Stamping.	131
139. A Grimace of Masks	Unattributed.	132
140. A Pair of Shoes	From Beeswax Rubber Stamping.	132
141. A Plume of Feathers	18th Century French Women's Hair and Hats by Hoey.	133
142. A Shear of Scissors	From a catalogue for the Great Exhibition of 1851.	135
143. A Set of Spoons	From 'Il Cuoco Segreto Di Papa Pio V' (The Private Chef of Pope Pius V), by Bartolomeo Scappi, Venice, 1570.	136
144. A Stack of Dishes	From a catalogue for the Great Exhibition of 1851.	136
145. A Vial of Perfume	From a catalogue for the Great Exhibition of 1851.	138
146. A Collection of Toys	By Grandville, title unknown.	139
147. An Affectation of Accoutrements	By Grandville 1844 'Fashionable people represented in public by their accoutrements', from Un Voyage d'Avril.	140

148. A Coven of Kettles	Illustration by J J Grandville from Un Autre Monde Paris: H. Fournier, (1844).	140
149. A Vernissage of Brushes	By Grandville, from 'Le Royaume des Marionettes'.	141
150. A Line of Washing	From Childland by Oscar Petch, Project Gutenberg.	141
151. A Superfluity of Cooks	By Daumier, title unknown.	142
152. A Chalder of Barley	From Medieval Life Illustrations.	143
153. A Batch of Bread	From Medieval Life Illustrations.	143
154. A Schooner of Beer	Tapping a keg; drawing based on a Medieval misericord wood carving. From Medieval Life Illustrations.	144
155. A Churn of Butter	From Medieval Life Illustrations.	145
156. A Cornucopia of Food	From Medieval Life Illustrations.	145
157. A Firkin of Ale	From Medieval Life Illustrations.	146
158. A Frail of Figs	A basket of figs; from an anonymous broadside, Strasbourg, 1500.	147
159. A Mutchkin of Ale	From Medieval Life Illustrations.	149
160. A Rose of Pilchards	From Medieval Life Illustrations.	150
161. A Punnet of Strawberries	Strawberry Picking, woodcut by Clare Leighton, 1935.	151
162. A Tailpiece	Tailpiece, from 'Household Stories' by Brothers Grimm, illust. Walter Crane 1886 Project Gutenberg.	152
163. A Joint of Meat	Tailpiece, from 'Household Stories' by Brothers Grimm, illust. Walter Crane 1886 Project Gutenberg.	153
164. A Cast of Oysters	'Term Time', By Cruikshank; 'Gentlemen, it was a very fine oyster. The Court awards you a half each', 1827.	154
165. A Burst of Bubbles	By Grandville, The Primum Mobile, from The Mysteries of Infinity in Un Autre Monde. God is seen as a magician creating matter by blowing bubbles.	154
166. A Newton of Apples	By Grandville, title unknown.	155

167. A Gargantua of Greed	By Daumier - 'Gargantua'. Daumier transformed Rabelais's 'Gargantua' to King Louis Philippe, (for which he served six months in prison at Ste-Pelagie). Senators feed the King taxes extracted from the poor and he craps honorary titles for his toadies.	156
168. A Line of Dominoes	By Daumier, title unknown.	156
169. A Den of Gamblers	19th century cartoon. Unattributed.	157
170. A Brood of Chess Players	A royal game of chess; frontispiece to Cessolis, Libro di Giuco di Scacchi, Florence 1493-94.	158
171. A Chimera of Kites	Kite flying at Hae-Kwan on the 9th Day of 9th Moon. Thomas Allom (1804-1872).	158
172. A Deck of Cards	By Grandville, from "Un autre monde".	161
173. A Dabble of Paddlers	By Daumier, title unknown.	162
174. A Tumble of Gymnasts	By Daumier – 'Comme quoi la gymnastique forme les membres, mais deforme le nez' ('This is how gymnastics forms strong bodies, but deforms the nose') (1845). From the series Professeurs et Moutards.	162

Chapter 9: A Play of Words – Theatre, Music, Dance, Religion

175. A Harlequinade of Clowns	Unattributed.	163
176. A Show of Hands	By Grandville, 'Apocalypse du Ballet', from "Un autre monde".	164
177. A Tableau of Actors	Peasants frolicking; detail of a page from Horae, Paris, 1506.	164
178. A Salvo of Bravos	By Daumier, 'One says that the Parisians…'; 1864.	165
179. A Cast of Characters	From Medieval Life Illustrations.	165
180. A Set of Scenery	Unattributed.	166
181. An Ogle of Spectators	By Grandville, from "Un autre monde".	167
182. A Quadrille of Dancers	Unattributed – 19th century engraving.	167

183. An Ensemble of Musicians	By Grandville, from "Un autre monde".	168
184. An Arpeggio of Notes	By Grandville, 'Baoum, baoum, baoum, la la la, tchinn!'	168
185. An Array of Instruments	From Clipart Etc website (see p265).	169
186. A Band of Musicians	Egyptian street musicians, from ClipArt Etc	171
187. A Tintinnabulation of Bells	Cartoon of Henry Irving by Alfred Bryan – 'Know how to play 'the bells'. Well, I ought to, after twenty-five years' practice'. From "The entr'acte," December 5th, 1896.	172
188. A Consort of Musicians	Painting by Abraham Bosse, 'Musical Society', France, 1635; from Wikimedia Commons.	172
189. An Alphabet of Letters	From 'Child-Land, by Oscar Petch & M Rictor, Project Gutenberg.	173
190. A Stack of Books	From ClipArt Etc.	173
191. An Olio of Miscellaneous Pieces	From ClipArt Etc.	174
192. A Library of Books	From ClipArt Etc.	175
193. A Scroll of Parchment	From ClipArt Etc.	176
194. A Screed of Writing	Unattributed.	177
195. A Tailpiece	Children reading, from ClipArt Etc.	177
196. The Age of Intellect	Teaching your grandmother to suck eggs, by George Cruikshank – 'The Age of Intellect – Teaching one's aged progenitress the proper way in which to do the thing' (1829). Humorous take on a proverbial phrase. Notice that the tyke has Shakespeare, Halley, Bede, Hume, Gibbon, Flamsted, Milton, Bentley, Boyle, Newton, & Euclid in her toy-basket, and Theology, Algebra, Bacon, & Locke on the floor (& scientific apparatus on the table), while grandma is reading "Who killed Cock Robin?"	178

Part Three: A Ragbag of References

197. An Invasion of Aliens	By Grandville, from "Un autre monde".	178
198. A Cult of Celebrity	By Grandville, '..the Queen of the Flowers, the Rose...', from Un Autre Monde.	180
199. An Army of Angels	By Albrecht Durer – 'The Revelation of St John: 8. The Battle of the Angels'. 1497-98 Woodcut.	181
200. An Abomination of Monks	From Medieval Life Illustrations.	182
201. A Skulk of Friars	From Medieval Life Illustrations.	183
202. A Congregation of Worshippers	A religious festival at St Petersburg, from USA Library of Congress Prints and Photographs Division Washington, D.C.	185
203. A Pantheon of Gods	Image of Olympians, by Stephane Mallarmé, from Les Dieux Antiques, nouvelle mythologie illustrée. Paris, 1880.	186
204. An Enchantment of Fairies	'Lily's Ball' – painted by J A Fitzgerald, The Illustrated London News in 1863, with a sentimental poem by D'Arcy Thompson, which began with the verse: 'Lucy gave a party, And her little playmates all, Gaily drest, came in their best, To dance at Lily's ball.'	186
205. A Flight of Dragons	From 'Abraham Eleazar', Nicholas Flamel 1399.	187
206. A Swarm of Sprites	Tailpiece, from 'Household Stories' by Brothers Grimm, illust. Walter Crane 1886 Project Gutenberg.	188
207. A Mischief of Elves	From 'The Shoemaker & the Elves', ClipArt Etc.	188
208. A Charm of Fairies	By George Cruikshank, 'Or on the Sundial's Polished Face.' Illustration for 'Poems by the Knight of Morar', by William Fraser. (1869).	189
209. A Flight of Witches	From ClipArt Etc.	189
210. A Horde of Demons	By Hans Holbein the Younger, from 'Historiarum Veteris Testamenti Icones', printed by Johan and Franciscus Frellon, Lyons, 1543.	190

Gallimaufry

Chapter 10: A Comedy of Errors – Ideas, Language, Emotions

211. A Montage of Images	By Boilly, 'Les Grimaces'.	191
212. A Distribution of Largesse	By Daumier – 'Tiens, peuple, tiens, bon peuple, ens veux-tu, en voila.' Lithograph.	192
213. A Dance of Death	By Michael Wolmegut, 'Orchestra of the Dead'. Woodcut, from Hartmann Schedel's Liber Chrnicarum, printed by Anton Koberger, Nuremberg, 1493.	194
214. A Drift of Shadows	My Shadow, from 'A Child's Garden of Verses', Robert Louis Stevenson, illust. Charles Robinson, 1895. Library of Congress Rare Books Digital Edition.	195
215. A Finger of Fate	By Grandville, 'A great sculptor finishing his masterpiece, 'The Finger of God'', wood engraving, from Un Autre Monde, Paris, (1844).	196
216. A Leap of Faith	By Grandville, from Le Royaume des Marionettes.	197
217. A March of Progress	Marching Song, from 'A Child's Garden of Verses', Robert Louis Stevenson, illust. Charles Robinson, 1895. Library of Congress Rare Books Digital Edition.	199
218. A Tree of Life	From ClipArt Etc.	201
219. A Sense of Proportion	By Grandville, 'Chien promenant son maître' ('Dog Walking His Master'). From 'Un Autre Monde'.	203
220. A Web of Intrigue	By Daumier, Types Parisiens Series - "Oh! absolument comme si on y était; la grande ôte son corset, et la petite chereche une puce." 1841 ("Oh! Absolutely as if one were there; the fat one removes her corset, and the small one is looking for a flea.").	203
221. A Bastion of Support	By Daumier, 'Ou Allons Nous, Ou Allons Nous?' (What are we coming to, what are we coming to? We're walking on a volcano...') 1834, from 'La Caricature'. The figure on the	204

Part Three: A Ragbag of References

	right and most of the prints in the window of Aubert's shop represent Le Constitutionnel, a liberal journal which was suffering a severe decline, hence was personified by a dotard. He shares views with Charles Etienne, his owner-editor.	
222. An Orgy of Violence	By Daumier, 'Rue Transnonain' - portrays a dramatic event of the insurrections of April 1834, which involved the slaughter of a house full of people in Transnonain Street. This lithography has become very rare because hundreds of its copies were destroyed.	204
223. A Sea of Faces	By William Hogarth: 'Characters and Caricaturers' (1743).	205
224. A Tirade of Abuse	By Daumier, 'Un Cause Célèbre', ('A Famous Motive'). 1862-65.	205
225. A Rosetta Stone of Languages	Unattributed.	207
226. A Eulogy of Praise	19th-century man and woman lightly flirting (illustration from Sep. 23 1882 Police Gazette).	207
227. A Titbit of Gossip	Three men looking over a wall; detail of a page from Horae, London (Pynson), 1497.	208
228. A Babel of Tongues	Unattributed.	209
229. A Declaration of Love	By Grandville, 'The True Cupid', from Un Autre Monde, 1850.	210
230. A Barrage of Criticism	By Daumier, 'Le Carcan', ('Pillory') from La Caricature (Journal) No. 219, published 15 January 1835. This lithograph represents the National Assembly where the deputies are bored and asleep. They cannot say anything because of what is written on the board on the left: "censorship".	210
231. A Stroke of Genius	By Grandville, Master artist and students, from 'Le Royaume des Marionettes'.	211
232. An Ambiguity of Expression	By Daumier, 'The Past, the Present, the Future' Plate 349, La Caricature, no. 166, 9 January (1834).	211

Gallimaufry

233. A Well of Despair	By Cruikshank, 'An Execution Sweeps Off the Greater Part of Their Furniture', from the publication 'The Bottle', on the perils of drink (1847).	212
234. A Cocoon of Love	By Dante Gabriel Rossetti, 'Golden Head by Golden Head' – an illustration for a book of poems by his sister, Christina Rosetti.	213
235. A Threnody of Grief	By John Everett Millais, title unknown.	214
236. A Prick of Conscience	One of the most well-known Gibson Girls, created by Charles Dana Gibson circa 1900.	215
237. A Vale of Tears	Pre-Raphaelite style illustration by Helen Stratton (active 1891-1925).	216
238. A Feeling of Pressure	By Daumier, 'Ha! So you wish to mess with the press?' 1833.	217
239. A Wave of Ennui	By Daumier, 'In the Omnibus', 1864.	218
240. An Air of Disdain	By Daumier, 'The Clinic of Doctor Macaire'.	218
241. A Test of Time	Front view of a large quarter clock by Sir E. Beckett, Encyclopedia Britanica, 1893.	219
242. An Eternity of Time	By Grandville, Un autre monde.	220

Chapter 11: A Compound of Collectives – Science, Technical, Legal

243. A Head of Hair	French Hair-dress of the 1770's from Stibbert,	221
244. A Phalanx of Noses	By George Cruikshank. "A Chapter of Noses." Etching, (1834). From Cruikshank's Sketches.	222
245. A Flounce of Curls	From a 17th century engraving of a Hurluberlu (scatterbrain) hairstyle, ca. 1671. L'Âge d'Or and Kirke's Lambs (see notes)	222
246. An Assemblage of Bones	Unattributed.	222
247. An Expanse of Belly	By Daumier, 'Le Cauchemar', 'The Nightmare', 1832. Lithograph.	224
248. A Helix of Springs	Grandville, 'Une fusée élastique' An Undersea Message from Krackq Arrives by Spring in: Un autre monde: Fournier, (1844). Grandville's woodcarving shows a letter shooting up from the sea on a spiralling cable, re. the first submarine telegraph cable.	224

Part Three: A Ragbag of References

	In 1844 Samuel Morse stated 'a telegraphic communication line could certainly be established across the Atlantic Ocean'. Over 20 years later he was proved right.	
249. An Alloy of Metals	From Medieval Life Illustrations.	225
250. A Compass Rose of Directions	Unattributed.	226
251. A Bouquet of Multi-Media Services	By Grandville, title unknown.	228
252. An Epidemic of Disease	By Daumier, 'The Physician' 1833 litho of the 1831-32 Cholera Epidemic. "How the devil does it happen that all my patients succumb? . . . I bleed them, I physic them, I drug them. . . . I simply can't understand it."	229
253. A Cocktail of Drugs	From Medieval Life Illustrations.	230
254. A Vial of Medicine	Woman visiting a doctor, who examines her urine flask; Mer des Hystoires, Paris 1488-89.	231
255. A Bout of Sickness	By Daumier, 'Le malade imaginaire'. ('The Imaginary Illness').	231
256. A Team of Doctors	By Grandville, 'Les Medecins' from the Fables de Jean de la Fontaine.	232
257. An Odium of Politicians	By Daumier, 'Masks of 1831'.	232
258. An Eloquence of Lawyers	Adapted from 'Chaucer Colouring Book', Bellerophon Books, 1992.	235
259. A Ship of State	Unattributed.	237
260. A Tailpiece	Rampions, a tailpiece, from 'Household Stories' by Brothers Grimm, illust. Walter Crane 1886 Project Gutenberg.	238
261. An Array of Attorneys	By Daumier, 'Les Avocats et Les Plaideurs', (Lawyers and Litigants)'.	239
262. A Line-up of Suspects	By C. J. Grant, 'The March of Roguery', 1830. State (king, holding sceptre): "I Rule"; Church (bishop, with "£10000" in the crook of his arm): "I Pray"; Farmer (in smock): "I Work for Both"; Merchant: "I Cheat you Three"; Lawyer: "I Fleece you Four"; Doctor: "I Poison you Five", Devil: "I'll have all Six".	240

Part Three: A Ragbag of References – Bibliography, Images, Index

263. A Drunkship of Collective Noun Collectors	A student's drinking bout, from Directorium Statuum, Strassburg, about 1489.	241
264. List of Illustrations	From 'Household Stories' by Brothers Grimm, illust. Walter Crane 1886 Project Gutenberg	246
265. A Bevy of Alcoholics	From "Images d'Épinal", popular prints created by the Imagerie d'Épinal in France. These stencil-coloured woodcuts of military subjects, Napoleonic history, storybook characters & other folk themes were widely distributed throughout the 19th C.	264
266. A Worship of Writers	Woodcut of a woman reading, circa 1810.	296

'a bevy of alcoholics'

Part Three: A Ragbag of References

Sources used for illustrations include:

- 'Medieval Life Illustrations', Dover Publications Inc. 1995; ISBN 0-486-28862-5
- 'Curious & Fantastic Creatures', Dover Publications Inc. 1995; ISBN 0-486-28463-8
- 'Curious Woodcuts of Fanciful & Real Beasts', Dover Publications Inc 1971; ISBN 0-486-22701-4
- 'Daumier: 120 Great Lithographs' by Charles F Ramus; Dover Publications Inc. 1978; ISBN 0-486-23512-2
- 'Grandville's Animals', Thames & Hudson 1981; ISBN 0-500-23340-3

I am particularly indebted to the following **websites** for some of the images:

- USA Library of Congress has an excellent archive of images, many in the public domain: http://www.loc.gov/pictures/
- For all manner of wonderful images from old books, Project Gutenberg: http://www.gutenberg.org/wiki/Category:Bookshelf
- The Public Domain Review – a joy to browse through: http://publicdomainreview.org/2012/09/24/an-alphabet-of-celebrities-1899/
- For medieval illustrations – 'A Boke of Gode Cookery', at http://www.godecookery.com/
- For 17th century images – L'Âge d'Or and Kirke's Lambs, at http://www.kipar.org/index.html
- Rattlesnake Jack's Old West Clipart Parlour, at: http://members.memlane.com/gromboug/P3TofC.htm#Images
- For vintage clipart images, Webster's New International Dictionary of the English Language, 1911: http://srufaculty.sru.edu/david.dailey/public/public_domain.htm
- A huge range of Historical clipart is available from: http://www.clipart-history.com/index.php?id=73&Subcategory=
- ClipArt Etc: Superb ad-free quality clip art site: http://etc.usf.edu/clipart/

Notes on the principal illustrators:

Louis-Léopold Boilly (French, 1761-1845). Portrait and genre painter whose work illustrated everyday life during the French Revolution and Napoleonic Empire. Sensitive command of media, colour, and composition. Boilly's only teacher was his father, Arnould Boilly, a wood-carver. Boilly came to Paris for the first time in 1785, and remained there permanently. He is said to have painted over 5000 portraits, besides other works. (Biography from Fine Art Museums of San Francisco).

Walter Crane (1845–1915) was an English artist and book illustrator. He is considered to be the most prolific and influential children's book creator of his generation and, along with Randolph Caldecott and Kate Greenaway, one of the strongest contributors to the child's nursery motif that the genre of English children's illustrated literature would exhibit in its developmental stages in the latter 19th century. His work featured some of the more colourful and detailed beginnings of the child-in-the-garden motifs that would characterize many nursery rhymes and children's stories for decades to come. He was part of the Arts and Crafts movement and produced an array of paintings, illustrations, children's books, ceramic tiles and other decorative arts.

George Cruikshank was born in London on 27th September, 1792. His father, Isaac Cruikshank, was a caricaturist who died as a result of his alcoholism in 1811. After a brief education at an elementary school in Edgeware, Cruikshank set himself up as a caricaturist in London. An early influence on Cruikshank was James Gillray, Britain's leading caricaturist at the time. Cruikshank was soon selling his drawings to over twenty different print-sellers; these early drawings included attacks on the royal family and leading politicians. In 1836 Cruikshank met Charles Dickens and the two men worked on several projects together, principally with Cruikshank providing the illustrations for Sketches by Boz (1836) and Oliver Twist (1838). Cruikshank was a strong supporter of the Temperance Society and in 1847 produced *The Bottle* which sold almost 100,000 copies. He died on 1st February, 1878.

Honoré Victorin Daumier, French (1808-1879). French caricaturist, painter, and sculptor. In his lifetime he was known chiefly as a political and social satirist, but since his death recognition of his qualities as a painter has grown. In 1830, after learning the still fairly new process of lithography, he began to contribute political cartoons to the anti-government weekly *Caricature*. He was an ardent Republican and was sentenced to six months' imprisonment in 1832 for his attacks on King Louis-Philippe, whom he represented as 'Gargantua swallowing bags of gold extorted from the people'. On the suppression of political satire in 1835 he began to work for *Charivari* and turned to satire of social life, but at the time of the 1848 revolution he returned to political subjects. He is said to have made more than 4,000 lithographs, wishing each time that the one he had just made could be his last. In the last years of his life he was almost blind and was saved from destitution by Corot. Daumier was one of the greatest draughtsmen of the 19th century. He had an insight into character and an ability to observe gesture, atmosphere and human nature which has seldom been matched. With just sufficient exaggeration to make his point more visually powerful he also used realism to bitter effect.

Albrecht Dürer –, Born May 21, 1471, in the Imperial Free City of Nürnberg, Germany, he was the third son of the Hungarian goldsmith Albrecht Dürer. He began as an apprentice to his father in 1485, but his earliest known work, one of his many self-portraits, was made in 1484. German painter, printmaker, draughtsman and art theorist, he was generally regarded as the greatest German Renaissance artist. His vast body of work includes altarpieces and religious works, numerous portraits and self-portraits, and copper engravings. His woodcuts, such as the *Apocalypse* series (1498), retain a more Gothic flavour than the rest of his work. Dürer died on April 6, 1528, in Nürnberg.

Jean-Jacques Grandville – His name was actually Jean Ignace Isidore Gérard. He was born in Nancy on September 15, 1803 and died March 17, 1847 in Vanves near Paris. His adopted artist's name was Grandville, however, and as such he is widely known among the lovers of caricatures and pointed political sarcasm. Grandville contributed to *Le Charivari* and *La Caricature*, France's most prominent satirical magazines in the 19th century. His way of drawing people with the heads of animals and vice versa contributed to the fine line of irony for which his art is famous. *Les Métamorphoses du Jour* appeared in 1829, *Les Animaux* in 1842, *Petites Misères de la Vie Humaine* in 1843 and *Un Autre Monde* in 1844. He is just as famous for his book illustrations – the Fables of La Fontaine, Balzac, Hugo, *Gulliver* and *Robinson Crusoe* are his most prominent works.

William Hogarth - (10 November 1697 – 26 October 1764) was an English painter, printmaker, pictorial satirist, social critic and editorial cartoonist who has been credited with pioneering western sequential art. His work ranged from realistic portraiture to comic strip-like series of pictures called "modern moral subjects". Knowledge of his work is so pervasive that satirical political illustrations in this style are often referred to as "Hogarthian."

Part Three: A Ragbag of References

Index of collective nouns

(with Chapter # - and from which you learn that the most widely used collective noun is a Cluster!)

A

A-list	5
Aarmoury	1
Abandonment	5
Abominable sight	9e
Abomination	9e
Abscondance	3a
Absence	5
Abundance	10a,10c
Abyss	7b
Academy	5
Acceleration	10a
Accolade	10b
Accumulation	11d
Acknowledgement	10b
Acne	5
Acre	7a
Act	9e,10a
Address book	11b
Aeon	10d
Affiliation	11d
Age	10d
Agenbite	10c
Agenda	10a
Agglomeration	7c
Agony	10c
Air	10c
Album	8a,9b
Alignment	7a,7b,11d
Allocation	10a,11d
Allotment	7a,11d
Allowance	11d
Alloy	11b
Alluvium	7c
Almanac	9c
Alphabet	9c
Amalgam	11b

Amalgamation	5,11d
Ambiguity	10b
Ambivalence	10b
Amble	5
Ambuscade	5
Ambush	1,5
Amount	11b
Amphora	8b
Amplification	9b
Ampoule	11c
Ampulla	8b
Annal	10a
Annoyance	11b
Anorak	5
Anthology	5,9c
Antiphony	9d
Antiphonary	9e
Apiary	3a
Aquarium	3b
Aqueduct	7a
Aquifer	7c
Arboretum	4
Arbour	4
Arc	8a
Arcade	7a,8c
Archipelago	7c
Archive	9c,11b
Are	7a
Arena	5,10a
Argosy	6a,10a
Arm	11d
Armada	6a
Armament	1,6a
Armamentarium	11c
Armoury	6a,10a
Army	3a,3b,3c,5,6a,9e,9f

Aroma 5
Arpeggio 9b
Arran 3b
Arrangement 4
Array 1,3b,5,6a,7b,7d,9a,9b,10a
.... 11b,11d
Arsenal 6a,8c
Ascension 2
Ascent 5
Assemblage 9e,11a,11b
Assemblé 9a
Assembly 5,9e,11b
Assessment 10a
Assignment 10a
Assimilation 10a
Association 8c
Asterism 7b
Asylum 2
Athenaeum 9c
Atlas 9c
Atmosphere 10a
Atomiser 8a
Attack 10c,11c
Attitude 5
Attraction 10a
Auction 10a
Audience 5,9a
Audit 11d
Audition 9a
Aura 10a,10c
Aurora 1
Autocade 6b
Avalanche 7d,10a
Avenue 4,6a,7a
Aviary 2
Awe 7d
Axis 10a

B

B-list 5
Babble 5,9b
Babel 10b
Bacchanal 5
Backlog 10a
Backup 11b

Badelynge (or badling) 2
Badinage 9a
Bag 1,2,8a,8b
Balance 6a,7d,11d
Balcony 9a
Bale 3b,3c,4,8a,9c
Ball 7d,8a,10a
Ballet 2
Balloon 8b
Ballot 11d
Bally 3b
Balthazar 8b
Band 1,2,5,7c,8a,9b,9e
Bandolier 6a
Bank 2,4,7d,8a,9a,10a,11b
Banner 5
Banquet 8b
Baptism 10a
Bar 8a,8b,9b
Baring 5
Baron 8b
Baronage 5
Baronetcy 5
Barrage 6a,10b
Barratry 11d
Barrel 1,6a,8a,8b,10c
Barrel-full 10a
Barren 1
Barricade 6b,8a
Barrow-load 8a
Basin 8a
Bask 3c
Basket 8a,8b,11d
Bastion 10a
Batch 8b
Bath 8a
Batholith 7c
Batt 8a
Battalion 6a
Batten 9a
Batterie 8a
Battery 2,3b,6a,9b,11b
Battle 10a,10b
Battlefield 6a
Baulk 3b

Part Three: A Ragbag of References

Bavin 8a
Bazaar 2,7a
Beacon 7d
Beat 4
Bed 3a,3b,3c,4,8a
Belfry 1
Bellow 1
Bellowing 2
Bellyful 5,8b,10c
Belt 6a,7b
Bench 1,8c,9e,11d
Benchmark 10a,11b
Beowolf cluster 11b
Berry 8a
Bestiary 9f
Bevy 1,2,5
Bew 2
Bibliography 9c
Bike 3a
Bill 11d
Billet 6a
Billow 5
Bind 3b,9c
Binder 5
Binge 8b
Biosphere 10a
Bit 10b,11b
Bite 3a
Bivouac 7a
Blackening 5
Blacklist 11d
Blanket 7d,8a
Blarney 5
Blast 5,6a,8c,9b
Blaze 5,7d,10a
Blazon 8c
Blazonry 6a,7d
Bleach 5
Bless 5
Blessing 9f
Blight 7a
Blister pack 11c
Blitz 6a
Blitzkrieg 6a
Blizzard 7d

Bloat 1
Block 7a,8a,8b
Blockade 5,6a
Bloom 3b
Blunder 5
Blur 5,10a
Blush 5
Board 5,11d
Boast 6a
Bob 2
Bobbery 1
Body 5,7c,7d,9c,9e,10a,10b,11d
Boil 2
Boll 4,8b
Bolt 8a
Bolting 4
Bombardment 6a
Bonanza 10a
Bond 5
Bone 10a
Boogle 1
Book 8a,8c,9c
Booly 5
Bored 5
Boredom 11d
Botnet 11b
Bottle 4,8b,11b,11c
Boughpot 4
Bouquet 2,4,5,8a,11b
Bout 8b,8c,10c,11c
Bovate 7a
Bow 1
Bowl 3b,8b,8c,10a
Box 6a,8a,8b,8c,9a
Brace 1,2,6a,9a,10d,11c
Bracelet 8a
Braid 11a
Brain drain 11d
Branch 6a,10a,11b,11c
Bray 10c
Breach 6a,10a
Breakdown 6a,11d
Breaking-school 3b
Breath 7d
Brew 8b

271

Bridge 6a
Brigade 5,6a
Brimming 3b
Broadside 6a
Brood 2,3b,5,8c
Brook 2
Brotherhood 5
Browse 4,11b
Browss 8a
Brouhaha 10b
Brushful 8a
Bucket 3b,8a
Budget 8a,11d
Buffoonery 1
Building 2
Bulb 8b
Bulk 8b
Bully 9e
Bunch 1,2,4,5,8a,8b,11a
Bundle 5,6a,8a,8b,9c
Bunker 8a
Burden 1,4,9b,10a
Burgeoning 10a
Burn 8a,8b
Burrow 1
Burst 7d,9a,8b,10a,10b
Bury 1,8a
Bush 3b
Bushel 3a,8a,8b
Business 1,3a
Busyness 1
Butt 3a,8a,8b
Buttonhole 4
Buzz 5
Byre 1

C

C-list 5
Cabal 5
Cabinet 8a,8b,10a,11c,11d
Cable 8a
Cache 8a,11b
Cackle 1,10c
Cacography 9c
Cacophony 9b

Cade 8b
Cadence 9b
Cadenza 9b
Cadre 6a
Cafetiere 8b
Cage 1
Cairn 7a
Caisson 6a
Cajolery 5
Calendar 9e,10d
Call 10a
Calyx 4
Camarilla 5
Camp 5,10a
Campaign 6a,10b,11d
Can 8b,10a
Canal 7a
Cancellation 6b
Candle 1
Canister 8a
Cannonade 6a,7d,10b
Canon 9c,9e,10a
Canopy 4,7b,7d
Canteen 8a,8b
Canto 9b,9c
Canton 7a
Caper 5
Carat 8a
Caravan 1,10a
Caravanserai 5
Carbonade 8b
Carboy 8a
Card 8a
Cargo 2
Carillon 9b
Carp 10b
Carpet 2,4
Carrot 8a
Cartel 5,11d
Cartload 1
Carton 8b
Cartouche 9c
Cartridge 8a
Cartulary 11d
Carucate 7a

Cascade	4,7c,8a,11b
Case	6a,8b
Caseload	11c
Casino	8c
Cask	8b
Casket	8a
Cast	1,2,3b,8b,9a
Caste	3a,5,6a,8a,8b,9e
Catalogue	5,10a
Catch	3b,5
Catch-all	10b
Catchment	7a
Category	3a
Catharsis	10c
Caucus	2,11d
Cauldron	8c
Cavalcade	6a,6b
Cavalry	6a
Cavayard	1
Ceilidh	9b
Cell	5,6a
Cellar	8b
Cemetery	7a
Cenoby	9e
Centenary	10d
Centre	10a
Century	8c
Cesspit	8a
Cete	1,2
Chain	2,4,5,6a,7a,7c,8a,10a,10b
Chalder	8b
Chaldron	8a
Chamber	9a,11d
Chameleon	7d
Change	9a,9b
Channel	7c
Chantry	9e
Chapbook	9c
Chapel	9c
Chapter	5,9e,10a
Charge	6a,6b,9e
Charlotte	11b
Charm	2,5,7b
Charnel-house	11a
Chart	9d
Chartulary	9e
Chase	9c
Chatelaine	8a
Chatter	2
Chattering	2
Cheat	5
Chest	8a
Chicane	7a,8c
Chiliad	10d
Chiliarchy	5
Chime	2,9b
Chimera	8c,10a
Chine	1
Chirm	2
Chit	3a
Choir	9b
Chopin	8b
Chopine	8b
Chorale	9b
Chorus	3a,3c,9a,9b,9e,10a
Chrestomathy	9c
Chronicle	9c,10a
Chronology	10a
Chub	8b
Churn	8b
Chyne	2
Cinerarium	8a
Cipher	9c
Circle	5,6b,7a
Circus	1,2,3a,6a,9a
Cistern	8a
Citadel	1
City	7a,10a
Civilisation	9d
Clamour	2,5
Clan	1,2,5
Clank	6a
Clap	7d
Claque	5
Clash	1,9b,10a,10b,10c
Class	3a,5
Classification	3a,9c
Clat	3a
Clatch	2
Clatter	6a

Gallimaufry

Clattering 2
Clearance 8a
Cletch 2
Clew 3a,8a
Click 5,11b
Climate 10b,10c
Clip 6a
Clipping 1
Clique 5
Cliterati 9c
Cloak 7d
Clod 4,8a
Closet 8a,11a
Closing 5
Clot 11a
Cloth 8b
Cloud 1,2,3a,3b,5,6a,8a
Cloudburst 7d
Clouder 1
Clove 8b
Clowder 1,5
Club 5
Clump 3b,4
Cluster 1,2,3a,3b,4,5,6a,7a,7b
 .... 7c,7d,8a,8b,9b,9c,11b,11c
Clutch 2,5,8a,8b,8c,10c,11a
Clutter 1,2,3a,8a
Coach-load 5
Coagulum 10a
Coalition 1,11d
Coat 8a
Coating 8a
Coble 8a
Cobweb 10b
Cockade 8a
Cocktail 8b,10b,11c
Cocoon 3a,10c
Code 10a
Codex 11c
Coffer 8a
Coffle 1,5
Cognoscenti 5
Cohort 1,5,6a
Coign 10a
Coil 2,8a

Collaboration 5
Collage 8a
Collation 9c
Collection 8a,9b,9c
Collective 5,9c,9d
College 5,9e,11d
Colloquium 5
Colluvium 7c
Colonnade 7a
Colony 1,2,3a,3b,4,5
Colt 3a
Columbarium 2
Column 1,2,5,6b,8a,11d
Comb 8b
Combination 8a,8c10a
Comedy 6b
Comfort 8a
Command 6a
Commission 5
Committee 5
Commonality 10a
Commonwealth 11d
Commotion 2
Commune 5
Communion 9e
Community 1,3a,4,5,9e,11d
Compact 8a
Companion set 8a
Company 1,2,3b,5,6a,9a,11d
Compass rose 11b
Compendium 8c,9c
Compilation 9c
Complement 5,8a
Complex 5,7a
Composite 10a
Compound 7a,11b
Compurgation 11d
Concatenation 11b
Concelebration 9e
Concentration 2,10a,10b
Concertino 9b
Concerto 9b
Concert party 9a,11d
Conclave 9e
Concoction 8b

Concord	9b
Concordance	9c,9e
Concourse	2,5
Concretion	8a
Condescension	9a
Condominium	7a
Cone	10a
Confederacy	5,11d
Conference	9e,11d
Conflagration	5
Conflict	10c
Confluence	7c
Confraternity	9e
Confusion	1
Congeries	9b
Conglomerate	5,7c
Congregation	2,3b,3c,7d,9e
Congress	1,5,11d
Conjugation	9c
Conjunction	5,7b
Consensus	10b
Conservatory	4
Consistory	9e
Consolidation	10a,10b
Consonance	9b
Consort	9b,9c
Consortium	11d
Conspiracy	2,6b,10a
Constable	2
Constabulary	11d
Constellation	3b,7b
Consternation	5
Constituency	11d
Construct	10b
Construction	9c
Contagion	11c
Continuum	7b
Conurbation	7a
Convent	9e
Conventicle	9e
Convention	5,9d
Convergence	10b
Converting	9e
Convocation	2,9e
Convoy	6a,6b
Cookbook	8b
Co-operative	5
Copse	4
Cord	4,8a,9b
Cordage	6a
Cordon	5,6b
Cordillera	7c
Core	8c
Cornucopia	3a,8b,10a
Corolla	4
Corona	7d
Corps	1,6a,9a,9b,11c
Corpus	9c,9d
Corral	1,6b
Corridor	6a
Corroboree	2,5
Corsage	4
Cortege	5,6b
Cote	2,3a
Coterie	1,4,5
Council	2,9e,11d
Coup	6a,9a,10a
Couple	1
Course	11c,11d
Court	1,11d
Coven	5,8a,9f
Cover	7d
Covert	2
Covey	2,9b
Cowardice	1
Cowel	8b
Crack	7d
Cracker	8a
Cradle	7a
Cran	3b,8b
Crash	1,3a
Crate	8b
Creaght	1
Crèche	1,2,5,6a
Credence	5
Creel	3b
Creep	3c
Crescendo	8c,9b
Crescent	7a,7c
Crew	6a,8c,9a

Gallimaufry

Crib-list 10a
Crisis 10c
Croak 3c
Crock 8a,10a
Crocodile 5
Croft 7a
Crop 2,4,5,7b,11a
Crowd 2,4,5,9c
Crucible 10a,11b
Cruet 8b
Cruft 11b
Crumb 8b
Crunch 8c
Crusade 5
Cruse 8a
Crush 5
Crust 8b
Cru 7a
Cry 1,9a
Cube 8b
Cuddle 1
Culch 3b
Cull 1
Cult 9d,9e
Culture 3a,10a
Cumulus 7d
Cup 8b,10c
Curie 11b
Curiosity 1
Current 7c,7d
Curriculum 8a
Curse 5
Curtain 7d
Cushion 7d
Cut 8b
Cutch 8a
Cutting 5
Cycle 5,6a,9c,10a
Cylinder 8a

D

Dab 8a
Dabble 8c
Daub 8a
Damning 11d

Damocles 7c
Dance 3a,10a
Darkening 2
Dash 5,10c
Database 11b
Day 10a
Day's work 7a
Dazzle 2,5,7d
Deal 10a
Debauchery 5
Decade 10d
Decanter 9e
Deceit 2
Deck 9d
Decline 10a
Decorum 9e
Deck 6a,8c
Defilade 6a
Degree 10a
Delegation 11d
Délicatesse 5
Delicatessen 5
Delight 3b
Delirium 3a,5
Delivery 8a
Delving 9f
Demesne 7a
Demi 8b
Demijohn 8b
Demonstration 5
Den 1,3b,3c,5,8c,10a
Denier 8a
Deployment 6a
Derecho 7d
Descent 2,5,9d
Desert 2
Desperation 5
Destruction 1
Detachment 6a,11d
Detritus 4
Devoutness 9e
Diary 10a
Diaspora 5
Diatribe 10b
Dictionary 9c

Diet	4
Dignity	9e,9f
Dilation	5
Diligence	5
Diminution	9b,10a
Directory	9c,11b
Disagreement	11d
Discography	8a
Discretion	9e
Disguising	5
Display	3b,5,8a,10c
Dissent	5
Dissimulation	2
Distribution	8a
Disworship	5
Divan	9c,11d
Division	4,5,6a,8a,9b,11d
Doading	2
Doctrine	9e
Dole	2
Domain	7a,7c
Don	1
Donut	11b
Doom	9d,9f
Dopping	2
Dormitory	8a
Dose	5,11c
Dossier	9c,10a
Double couple	1
Double helix	11b
Double magnum	8b
Dout	1
Down	1,7d,8a,8c
Downpour	7d
Dowt	1
Doylt	1
Draft	3b,6a,11d
Dram	8b
Draught	3b,5
Drave	3b
Dray (or drey)	1
Dread	2
Dream	3
Drear	7d
Dribble	5,7c

Drift	1,2,3a,4,5,7c,7d,8a,8c,10a
Drive	1
Dronkship	5
Dropping	2
Drought	3b
Drove	1,5
Druck	5
Drum	2
Drumming	2
Duet	2
Dun	1
Dune	7c
Duo	9b
Duplet	9b
Durante	1,2
Dusting	7d,11a
Dynasty	5

E

Earth	1
Echelon	6a,11b
Eddy	7c,7d
Edition	9c
Eight	8c
Eisteddfod	9b
Eldorado	8a
Electoral roll	11d
Element	10a
Elint	11b
Ell	8a
Eloquence	11d
Eluvium	7c
Embarras	10a
Embarrassment	2,10a,11a
Embassy	11d
Embodiment	10a
Embruing	5
Emporium	8a
Encampment	5,7a
Enchantment	9f
Enclave	5
Enclosure	7a
Encyclopaedia	9c
Enfilade	6a
Enigma	10a

Ennead 9e
Ensemble 9b
Enterprise 9d
Entourage 5
Entrance 9a
Ephemeris 7b
Epidemic 11c
Epoch 10d
Equivocation 11d
Erg 7c,11b
Error 10a
Erst 3a
Erudition 5
Eruption 7c,10c,11a
Escadrille 6b
Escalade 8a
Escalation 6a
Escargatoire 3a
Escheat 11d
Essay 5
Estate 7a
Eternity 10d
Etui 8a
Eulogy 10b
Euphony 9b
Eureka 10a
Evensong 9e
Ewer 8b
Exaggeration 5
Exaltation 2
Example 5
Execution 6a
Exhibition 8a
Expanse 4,7c,11a
Expression 10c
Extreme unction 5
Eye 2
Eyrar 2
Eyrie 2

F

Faction 5
Faculty 5,10b
Faggot 6a,8a
Faith 5

Fall 1,2,5,7d,9e
Family 1,3b,5
Family tree 5
Fanfare 9b
Fardel 8a
Fare 1
Farm 3a,7a
Farmyard 1
Farrago 10b
Farrow 1
Fascicle 4,9c,11a
Fascine 8a
Fat Quarter 8a
Feast 5
Federation 11d
Feeling 10c
Fellowship 5,9e
Fesnying 1
Festival 5,9d
Festoon 8a
Festschrift 9c
Fever 3b
Fez 1
Fichu 8a
Fid 8a
Fidget 5,9e
Field 1,4,5,7b,6a,7a,8c,10a,11d
Fifteen 8c
Fighting 5
Figment 10a
Figure 10a,10b
Filette 8b
Fillet 8b
Filth 2
Finger 10a
Fire 10c
Firkin 8b
Firlot 8b
Firm 11d
Firmament 7b
Fistful 8a
Fit 10c
Fix 9d
Fizz 8b
Fizzle 8a

Part Three: A Ragbag of References

Flagon	8b
Flamboyance	2
Flange	1
Flap	9e
Flash	7d,10c
Flask	8b
Flat	8a
Fleece	8a
Fleet	1,2,3b,5,6a,6b,8a
Flick	1
Flicker	7c,7d,10a
Flight	2,3a,5,6a,6b,7a,8a,8c
	9a,10a,10d,11d
Fling	2
Flink	1
Flirtation	8a
Flitch	8b
Float	3b,3c,9a
Flock	1,2,3a,5,9e
Flood	5,7c,8a,10b,10c
Floodgate	10c
Flote	1,3b
Flotilla	3a,3b,6a,7c
Flotsam	5,8a
Flounce	8a,11a
Flourish	5,9b,9c
Flow	7c,10b
Flurry	2,4,6a,7d,8a,10a,11d
Flush	2,5,6a,8c
Fluther	3a,3b
Flutter	3a,8a,11c
Focus	10a
Fold	1,5
Folkmoot	5
Force	5,6a,7d,11b,11d
Foreboding	10c
Foresight	5
Forest	3b,4,7a,9c
Formality	2
Formation	6b
Formicary	3a
Forpet	8b
Fortress	1
Forum	5
Fount	9,10a

Fountain	7c,9
Four	8c
Frail	3b,8b
Frame	10a,10c
Franchise	7a
Fraternity	5
Fraunch	5
Fray	3b
Freedom	10b
Freefall	2
Frisson	10c
Frost	5
Froufrou	8a
Fry	3a,9c
Fullness	10d
Furore	9b
Fusillade	6a
Fusion	10a,10b

G

Gaggle	2,5,11b
Gala	8c
Galaxy	5,7b
Gale	7d,10c
Galère	5
Galimatias	10b
Galleria	7a
Gallery	5,8a
Galley	5,9c
Gallimaufry	8a
Gallipot	11c
Gallon	2
Gallop	1
Gam	1,3b,5
Gambit	8c
Gambol	1
Game	2,8c
Gammon	8b
Gamut	7d,10c
Gang	1,2,5,6b,8c,9b,9d,11b
Ganglion	11a
Gangue	7c
Garb	4,6a
Garble	9c
Garboil	9f

Garden	3b,4,10a	Google	9d
Gargantua	8b	Googol	8
Garland	4,9b	Googolplex	8
Garner	8b	Goring	5
Garrison	6a	Gossip	5
Gasconade	10c	Gout	7c
Gate	8a	Government	9e,11d
Gather	8a	Gowpenful	8b
Gathering	5,9c	Grace	9f
Gatling	2	Graft	5
Gaze	1	Grain	8b,10a
Gazetteer	9c	Grapevine	10b
Geek	5	Graveyard	7a
Generation	3c,5	Great bevy	1
Genre	9d	Great herd	1
Genus	1,4	Greenhouse	4
Geode	7c	Grid	5,8a,11b
Get-together	5	Gridlock	6b
Geyser	7c	Grimace	8a,9a
Ghetto	5	Grimoire	9f
Gift	10b	Grind	3b
Giggle	1,5	Grinder	8b
Gild	5,9a	Grip	5,10c
Glade	4	Grist	3a
Glaring	1	Grope	5
Glaze	5,7d	Grotto	4
Gleam	5	Grouch	5
Glean	3b	Group	1,5,9a,11b,11d
Glide	3b	Grove	4,5,6a
Glimmer	10c	Grumble	1
Glint	3b,5,8a	Guard	5,6a
Glister	2	Guarantee	10a
Glitch	9f	Guess	11c
Glitter	6a	Guffaw	10c
Glitterati	5	Guild	5
Glorying	1	Gulag	5
Glossary	9c	Gulp	2
Glow	10a	Gun	8b
Glozing	5	Gush	5
Glut	3b,8a,8b	Gust	7d
Gnome	10a	Gut-full	8b
Gob	11a	Guzzle	11d
Gobble	2	Gymkhana	6b
Goggle	5	Gyre	7c
Goldmine	10a		

Part Three: A Ragbag of References

H

Haboob 7d
Hack 5
Haggle 5
Hagiography 9e
Hagiology 9e
Hail 6a,10b
Hailstorm 6a
Halcyon 2
Halfendale 8a
Hall 7a
Halo 7d
Hamper 8b
Hand 8b,8c
Handful 5,8a
Hang 4
Hang-out 5
Hank 8a,11a
Harangue 10b
Harem 3b,5
Harlequinade 5
Harras 1
Harvest 3b,4,9e
Hastiness 5
Hatch 2
Hatchery 3b
Hatful 6a
Hat-trick 8c
Haunch 8b
Haven 10c
Haze 7d
Head 2,3b,4,7c,8a,8b
Headcount 11a
Heap 8a
Hectare 7a
Heep 5
Helix 11b
Helotry 5
Hennery 2
Herbarium 4
Herd 1,2,3a,5,9c,10a
Herpetarium 3c
Hide 1,7a
Hike 8a

Hill 2,3a,7a,10a
Hint 10a
Hirsel 1
Hive 3a,3b,9d,10a,11d
Hoard 2,8a
Hoarding 8a
Hod 8a
Hogshead 8b
Hold 6a,8a
Hold-all 8a
Holiness 9e
Homage 5
Honeycomb 7a
Hood 9d
Hoover 1
Hope 9d
Hope chest 8a
Hopper 8b
Horde 1,3a,5,9f
Horn 6a,10a
Host 2,3b,4,5,9e,10c
Hostel 5
Hotbed 10a,10b,10c
Hotchpotch 10b
Hothouse 4
House 5,10a,11d
Hover 2,3a,3b,6b
Howl 7d,10b
Huddle 1,2,3b,5,11d
Hug 8a,9a
Huggermugger 10a
Hully 8b
Hum 3a
Humidor 8a
Hurly-burly 11a
Hurtle 1
Husk (or huske) 1
Hutch 1

I

Ibiza 9d
Illusion 5
Imbroglio 10a,10b
Immersion 9e
Impatience 5

281

Impedimenta 6a
Imperial 8b
Impertinence 5
Impi 5
Implausibility 1
Improbability 2
Incantation 5,9f
Incredibility 5
Incredulity 5
Index 9c,11d
Indifference 5
Inferno 7c
Infestation 3a
Infinity 7b
Ingot 8a
Ingratitude 5
Inheritance 11d
Injection 11d
Inn 11d
Insectarium 3a
Institution 5
Intake 5,10c
Intensity 10c
Interplay 7d,10b
Interval 10d
Intrigue 1,11d
Intrusion 3a
Invasion 9d
Inventory 8a
Iota 10a
Isthmus 7c
Itinerary 10a

J

Jam 5
Jamboree 5
Jar 8b
Jardinière 4
Jeroboam 8b
Jerusalem 5
Jet 7c
Jetsam 8a
Joie 10c
Joint 8b,11c
Jorum 8b

Jot 10a
Journal 10a
Journey 1,8a
Jubilee 10d
Junction 7a
Jug 2,8b
Jumble 8a,9c,10c
Junta 5
Jungle 4
Jury 5

K

Kahuna 2
Kaleidoscope 3a,7d
Keg 6a,8b
Kennel 1
Kernel 10a
Kettle 2,10a,11d
Keyboard 11b
Kilderkin 8b
Kindle 1
Kindness 5
Kine 1
Kiss 10a
Kit 2,5a
Kitchen cabinet 11d
Kitsch 5
Knab 3c
Kneeling 5
Knitch 4
Knob 2
Knot 3a,3b,3c,5,7d
Knuckle 5
Kraal 1,7a

L

Laboratory 1,11b
Labour 1
Labyrinth 7c
Lack 5,10c
Lacuna 9c
Lake 7c,8b
Lamentation 2
Land 10a
Landfill 8a

Lane	3b	Live tuck	8b
Lap	3b	Load	8a,10a
Larder	8b	Loaf	8b
Lash	3b,5	Lobby	11d
Laughter	5,8b	Lock	4,8a,11a
Laura	9b	Lode	7c,8a
Lavender list	11d	Lodge	1,5
Lavra	9b	Loft	2
Lawn	4	Log	10a
Layer	7c,8a,10b	Logbook	10a
Layette	8a	Logjam	4
League	5,8c	Loomery	2
Leap	1,5,10a	Long hundred	3b,8a,8b
Lease	1	Lorry-load	1,8a
Leash	1,2,3b	Loss	10c
Lectionary	9e	Lot	5
Leer	5,7a,8a	Lounge	3c
Leg	8b	Loveliness	3a
Legacy	11d	Luck	3a
Legion	5,6a	Lud	8a
Lek	2	Lump	3c,8a
Lepe	1	Lurch	6b
Leprosarium	5	Lying	5
Levee	5		
Levy	6a,11d		

M

Lexicon	9c	Macaroni	10b
Liaison	5	Macedoine	8b
Library	9b,9c,9d	Machination	1
Lick	7c,8a	Madder	5
Lie	1,8c,11d	Madness	1
Life	10a	Maelstrom	7c,10a,10c
Lifetime	8a,10a,10c	Magazine	6a
Lightness	10c	Magnum	5,8b
Limerick	9f	Malapertness	5
Line	3b,6a,8a,8c,9d	Mall	7a
Line-up	5,8c,9a,11d	Manifest	8a
Lippie	8b	Maniple	6a
List	9a,10a	Manner	10d
Listing	8a	Manual	9c
Litany	9e,10a,10b	Manuscript	9b
Litter	1	March	5,10a
Little herd	1	Mardi Gras	5
Liturgy	9e	Margin	10a
Livery	5	Marie Jeanne	8b
Live-tank	3b	Marina	6b

Gallimaufry

Marinade 8b
Mark 2
Mask 1
Masquerade 5,7a
Mass 4,7c,9e,10a,10b,11a
Match 2
Matter 10d
Matrix 7c,11b
Maul 1
Mawn 8b
Maze 7a,7c
Meadow 4
Mease 8b
Measure 8c,9a,10a
Medley 9b
Medusa 3b
Meet 1,5,8c
Meeting 9e,10a,10b
Meinie 1,2,7c
Meiny 5,8c
Melchior 8b
Meld 8c,10a
Mêlée 5
Melody 9b
Melting pot 10a,10b
Membership 9e
Menace 1
Ménage 1,5
Menagerie 1
Menu 8b,11b
Merger 11d
Mess 3c,5,6a,8b,11d
Methusaleh 8b
Mews 2,7a
Miasma 7d,10a
Midden 8a
Middle bevy 1
Middle herd 1
Migration 1
Millennium 10d
Millrace 7a
Mine 10a
Minefield 10a
Minstrelsy 9b
Mint 8a

Minutiae 10a
Minyan 9e
Misbelieving 5
Miscellany 8a
Mischief 1
Mishmash 10c
Mission 1
Mixture 8b
Mob 1,2,5,8b,10a
Mobilisation 6a
Mode 6b
Model 10c
Modicum 10a
Moiety 5,8a
Mole 11b
Moment 10c
Monastery 9e
Monopoly 11d
Monotony 10a
Monsoon 7d
Montage 10a
Montgolfier 8c
Month 10d
Moraine 7c
Morass 10a
Morbidity 6a
Morgen 7a
Morsel 8b
Mosaic 8a
Motorcade 6b
Motor-pool 6b
Mound 3a,7c,8a
Mountain 8a,8b
Movement 1
Mug 8b
Mulada 1
Multiplying 5,9e
Multitude 5,9e,10a,10c
Mumble 1
Murder 2
Murk 7d
Murmur 10b,10c
Murmuration 2
Muscle 6a
Muse 9c

Part Three: A Ragbag of References

Museum 8a,9a
Muster 1,2,6a
Mutation 2
Mutchkin... 8b
Mute 1
Mutter 5

N

Nation 5
Navy 6a
Nebuchadnezzar 8b
Nebula 7b
Neck 4,7c
Necropolis... 7a
Nerve.. 5
Nest 1,2,3a,3c,6a,8a,11b,11d
Net 3b,8c
Netfull 5
Network....................................5,7a,11b,11d
Neverthriving... 5
Newton 8b,11b
Nide... 2
Nieveful 8c
Nine 8c
Nobility... 1
Nod 3c
Noggin 8b
Noil... 8a
Nonet... 9b,9c
Nosegay 4
Nuance 10b
Nub..3b
Nucleus 5
Nugget 8a
Number.. 8a
Nursery 1,4
Nye 2

O

Oasis 10a
Obeisance... 5
Obscuration 5
Observance 5,9e
Obsolescence 8a
Obstinacy 1

Ocean 10c
Oceanarium 3b
Octet... 9b
Odium 9e,11d
Odour 9e,10c
Oeuvre 9c
Ogle 5
Ohm 5
Oligarchy.. 11d
Olio 8b,9b,9c
Omnibus.. 9c
Omnium-gatherum 8a
Opus 9b
Orchard 4
Orchestra.. 3a,9b
Order 1,5
Ordinance 6a
Orgy 9d,10a
Orrery 7b
Ossuary 11a
Ostentation 2
Ounce 10a,10c
Outbreak 6a,7d,11c
Outburst 10c
Outcrop 7c
Outfit 8a
Outpouring 10c
Overdose 9d,11c
Overload 10a
Oxgang 7a

P

Pace... 1
Pack 1,2,3b,4,5,6a,8a,8b,8c,10b
Package 11d
Packet 8a
Pad 8a
Paddling 2
Pageant... 5,6b
Paideia 9c
Pail 3a,8b
Pair 8a,11d
Palette 7d
Palisade 7a,7c
Pall 8a,10a

285

Gallimaufry

Pallor 5
Pan 5
Panache 8a
Pancake 7c
Pandect 11d
Pandemic 11c
Pandemonium 1,2
Pander 5
Pandora's box 10a
Pane 8a
Panegyric 10b
Panel 5,8a,11d
Pang 10c
Panic 9a
Panicle 4
Panoply 1,6a,7b,9a
Panorama 10a
Pantheon 9e
Pantry 8b
Paper 8a
Paper-trail 9c
Parade 1,2,5,6a,6b
Paradigm 9c,10b
Paragon 10c
Paraison 8a
Paraphernalia 8a
Parcel 1,2,7a,7d
Parenthesis 9b
Parish 2
Park 6a,6b
Parlay 8c
Parliament 2,5
Paroxysm 10c
Party 2,3b,5,9e
Parure 8a
Pascal 11b
Passage 10d
Passel 1,5
Pat 2,8b
Patch 3b,4,7a,7d,11b
Patchwork 7a,7d
Path 6a
Pathos 5
Patina 10a
Patrol 1,5,6a

Patter 8a
Pavane 5
Payload 6a
Peal 5,7d,9b,10c
Pearl 10b
Peck 8b
Peep 2,10b
Pellet 7d
Pen 1
Pencil 7d,8a
Peninsula 7c
Penitentiary 5
Penny-pot 8b
Pentad 10d
Penumbra 7d
Period 10a,11d
Persistence 5
Petition 11d
Phalanx 2,6a,11a
Phantasmagoria 10a
Pharmacopœia 11c
Phial 11c
Phratry 5
Phut 8a
Phylactery 9e
Phylum 1,10b
Pi 9c
Picket-line 5,11d
Pickle 3b
Picolo 8b
Picture 10c
Piddle 1
Piece 8a,8c,10a
Pil 2,3b,8a
Pile 6a,8a,10a,11c
Pile-up 6b
Pilgrimage 9e
Pillar 7d
Pilmer 2
Pinch 8a,8b,10a
Pinetum 4
Pinnacle 10a
Pipe 8b
Pipeline 8a
Pit 3c

Pitch	2	Pop	1
Pitcher	8b	Porringer	8b
Piteousness	2	Portfolio	8a,11d
Pitfall	9c	Portion	8b
Pitter-patter	7d	Portmanteau	10b
Pity	5	Posse	2,5,11d
Pitying	2	Postponement	6b
Pladge	3a	Posy	4
Plagiary	5	Pot	8a,8b
Plague	1,3a	Potpourri	8a
Plait	11a	Pounce	1
Plan	6a,11	Pound	3b,9b
Planetarium	7b	Poverty	9b
Plank	8a	Powerhouse	10a
Plantation	4	Practice	5,11c
Platform	5,11d	Prance	5
Platoon	6a	Pratfall	5
Play	3a,7d	Prattle	2
Plethora	10a	Pray	2,9e
Plight	5	Precinct	5
Plocke (or plucke)	5	Presage	6a,10c
Plot	7a,9a	Press	5,8a
Plug	6a,7c,8a	Prettying	2
Plum	3b	Prevarication	5
Plume	8a	Prey	9d
Plummet	2	Prick	10c
Plump	2,8a	Prickle	1
Pocket	1,6a,7d	Pride	1,2,4,5,9d
Pod	2,3b,3c,8b	Prism	7d
Pogrom	6a	Prison	5
Polarity	10b	Process	10a
Policy	10a	Procession	5,6b
Polyglot	10b	Profile	10a
Polyzoarium	1	Profundity	10c
Pomace	8b	Programme	9a,9b,10a
Pomade	8a	Progression	9b
Pomander	8a	Prolixity	9c
Pomp	1	Promenade	5
Pomposity	5,11d	Promise	5,10d
Pond	3b	Promontory	7c
Ponder	5	Protectory	5
Pontificality	9e	Protestation	10c
Pontification	9e	Proud showing	5
Pool	5,6b,7c,7d,8a,8c,10a,10c,11a,11d	Provision	5
		Prowl	1

Prudence 9e
Prunus 8b
Pryde 1
Psalter 9e
Puddling 2
Puff 8a
Pummel 5
Punnet 8b
Purgatory 7d
Purple passage 9c
Purr 1
Pyrus 8b
Python 11b
Pyx 9e

Q

Quadrille 3b
Quadrumvirate 11d
Quagmire 7c,10a
Quake 5
Quality 10a
Quango 11d
Quantity 3b
Quarrel 2
Quartet 9b
Quatrain 9c
Quaver 9b
Quest 5
Queue 5,6b
Quid 8a
Quiddity 9c,10a
Quill 8b
Quincunx 4,7b,8a
Quintet 9b
Quire 9c
Quiver 3b,3c,6a,8a,8c,11d
Quiz 8a
Quorum 11d
Quota 3b

R

Rabbitry 1
Rabble 1,3a
Race 5,8c,9d,9f
Rack 1,6b,8a,8b,11a

Radiance 2,7d,10c
Rafale 6a,9b
Raffle 2,8a
Raft 2,3b,7c,8c,11d
Rafter 2
Rag 1
Ragbag 8a,10b
Rage 5
Rain 1,8c,10b
Rainbow 3a,7d
Rake 1
Rally 5,6a,6b,8c,10a
Rampage 1
Ramuda 1
Rangale 1,5
Range 7c,7d,8a,9a,10a,10b
Rant 9d
Rascal 5
Rash 9c,11a,11c
Rasher 8b
Rasp 2
Ratchet 11d
Ration 8b
Rattle 6a,11a
Ray 7d,10c
Rayful 5
Reading 9c
Ream 9c
Reassurance 7d
Recipe 8b
Recital 9b,9c
Record 10a
Redd 3b
Redoubling 10a
Reef 3b
Reel 8a
Referendum 10b
Reflection 5
Refugium 1
Regalia 8a
Regatta 2
Regime 10a
Regiment 2,5,6a
Register 11d
Regular army 1

Part Three: A Ragbag of References

Rehoboam 8b
Reign 6a,10a
Relay 1,10b
Remnant 8a
Remuda 1
Renaissance 10a
Rendezvous 5
Repertoire 9b
Repository 8a,10a,11b
Reserve 1
Reservoir 7a,10a
Reticule 8a
Retinue 5
Reunion 5
Reverberation 9b
Revolt 11d
Rhapsody 9b
Rhumba 3c
Rick 4
Richesse 1
Richness 1
Riddle 8b,9f
Ridge 7c,7d
Riffraff 5
Rime 7d
Ring 1,4,5,6a,7a,7c,8a,9b
Ringlet 11a
Riot 7d,9a
Ripple 9a,10c
Rite 10a
River 7c,11a
Rivulet 7c
Roar 9a,10c
Rolag 8a
Roll 8a
Roller coaster 10a, 10c
Romp 5
Rookery 2,3b
Rope 8a,8b
Rosary 8a
Rose 8b
Rosetta 10b
Roster 5
Rota 5
Rouleau 8a

Round 8b,9a
Round robin 8c,9c
Roundup 1
Rout (or route) 1,3a,5
Round 6a,8c
Roving 8a
Row 6a,7a,8a,8c
Rubber 8c
Ruck 8a,8c
Ruffle 8a
Rule 10a
Rumble 6a,7d,9b
Rumpus 1,10a
Run 1,2,3b,5,9a,10a
Rush 2,4,7c,7d,10c

S

Sabbat 9f
Sachet 8a
Sack 8a,8b
Saddle 8b
Safe 2
Safeguard 5
Saga 9c
Sail 2
Sale 8a
Salmagundi 8b
Salmanazar 8b
Salon 1,5
Salvo 6a,9a,10b
Samovar 8b
Sample 5,8a,11c
Sanatorium 11c
Sanctuary 1,2
Satchel 8a
Saturnalia 5,8a
Saucer 8b
Sault 1
Saunter 5
Sawt 1
Scabard 3b
Scale 3b,9b
Scamper 2
Scattering 7d
Scenario 10a

289

Gallimaufry

Scene	6a
Scheme	7d
School	2,3b,5,8c,9c,10a,10c
Schooner	8b
Scintilla	10a,10c,11d
Scolding	2,5
Scoop	5
Score	5,9b
Scourge	2,3a
Scrap	8a
Scrapbook	8a
Scraw	3a
Scream	5
Scree	7c
Screech	2
Screed	8a,9c
Screw	2,8a
Scroll	9c
Scrum	8c
Scud	7d
Scurry	1
Scuttle	3a,8a
Sea	7c,9c,9e,10a,10c,11d
Seam	7c,8a,8b
Seat	5
Sebbard	8b
Sect	9e
Sedge	2
Seed-bed	5
Selection	8b,9c
Sense	10a,10c
Sentence	11d
Septet	9b
Sequence	7c,8c,11b
Seraglio	5
Serge	2
Series	6a,7c,8a,9a,10a,11c,11d
Serpent's tooth	5
Service	8a
Serving	8b
Sestet	9c
Set	3b,5,7c,8a,8c,9a,9b,10a,11a,11b
Sett	1
Settlement	7a
Sextet	9b
Shadow	10a
Shaft	7d
Shag	8a
Shaker	8b
Shard	8a
Sheaf	4,6a,8a,8b
Shear	8a
Sheet	7d,8a
Shermer	3b
Shift	1
Shimmer	2
Ship	5,11d
Shipment	6a,8a
Shitload	9d
Shive	4
Shiver	3b
Shoal	2,3b
Shock	4,11a
Shoder	8a
Shop	9d
Shortage	9f
Shortlist	11d
Shot	8a,11c
Shovelful	8a
Show	6a,9a
Showcase	5
Shower	5,7b,7c,7d,8,10a,10b
Shred	10a
Shrewdness	1
Shrivel	5
Shuffle	5
Shush	5
Side	8b
Siege	2
Sigh	10c
Sign	10a
Signature	9c
Silo	8b
Simplicity	6a
Singular	1
Sirloin	8b
Sisterhood	5
Sitting	5,8b
Six	8c
Six-pack	8b,11a

Part Three: A Ragbag of References

Skein	2,8a	Span	1,10a,10d
Skeleton	11a	Spark	10c
Skep	3a	Spasm	10c
Skipful	8a	Spate	7c,10a,10b,11d
Skirl	9b	Spatter	7d
Skulk	1,5,9e	Spearhead	6a
Slant	5	Species	1
Slate	8c,11d	Specimen	11c
Slaver	5	Speck	8a
Sleuth	1	Spectrum	7d,10b
Slew	5,8a,10a,10b	Spell	8b,10c
Slice	8b	Spew	3a,9c
Slither	3b,3c	Sphere	5,10a
Sliver	8a	Spider	11b
Sloth	1	Spill	8a
Slouch	5	Spindle	3a,8a
Slough	10c	Spinney	4
Slumber	1,5	Spiral	11d
Smack	3b,8a	Spirit	10c
Smart	3a	Spit	7c
Smattering	9a,10a,10c	Spite	9a
Smear	5,8a,11c	Splash	7c
Smelting	5	Splendour	2
Smere	5	Splinter	8a
Smirk	5	Split	2
Smorgasbord	10a	Splurge	8a,11b
Smuth	3b	Spool	8a,11b
Sneak	1	Spoonful	8b,11c
Sneer	5	Spot	10a
Snicker	10c	Spray	4,7c
Snigger	10c	Spread	3b,6a,9c
Snippet	10b	Spree	8a
Snort	10c	Sprig	4,5,8b
Soar	10c	Spring	2,3b,7c
Society	1,9e	Springful	2
Sod	4	Sprinkling	5
Soiree	5	Spurt	7c,10a
Sonnet	9c	Squabble	2
Sord	2	Squad	5,6a,8c,11d
Sorority	5	Squadron	2,3b,6a
Sort	5,8b	Squall	2,7d
Sounder	1	Squat	2,5
Soupcon	10c	Squeal	5
Sownder	2	Squeeze	8b
Sowse	1	Stable	1,6b

Stack	4,5,6a,6b,7a,8a,8c,9c	Stud	1,8c
Staff	11d	Studk	3b
Stalk	5,8b	Sty	1
Stampede	1,5	Subtiltie	11d
Stand	2,4,5a,6a,10a	Suggestion	10a
Stanza	9c	Suit	2,6a,8a,8c
Staple	8a	Suitcase	8a
Stare	2,7b	Suite	7a,8a,9b,11b
Stash	9d	Sulk	5
State	3a,5,6a,10a,10c	Sum	10a
Statement	11d	Supercell	7d
Station	5	Superfluity	8b,9e,10a
Stave	4	Surfeit	1,3b
Steam	3b	Surge	10c
Stein	8b	Surgery	5,11c
Stench	1	Surplus	8b
Stick	3b,6a	Survey	10b
Stint	11d	Sute	1,2
Stirring	10c	Swag	8a
Stock	3b,8a,11d	Swarm	1,3a,3b,5,7b,9e,9f
Stockade	6a	Swatch	8a
Stockpile	6a	Swathe	4,6a,8a
Stock-take	8a	Sweet smell	10a
Stook	4	Swish	5
Stoop	5	Syllabary	9c
Store	5,8b	Syllabus	10a
Storm	6a,7b,7c,7d,10b,10c	Symmetry	10a
Storytelling	2	Symphony	9b
Strain	3a	Symposium	5,9c
Strake	6a	Syndicate	11d
Strand	2,8a,11b	Synergy	10b
Strangle	5	Synod	5,9e
Strata	7c	Synthesis	10b
Stratum	10a	System	6a
Streak	1,7d,10c	Syzygy	11b
Stream	2,3b,5,7c,7d,10a,10b		
Street	7a		
Stretch	1		
Strike	4		
String	1,8a,8b,9b,10a,10b,11d		
Strip	5,7c		
Stripe	1		
Stroke	10a,10c		
Stroll	8a		
Stubbornness	1		

T

Tabernacle	5
Table	8c,9c
Tableau	8c,9a
Take	3b
Talent	8c
Tally	3b,8c,11a,11d
Tangle	3b,4,5,6b,8a,10a,11a
Tank	3b,3c,8a

Part Three: A Ragbag of References

Tanker	8a,8b
Tantrum	5
Tapestry	7d
Tariff	8a
Taste	10a
Tattoo	9b
Team	1,2,3b,5,8b,8c,11c,11d
Tedium	8c
Teeme	2
Temperance	5
Tenet	9e
Tenor	10d
Term	11d
Terrace	7a
Terrarium	4
Terrine	8b
Terror	1
Test	10d
Testimony	10a
Thatch	8a,11a
Theatre	6a,9a
Thermos	8b
Thesaurus	9c
Thicket	4,5
Think-tank	5
Thought	5
Thrave	5
Thread	8a,10b
Threatening	5
Threnody	10c
Thrill	5
Throng	5
Throw	3b
Thunder	1,9a
Thunderhead	7d
Tidal wave	11d
Tide	10a,10b,10c,11d
Tiding	2
Tier	8b,9a
Tierce	8b,8c
Tilt	7a
Timeline	10d
Timetable	8a,9a,10a
Tin	8a
Tincture	7d,8a,11c

Tinkle	10c
Tintinnabulation	9b
Tirade	10a,10b
Tissue	10b
Titbit	10b
Tithe	8a
Tittering	2
Toby	8b
Tod	4,8a
Tok	2
Token	10a
Tolling	9b
Tongue	7c
Top	8a
Topple	8c
Torque	5
Torrent	7c,10a,10b
Torsade	8a
Tot	8b
Totter	1
Touch	10c
Tour	6a,10a
Tournament	8c
Tourney	5
Tow	8a
Tower	1,7c,10a
Town	1
Trace	1,10a
Tracery	8a,11a
Tract	7a,7c
Traffic jam	6b
Tragedy	6b
Trail	3a,6a,8a,10a
Train	1,2,5,6b,7c,10c
Trance	5
Transplant	5
Trap	3b
Trawl	11b
Tray	8b
Treasure trove	10a
Tree	10a
Trembling	2
Tress	11a
Triad	7d,9b,11b
Tribe	1,2,5,9f

Tribulation	5
Tribute	8a
Trick	8c
Trickle	7c,10b
Trill	9b
Trimming	2
Trine	5
Trinity	9e
Trinket	5
Trio	9b
Triolet	9c
Trip	1,2,5,9d
Triplet	9b
Triplex	11b
Trogle	3c
Trolley	8a
Troop	1,3b,4,5,6a,11d
Trooping	6a
Troubling	2,3b
Trough	7d,8a
Troupe	5,9a,9b
Trousseau	8a
Truckload	1
Truculence	5
True love	2
Trug	8b
Truss	4,7a
Truth	5
Trynket	5
Tryst	5
Tub	8b
Tube	8a,11c
Tuft	4,8a
Tumble	8c
Tumult	9b
Tun	8b
Tureen	8b
Turmoil	3b
Turn	3b,3c,10a,10b
Tussock	4
Twaddle	5
Twelve	8c
Twinge	10c
Twinkle	7d
Twinkling	10d
Twirl	7d,8a
Twist	8a
Twitch	11b

U

Ubiquity	2
Ugly	3b
Ululation	5
Unanimity	10b
Unction	5
Unease	10a
Unemployment	5
Unhappiness	5
Union	5
Unit	6a
Unkindness	2
Untruth	5
Updraft	7d
Urn	8a,8b

V

Vagary	10a
Vale	10c
Vanguard	5,6a
Varia	9c
Variety	10a
Vase	4
Vat	8a,8b
Veil	7d,10c
Vein	2,7c
Veneer	10a
Verse	9c
Verticil	4
Vespiary	3a
Vial	8a,11c
Village	5
Vinery	4
Vineyard	4
Vintage	8b
Virgate	7a
Vision	10a
Vista	10a
Vivarium	1,3c
Vocabulary	9c
Volary	2

Part Three: A Ragbag of References

Volery	2
Volley	6a,10b
Vortex	7d
Voyage	10a

W

Wad	8a
Waddle	1,2
Wail	9f
Walk	2,3a,10a
Wake	2
Wall	10a
Wandering	5
War	10b
Ward	11c
Wardrobe	8a,9a
Warp	8b
Warren	1,2,7a,7c
Watch	2,6a
Wave	5,6a,9a,10b,10c
Way	10a
Waywardness	5
Wealth	3b,9c,10a
Weapon	6a
Web	9c,10a,11a
Web-ring	11b
Web-site	11b
Wedge	2,7d,8b
Weel	8b
Weight	10a
Well	10c
Welter	8a,10a,10c
Whale	10d
Wheeze	8c
Whiff	10b,10c
Whine	9b
Whinge	5
Whirl	10a,10c
Whisper	10b
Whistle	11b
Whiteness	2

Whoop	1
Whorl	4,7d
Who's who	5
Wiggle	3c
Wilderness	1
Wiliness	1
Wince	5
Wind	10a
Window	10a
Wing	2,3b,6a
Wisdom	1,2,5
Wisket	8b
Wisp	2,3b,8a,10b
Withdrawal	11d
Wobble	6b,7d
Wolfpack	6a
Wood	4
Woodchoir	2
Word	10b
Work	9c
Workforce	5
World	10a
Worship	5,9c
Wrack	1
Wrangle	5
Wrap	9d
Wreath	4
Wreck	2
Wriggle	3a
Wunch	5

Y

Yard	8a,8b
Yield	3b
Yoke	1

Z

Zeal	1
Zodiac	7b
Zoo	1

Gallimaufry

'a worship of writers'